Drunk Driving

Studies in Crime and Justice

Drunk Driving

An American Dilemma

James B. Jacobs

Foreword by **Franklin E. Zimring**

The University of Chicago Press
Chicago and London

The University of Chicago Press, Chicago 60637
The University of Chicago Press, Ltd., London

© 1989 by The University of Chicago
All rights reserved. Published 1989
Printed in the United States of America

98 97 96 95 94 93 92   5 4

Library of Congress Cataloging-in-Publication Data

Jacobs, James B.
    Drunk driving : an American dilemma / James B. Jacobs ;
foreword by Franklin E. Zimring.
        p.   cm. — (Studies in crime and justice)
    Bibliography: p.
    Includes index.
    ISBN 0-226-38979-0 (pbk.)
    1. Drunk driving—United States.   2. Drinking and traffic
accidents—United States.   I. Title.   II. Series.
HE5620.D7J29   1989
363.1′251—dc19   88-17383
                                                    CIP

This book is dedicated to the memory of Cornell sociologist
Professor Rose K. Goldsen
valued colleague, respected intellect, and dear friend

Contents

Foreword

Social control of the drinking driver, a persistently important policy issue in the United States, has been chronically understudied in the social sciences, in academic law, and in criminology. The policy significance of the problem has long been acknowledged because tens of thousands of lives lost each year in accidents and hundreds of thousands of arrests are hard even for the professoriate to ignore. But the jurisprudential and criminological issues have not been considered of sufficient intellectual status to concern those in the higher reaches of the American legal and criminological academies. Scholars from public health, alcohol studies, and sociology who were developing knowledge on this topic were regarded by many criminologists and criminal law scholars in much the same way that many regard chiropodists—as people doing useful but not very interesting work.

In the United States, no law professor in the postwar generation established a tradition of study involving drinking and driving to parallel the career of Johannes Andenaes in Norway. Meanwhile, postwar American criminology was preoccupied with theories of delinquency and with large-scale ideological battles. Even the general public paid little attention to the social cost of drunk driving in the United States during the 1960s and early 1970s, in part because of the pressures brought by sharp increases in the rates of other crimes.

Public perception of the importance of the social control of drinking drivers had changed dramatically by the late 1970s. Just as rates of street crime moderated in the United States, grassroots concern with the death toll from alcohol-related accidents increased and became a persistent presence in the media, in state and local legislative bodies, and in schools and other community institutions. And the new salience of drunk driving does not appear to be a short-lived phenomenon. Interest in control of the drinking driver has exhibited a one-directional dynamic in the past decade: new institutions and groups get involved, but there is no substantial example of levels of public concern or involvement diminishing.

Now, at last, the legal academy is catching up with its social environment. This book breaks new ground in law-related research and establishes its author as the first authentic academic legal authority on alcohol and traffic safety in the United States.

This study integrates the considerable learning currently available on both the many facets of drunk driving and the institutions that respond to the drinking driver. The range of disciplines and issues covered is large—from psychopharmacology to criminal procedure. Mastering so substantial a literature is one of the book's achievements.

And it turns out that social response to drunk driving is an absolutely fascinating case study in law and society. Much as geologists flock to live volcanoes to study the processes of land formation, the student of legal policy can examine drunk driving as an example of exceptionally fast change in the criminal law. And while many areas of vice control have become examples of decriminalization, the trend in the issue of drunk driving has been toward treating the behavior as a more serious threat and the offender as a more culpable actor. We are here witnessing the modern morality play of the process of criminalization. So this volume introduces the student of law and society to a laboratory of social and legal change that can teach much about the conditions under which such changes are likely to occur and more still about some consequences of criminalization.

This is one of two consecutive volumes in the Studies in Crime and Justice series that are devoted to the criminal law aspects of alcohol and traffic safety. The volumes are designed to complement each other. Michael Laurence, John Snortum, and I edited a volume of essays by subject-matter specialists on the wide range of areas relevant to the topic. The aim of that volume was encyclopedic; the aim of this volume is synthetic.

This is as well the second volume Jim Jacobs has contributed to the studies in Crime and Justice series. He is the fifth author to contribute more than one book to the series and is the youngest member of that distinguished bank of recidivists. It is one of the particular pleasures of this business to watch the personal development of scholars over time, as well as the accumulative impact of their scholarship in this series of books. Those of us associated with the progress of the series and the career of Jim Jacobs have reason to be doubly proud.

FRANKLIN E. ZIMRING

Acknowledgments

Over the many years that I have been laboring on this book and on several essays that have led up to it, I have been assisted immeasurably by family, colleagues, and critics. I owe debts of gratitude to two New York University faculty colleagues, Graham Hughes and Nadine Strossen. For two years Graham and I cotaught a law school seminar on drunk driving; as always, I benefitted immensely from his probing jurisprudential analyses. Nadine collaborated with me on an exhaustive legal analysis of drunk driving roadblocks. She pushed me to think much harder about this subject than I could possibly have pushed myself. I also owe a very large debt of gratitude to David Wasserman, a lawyer and fellow at our Center for Research in Crime and Justice who went over the final revisions of this book chapter by chapter and line by line. His criticisms, suggestions, and encouragement helped me immeasurably. My final revisions were also facilitated by the excellent research assistance of Julie Macht and the insightful comments of Andrew von Hirsch.

Two University of Chicago Press reviewers, Franklin Zimring and Phillip Cook, provided constructive and penetrating criticism that pushed me to my limits and beyond; they have contributed enormously to the development of this book. While this was my first experience with Professor Cook's incisive mind, I have been the beneficiary of Franklin Zimring's brilliant insights and incredibly generous assistance throughout my career, and I would like to take this opportunity to thank him publicly.

Throughout most of this project my secretary, Eileen Peters, provided the day-to-day office assistance that made it possible for me to function effectively. When she left to begin her family, Yvette Morales took over with skill and good humor. Throughout every day of this project, my wife, Jan Sweeney provided the constant support and encouragement that made it possible to complete the manuscript.

I would also like to acknowledge the generous support of the Filomen D'Agostino and Max Greenberg Research Fund of New York University School of Law, which provided summer support and a semester's research leave.

Chapter 10 appeared in Michael D. Laurence, John R. Snortum, and Franklin E. Zimring, *Social Control of the Drinking Driver*, in slightly different form. © 1988 by The University of Chicago.

Introduction

Drunk driving is the intersection of two American institutions: drinking and driving. Beverage alcohol plays a central role in American life and culture. It is an integral component of leisure activities and celebrations. From cocktail parties to sporting events, from dining out to wakes and christenings, from fraternity bashes to clambakes, beverage alcohol plays a well-defined role as an aid to and symbol of celebration, conviviality, camaraderie, and intimacy. Alcohol consumption and intoxication also serve important psychological functions. Individual drinkers seek reduction of tension, guilt, anxiety, and frustration and enhancement of fantasy, sensuality, aggressiveness, self-esteem, and escapism.

Per capita, Americans consume more alcoholic beverages than they do milk. On average, each person over fourteen years of age annually consumes the equivalent of 591 twelve-ounce cans of beer or 115 bottles (fifths) of table wine or 35 fifths of 80-proof whisky, gin, or vodka. Since a third of the population abstains, the drinking population consumes much more than the per-capita average. Daily alcohol consumption for the nonabstaining population fourteen years of age and older averages approximately three drinks per day. The most heavily drinking tenth of the population consumes half of the alcoholic beverages sold (U.S. Department of Health and Human Services 1983). The beer, spirits, and wine industry advertises aggressively, linking its products to positive cultural symbols and psychological needs (Jacobson, Atkins, and Hacker 1983).

While beverage alcohol lubricates social life and plays a positive role in the personal lives of most drinkers, it also is associated with many personal and social problems and with much human misery.[1] Alcohol abuse is involved in a quarter of all admissions to general hospitals, and it plays a major role in the four most common causes of death of men aged twenty to forty: suicide, accidents, homicide, and cirrhosis of the liver (Hyman et al. 1980; Vaillant 1983, P. 1). Frequently it is a factor in spouse and child abuse (Hamilton and Collins 1981).

The drunk driving story is also a transportation story. There is nothing discrete about Americans' love affair with the automobile (see Meyer and Gomez-Ibanez 1981; Lewis and Goldstein 1983). The car is a symbol of social status and personal life-style; for many people it fulfills deep psychological needs for power, aggression, fantasy, and control. There are more registered vehicles (171,690,733) and more miles of roadway (3,861,934) in the United States than in other nations. Americans show less interest in public transportation and drive greater distances between home, work, and play.

There would be no drunk driving without automobiles, and there would be no major drunk driving problem without the societal assumption that automobile ownership and operation should be nearly universal. Moreover, taverns, bars, restaurants, and liquor stores dot our roads. For those who are not alcohol abstainers, active participation in American social life practically ensures a high probability of at least occasional driving after drinking.

Recognition of a Social Problem

As long as there have been vehicles, there have been drunken drivers. During the nineteenth century, intoxicated railroad engineers surfaced as a serious problem. As early as 1843 the New York Central Railroad prohibited drinking by employees on duty (Borkenstein 1985). In 1904 the *Quarterly Journal on Inebriety* editorialized that "the precaution of railroad companies to have only total abstainers guide their engines will soon extend to the owners of these new motor wagons. . . . With the increased popularity of these wagons, accidents of this kind will multiply rapidly." Henry Ford declared that "booze had to go when modern industry and the motor car came in" (Lender and Martin 1982). New York State added a drunk driving offense to its traffic code in 1910 (King and Tipperman 1975).

The crucial impetus for mobilizing attention and resources for attacking the drunk driving problem was the Highway Safety Act of 1966. In effect, it federalized the issue by establishing the National Highway Safety Bureau, the precursor of the National Highway Traffic Safety Administration (NHTSA), and by authorizing the U.S. Department of Transportation's historic 1968 report *Alcohol and Highway Safety*. The 1968 report found that "the use of alcohol by drivers and pedestrians leads to some 25,000 deaths and a total of at least 800,000 crashes in the United States each year." The report warned that "this major source of human morbidity will continue to plague our mechanically powered society until its ramifications and many present questions have been exhaustively explored and the precise possibilities for truly effective countermeasures determined."

In 1970 NHTSA launched the Alcohol Safety Action Project (ASAP), the first major federal initiative against drunk driving. ASAPs were implemented in thirty-five communities around the United States at a cost of $88 million dollars. The goal was to achieve a significant reduction in drunk driving through a mix of intensive countermeasures (enforcement, rehabilitation, and public information) and a systems approach (coordinated efforts by police, courts, and treatment agencies). Arrests increased significantly in all ASAP jurisdictions, in some by more than 300 percent, and rehabilitation programs (especially drunk driver schools) provided treatment to tens of thousands of offenders. Nevertheless, a significant reduction of drunk driving could not be confirmed and the program was terminated in 1977 (Zador 1976; Levy et al. 1978; Nichols et al. 1978; U.S. Department of Transportation 1979; Voas 1981). By this time NHTSA had promulgated Standard 8, "Alcohol in Relation to Highway Safety," which set out a number of significant anti–drunk driving strategies that states had to meet in order to qualify for certain federal highway funds.

The Contemporary Anti–Drunk Driving Movement

The attacks on drunk driving did not wane with the demise of the ASAPs. During the late 1970s and early 1980s an extraordinary grass roots anti–drunk driving movement began organizing and lobbying across the United States. Remove Intoxicated Drivers (RID) was founded by Doris Aiken in Schenectady, New York, in 1978 after a drunk driver killed a local teenager. Mothers Against Drunk Driving (MADD) was founded in 1980 in Sacramento, California, by Candy Lightner, whose daughter had been killed by a drunk driver with a history of driving while intoxicated.

The time for organizing was propitious. The public health drive against alcohol abuse had already achieved significant success in defining alcohol abuse as a major social and health problem, and a vast network of federal, state, local, and private agencies, organizations, and programs had been established. These organizations all stood to benefit from a flow of referrals from the criminal justice system. Aiken and Lightner both obtained NHTSA grants to engage in organizing and in organization building. More important, perhaps, the media regularly featured the speeches and activities of the anti–drunk driving activists, particularly those of the charismatic Lightner. Dozens of newspapers and magazine articles reported on RID's and MADD's efforts to force an unresponsive criminal justice system to provide adequate punishment and deterrence for drunk drivers and justice to the victims and their families. In March 1983, NBC aired a documentary entitled "Mothers Against Drunk Driving: The Candy Lightner Story." After the airing of this movie, the growth of new MADD chapters almost doubled (Weed 1987).

Chapters of RID, MADD, and Students Against Drunk Driving (SADD) were formed in local communities all around the country.[2] MADD quickly grew to approximately 300 chapters, RID to 150. While MADD provides somewhat more direction and control, both organizations are highly decentralized. The national headquarters suggest organizing strategies and provide background materials on key issues for agenda formulation, but local chapters develop and set agendas according to the energies and aspirations of their own leaders. While legislative lobbying attracts the most media attention, these organizations are also actively involved in educational campaigns, victims services, and court monitoring.

While the anti–drunk driving movement calls to mind similar anti-alcohol campaigns of previous periods of our history (see Gusfield 1963), it should not be seen as a neo-Prohibitionist movement (but see Sheron 1986); in fact, Weed's (1987) survey found that local MADD officers believe that limiting the availability of alcoholic beverages is not a realistic solution or a morally appropriate strategy. The anti–drunk driving movement is closely related to the crime victims movement. It is significantly comprised of those whom drunk drivers have victimized, either directly or, more often, indirectly, by the killing of a family member. For the victims who comprise much of the leadership of the anti–drunk driving organizations, political action is a means of coping with personal tragedy and of accomplishing change. Like so many American movements, the anti–drunk driving groups place great emphasis on legislation; each year brings a new legislative agenda. Passing new laws is enormously important for sustaining and encouraging their activities (see Sheingold 1974).

During the early 1980s the anti–drunk driving groups brought drunk driving to the top of the social problems agenda. The issue made the cover of the leading newsmagazines and was the subject of several television specials and dramatizations. Anti–drunk driving messages appeared regularly on television public service announcements (PSAs), in magazines, on billboards, and in other media. Insurance companies, automobile manufacturers, and brewers, vintners, and distillers all supported public education campaigns.

Drunk driving soon achieved critical recognition at the federal level. Congress proclaimed a Drunk and Drugged Driving Awareness week each December and enacted two laws making federal highway funds contingent on, among other things, states (1) passing criminal statutes (per se laws) making it illegal for one to operate a motor vehicle when one's blood alcohol concentration (BAC) is greater than 0.10 and (2) raising their minimum drinking age to twenty-one. In 1982 President Reagan appointed a Presidential Commission on Drunk Driving, lending the moral and symbolic support of his office to the anti–drunk driving cause. Candy Lightner was one of the commissioners. The commission's Final Report, published in 1983, took stock of the political environment in which it was working:

In recent years, society has acted or reacted to the drunk driving problem in ways it has not in the past. A number of citizens groups have brought the problem of alcohol-related tragedies to the attention of the public and to officials at the local, state, and federal levels. The Presidential Commission is the culmination of a crescendo of voices—voices of victims and their families—who demand action. The demand for action is not new, but its intensity and extent have never been more dramatic. Such a national outcry presents an enormous opportunity and yet an enormous danger. (P. 2)

The enormous opportunity, according to the commission, arose "from the fact that the public is united in demanding solutions," while the enormous danger stemmed from the possibility that "either demands will be so unrealistic that any success will be virtually impossible, or that the Presidential Commission will bring forth a mixture of suggestions or recommendations that would create a serious credibility problem." The presidential commission proceeded to offer more than fifty recommendations, including encouragement for citizen action, joint citizen-government task forces at the local level, and a permanent national body "to ensure a continuing focus on efforts to combat driving under the influence."[3]

Since 1983 the legislative deluge of new anti–drunk driving laws has been continuous (U.S. Department of Transportation 1985), with states vying for the distinction of being toughest on drunk drivers. For the most part the new laws pick up where the ASAPs left off, attempting to reduce drunk driving through a combination of tougher criminal sanctions and intensified law enforcement (U.S. Department of Transportation 1985). Pressured by federal legislation linking highway funds to the passage of anti–drunk driving countermeasures, state legislatures have enacted mandatory jail terms, more-severe fines, and automatic and lengthier license suspensions and revocations. Some have restricted plea bargaining and added new sanctions, such as home detention with electronic monitoring.

Local police departments have given higher priority to drunk driving arrests; many have implemented nighttime roadblocks at which all drivers are stopped and scrutinized for the telltale signs of intoxication (Jacobs and Strossen 1985); between 1970 and 1986 arrests for driving while intoxicated (DWI) increased nearly 223 percent. The courts have endorsed almost all this activity and have added a few initiatives of their own, including (1) the availability of punitive damages against drunk drivers (e.g., *Taylor v. Superior Court*, 598 P.2d 854 [1979]) and (2) dram shop liability for commercial alcohol dispensers (e.g., *Lopez v. Maez*, 651 P.2d 1269 [1982]) and even for social hosts (e.g., *Kelly v. Gwinnell*, 426 A.2d 1219 [1984]). While the current programs give less emphasis to education and rehabilitation than did the ASAPs, many anti–drunk driving programs are linked in one way or another to alcohol abuse treatment programs and to drinking/driver schools to which massive numbers of drunk drivers are either diverted in lieu of prosecution or channeled after conviction.

While many systems of social control (treatment, education, private law, and insurance) have been mobilized, the dominant role of the criminal justice system has never been in doubt. From the mid-1970s to the mid-1980s drunk driving arrests increased by 50 percent, to 1.8 million per year. This makes drunk driving the most commonly prosecuted offense in our lower criminal courts. Strong citizen pressure along with (1) implied-consent laws which encourage (coerce) arrestees to provide breath samples (on pain of license forfeiture) and (2) restrictions on plea bargaining produce a very high conviction rate. The vast number of convictions create a challenge for our sanctioning systems. In some states, such as New York, drunk drivers are now the largest offender category on probation. Under mandatory sentencing laws, they are also becoming an increasing presence in many jails. Moreover, recidivist drunk drivers (convicted of felonies) are appearing in some state prison systems in significant numbers.

The enhanced attack on drunk activity is not likely to be a passing fad. In many localities and states, such as New York, anti–drunk driving programs have become institutionalized in special interest agencies or programs solely responsible for dealing with drunk driving. Moreover, initiatives such as New York State's "Stop DWI Program" channel fine money obtained from drunk drivers back to local anti-DWI programs; thus, some anti-DWI programs have become partially self-financing.

Drunk Driving Research: The Need for a Critical Synthesis

Robert Borkenstein (1985), for many decades one of America's leading drunk-driving researchers, traces American research back at least to the early 1930s. In 1934 Dr. Herman Heise collected data on automobile fatalities and found that a high percentage had significant alcohol in the blood. Heise's findings were confirmed by a major study in Evanston, Illinois, which over a three-year period, found that alcohol was present in significant concentrations in nearly half of 270 injured drivers; Dr. Richard Holcomb, Director of the Northwestern Traffic Institute, compared the alcohol concentrations of the Evanston accident-involved drivers with those of a random sample of road users by utilizing the Drunkometer, the first widely used breath-testing device. He found that 12 percent of road users had "significant blood alcohol concentrations" (Holcolm 1938).

From the beginning drunk driving research was pressed into the service of social control. The National Safety Council (NSC)(founded in 1914) Committee on Tests For Intoxication developed the "Standard Alcohol Influence" form in 1937. The first White House Conference on Highway Safety, convened in 1946, recommended that action be taken to curb drunk driving. Some pioneering work was carried out during the 1950s (see *Proceedings of the Second International Conference on Alcohol and Road Traffic 1955*) and early 1960s (e.g., Haddon, Suchman, and Klein 1964; Borkenstein et al. 1974). In 1957 the American Medical Association published its first *Manual on Alcohol and the Impaired Driver* and the Northwestern Traffic Institute published *Chemical Tests and the Law*. Despite these steps, however, most of the American research during the first two-thirds of the century was conducted by highway safety specialists, whose studies and findings did not achieve much recognition among university-based social scientists.[4]

Since the federalization of the drunk driving problem during the 1960s and 1970s, there has been an outpouring of government studies and reports, many funded by NHTSA. By itself, this corpus of research poses a prodigious challenge to someone seeking to determine the state of informed opinion about drunk driving. In addition to federal studies, there are scores of state and local evaluations, often proclaiming success even before a new program is fully operational. University-based research is also thriving in several disciplines. Highway safety experts continue to assay the extent of drunk driving, its contribution to traffic casualties, and the preventability of crash injuries and fatalities. Over the past fifteen years the federal government's National Institute of Alcohol Abuse and Alcoholism (NIAAA) has helped to generate an enormous body of research on drinking practices, alcohol abuse and alcoholism, and treatment modalities (see U.S. Department of Health and Human Services 1983). There are also several important university centers devoted to the study of alcohol problems (e.g., the Rutgers Center for Alcohol Studies and the UCLA Alcohol Research Center).

Psychologists are engaged in research to determine the extent of alcohol abuse among those convicted of drunk driving. H. Laurence Ross, a sociologist, has produced a steady stream of evaluations of deterrence initiatives in the United States, Europe, Australia, and New Zealand. Several economists have conducted sophisticated econometric studies to determine the effect, if any, of tough anti–drunk driving laws, of variations in beverage alcohol taxes, and of variations in minimum legal purchase age (Cook 1981; Males 1986). These diverse bodies of research are scattered in the journals of various disciplines. In fact, many of the most important studies in this field have not been published at all (e.g., Goldstein and Susmilch 1982).

Lack of Criminological and Jurisprudential Research

Oddly, drunk driving remains at the periphery of criminological and jurisprudential writing and research. The index of the tenth edition of Sutherland and Cressey's standard text, *Principles of Criminology,* contains only two index entries for drunk driving, and both refer to passages in which drunk driving is mentioned merely in passing. Only one article on drunk driving has appeared during the past ten years (1978–87 of *Crime and Delinquency,* a leading journal for theoretical and policy-oriented criminology). The situation in criminal law jurisprudence is no better. Despite an array of thorny theoretical and philosophical issues, the leading criminal law casebook–Kadish, Paulsen and Schulhoffer's *Criminal Law and Its Processes* (4th ed.)— does not contain a single case, and carries only a few brief notes, on drunk driving. While the law reviews have carried student notes and comments and a few faculty articles on implied-consent laws, drunk driving homicide, roadblocks, punitive damages, and BAC testing, the total amount of scholarship is very small.[5]

I can only speculate on why drunk driving has not yet excited the criminological appetite. One reason may be because drunk driving presents difficult research problems; the incidence of drunk driving cannot be determined from crimes reported to the police or from victims surveys, and evaluation of drunk driving countermeasures is frustrated by (1) inability to measure the amount of drunk driving and (2) inability to identify the separate impacts of simultaneous initiatives. A second reason may be that criminologists are uncertain about drunk driving's status as a "real crime." After all, the offense is usually found in the vehicle and traffic code, not in the criminal code; incidents of DWI do not figure in the FBI Crime Index or in the public's conception of America's crime rate.

A third hypothesis to explain lack of criminological interest is that drunk drivers do not conform to social psychological images of "crime." There are no ancient stereotypes of drunk drivers to rival those of murderers, thieves, and terrorists; in fact, drunk drivers are often depicted as feckless and humorous rather than as abhorrent and diabolical. A fourth and related hypothesis is that drunk drivers do not conform to sociological images of "criminals." For the most part, criminology has taken popular opinion and legislative emphasis on lower-class wrongdoing as a given. But drunk driving is not a crime associated with the poor and dispossessed. According to the FBI's Uniform Crime Reports (UCRs), drunk drivers have the highest percentage of white offenders (90 percent) of any arrest group.

A fifth hypothesis is that drunk driving does not make a critical case for liberal or conservative criminologists. It does not further either the liberal explanation of crime as a consequence of maldistribution of wealth, poverty, and unemployment or the neoconservative explanation of crime as rational economic behavior. Even traditional conservatives who believe that the root cause of crime is moral dissoluteness might find drunk driving troubling because of societal ambivalence toward alcohol and alcohol problems.

Whether or not my hunches about the reasons why drunk driving has been slighted are accurate, there is much that criminologists can gain by focusing on this offense. For example, the placement of DWI in the vehicle and traffic law, as well as its treatment as less serious than simple assault, larceny, or burglary, should itself be of criminological interest. Focusing on drunk driving should reinforce the criminological insight that there is nothing immutable about the content of the criminal code or the Crime Index. Moreover, an analysis of drunk driving's status as a hybrid traffic violation/criminal offense should draw attention to such questions as the following: (1) Why does a particular society choose to criminalize certain harmful behaviors but not others? (2) What leads criminal code drafters to regard certain offenses as serious and others as trivial? (3) What causes legislators at particular points in time to redefine a behavior as more serious and grave than previously? (4) Why and how does a society come to define its crime rate in terms of a small number of offense categories?

The study of drunk driving tests our capacity to overcome criminal stereotypes and to move toward a more rational and utilitarian criminal law that condemns behavior because of the harm or risk it creates, regardless of whether it is ancient and evil or contemporary and irresponsible. The criminal law should be conceived as one form of social control; the question criminologists should ask is whether criminal law enforcement can make a contribution to the control of a particular social problem and, if so, whether it is appropriate to employ it.

If criminologists focused more attention on drunk driving in their classes and writings, their very inquiries would help to break down the stereotypical image of criminals as poor blacks and Hispanics and of law-abiding people as middle- and upper-class whites. If this point were made often enough, it might help to convince the public that criminality is extremely widespread among all social classes and racial groups. While this would not *justify* the wrongdoings of poor people, it might help to encourage a more rational and restrained set of criminal justice policies.

I

The Anatomy of a Social Problem

The first four chapters of this book provide the essential background that is necessary to understand the anatomy of drunk driving as a social problem.

Chapter 1 places drunk driving in the context of America's relationship with alcohol and, more particularly, in the context of its alcohol abuse problem. Beverage alcohol plays a pervasive role in American social and economic life; DWI is a negative consequence of that role. Moreover, alcoholism and alcohol abuse are one of the nation's major health problems; DWI is but one manifestation of that problem.

Chapter 2 places drunk driving in the context of America's transportation system. That system provides unparalleled opportunity for individuals to move from place to place in pursuit of their individual and collective goals. Unfortunately, it also generates a toll in life and property that in magnitude can only be compared to casualties in warfare. In the rush to solve the drunk driving problem, we sometimes forget that the ultimate goal is to make the transportation system safer. Preventing and controlling drunk driving is but a subissue in the social control of vehicular traffic.

Chapter 3 focuses on drunk driving as a cause of highway casualties. To what extent are the drunk driving and highway safety problems identical—or at least overlapping? We will see that there is no simple answer to this question; and the question itself conceals several subtle assumptions that need to be examined. In any event, the magnitude of the drunk driving problem has been as much a subject of politics and politicization as of scholarly study and analysis.

Chapter 4 turns to the criminology of drunk driving, patterns of offending, and characteristics of offenders. What do we know about the frequency of this crime and about its offenders? Once again we will encounter a curious paradox: there is both too much and too little information, too many and too few studies. Nevertheless, there are some myths that can be readily dispelled and some basic facts that will prove useful in helping us to analyze the legal and public policy issues that are raised in Parts II and III.

1

Alcohol in American Society

Beverage alcohol plays a central role in American life and culture (see Lender and Martin 1982). It is an accompaniment of celebrations, leisure activities, fine dining, romance, and business deals. Its role is so pervasive and important that its absence in many social situations would be defined as inappropriate and deviant. In short, we Americans live in an alcohol-rich environment.

Alcohol consumption and intoxication also serve important psychological and emotional functions.[1] Drinkers seek reduction of tension, guilt, anxiety, and frustration. From personal experience and from viewing countless television and movie dramas, we have become accustomed to people turning to alcohol to cope with a hard day, family problems, or bad news. People also imbibe alcohol to loosen up, let down their hair, release inhibitions, and enhance fantasy and sensuality. Thus we are accustomed to drinking as a prelude to seduction or romance. In addition, people turn to alcohol to fortify confidence, enhance self-esteem, and increase aggressiveness. It seems normal for people to have a drink before proposing marriage, asking the boss for a raise, or going into battle.

The chemical ingredient that gives alcoholic beverages their intoxicating effect is ethyl alcohol (Olson and Gerstein 1985). Beer is generally 3–6 percent alcohol by volume, with light beer at the low end and malt liquor at the high end; wine is generally 10–20 percent alcohol, with table wine low and fortified dessert wine high; and spirits are generally bottled at 40 percent alcohol (80 proof). Despite these differences in alcoholic content per volume, alcoholic drinks generally contain approximately the same alcoholic content. A 12-ounce can of 4-percent beer, a 4-ounce serving of 12-percent wine, and a cocktail with 1.2 ounces of 80-proof spirits contain identical amounts of ethyl alcohol. One drink of any of these alcoholic beverages usually contains about one-half ounce of pure alcohol. While drinkers can and do become intoxicated by drinking all types of alcoholic beverages, wine drinking is more likely to be an accompaniment to meals and not a

3

means of intoxication. Spirits drinking, while by no means always associated with intoxication, provides a method of becoming intoxicated very quickly. Because beer so dominates the alcoholic beverage scene in the United States, it is not surprising that most alcohol abusers are beer abusers.

Patterns of Alcohol Consumption

Alcohol consumption is not unique to American society. In fact, the drinking practices that immigrants brought to America continue to be reflected in different ethnic drinking customs and patterns. Nevertheless, there are certain distinctive features of the American drinking environment—for example, a distinctive mix of spirits, beer, and wine; a large tavern and bar culture; and drunkenness as a social activity for certain segments of the population.

There are large differences in consumption patterns within the United States. The northeastern states show the highest per-capita rates of consumption, the south-central states the lowest. The mid-Atlantic states have the lowest proportion of abstainers, the southern Bible Belt states the highest. There are also wide differences in the rates of alcohol abuse among ethnic groups, with Jews and Italians showing far less dangerous drinking than the Irish.

The levels of consumption in colonial America have never been surpassed; for eighteenth-century Americans alcohol was considered safer and healthier than water. During the nineteenth century per-capita alcohol consumption declined from the astronomical rates of the colonial period. From 1850 to 1914 the per-capita consumption hovered around two gallons. Consumption decreased markedly during Prohibition, but since 1946 it has risen steadily to about 2.7 gallons per capita (Gerstein 1981; Malin et al. 1982) (see table 1.1). Per-capita alcohol consumption has increased approximately 35 percent since the

Table 1.1.   Alcohol Consumption per Capita 1950–86
(Gallons per Capita)

	Wine	Beer	Spirits
1950	.89	16.85	1.25
1960	.88	15.07	1.30
1970	1.25	18.48	1.82
1980	2.08	24.27	1.98
1986	2.42	23.98	1.63

Source: Distilled Spirits Council of the United States

early 1960s but has increased only slightly and perhaps has leveled off since the early 1970s. While wine drinking has increased somewhat, there has been a steady decline in the consumption of whiskey and other spirits. Today, in comparison with other Western societies, Americans are not problem drinkers. In per-capita alcohol consumption we rank far below the Italians, French, Portuguese, and Germans. Nevertheless, per capita, Americans consume more alcoholic beverages than they do milk; and the number of Americans either referring themselves or being referred by others to alcohol treatment programs has vastly increased over the past decade (Weisner and Room 1984).

While the other heavy-drinking countries consume most of their alcohol in beers and wines, Americans drink comparatively more whisky and other distilled spirits, although beer drinking exceeds the drinking of wine and spirits combined.

American alcohol consumption is unusual in the high percentage of abstainers in the adult population; approximately one-third of the population abstains completely, female abstainers (42 percent) outnumbering male abstainers (27 percent) by about three to two. Another third of the population reports drinking, on average, fewer than three drinks per week. The next fifth or so of the population averages about two drinks per day. About the next tenth of all adults averages three or more drinks per day. Finally, the remaining 1–4 percent of the population averages ten or more drinks per day (U.S. Department of Health and Human Services 1983; Olson and Gerstein 1985). Thus the per-capita alcohol consumption statistic is primarily affected by the drinking behavior of the heaviest 5–10 percent of drinkers, who account for more than half of all alcoholic beverages consumed.

The Business of Alcohol

Not surprisingly, alcohol is big business. The industry is composed of brewers (beer), distillers (whiskey), and vintners (wine); importers and distributors; and a vast infrastructure of liquor stores, taverns, bars, and restaurants. Like any other industry, its goal is to sell as much of its product as possible. A principle marketing strategy is intensive advertising, linking alcoholic beverages to positive cultural symbols and psychological needs (Jacobson, Atkins, and Hacker 1983). Another marketing strategy is to make drinking and drinking environments as desirable, attractive, and competitive as possible. All told, Americans annually spend $60 billion on alcoholic beverages.

Liquor advertising links beverage alcohol consumption to sex, power, success, esteem, patriotism, thrills, risk taking, relaxation, and practically every other positively valued cultural symbol (see Jacobson, Atkins, and Hacker 1983). Alcohol is suggested as a solution to life's stresses and disappointments. The alcohol industry, supported by a body of advertising research, has long claimed that alcohol advertising is meant to compete for the patronage of existing drinkers (brand loyalty), not to bring new drinkers into the fold or to increase the consumption of present drinkers. Whatever is meant by "meant," it is hard to take this claim seriously; but even if we do there is no reason to believe that advertising is so surgically precise that its messages can carefully bypass certain segments of the population and strike only intended subaudiences.

There is also reason to doubt that the industry has such limited goals. To the contrary, it is quite likely that many or most beverage executives consciously strive to increase both the number of drinkers and their consumption levels. Wine producers are the most explicit about their expansionist goals. They have frequently expressed the view that wine is directly competitive with tea, coffee, and soda and that it should become a staple of the American refrigerator and dinner table. A new generation of light (i.e., carbonated) wines is being marketed in six-packs, cans, and cardboard containers. The advertising campaign accompanying this effort attempts to convince the public that wine drinking need not await special occasions or even meals—that wine should be drunk, like soda, as an accompaniment to recreation or simply to quench thirst.

The impact of advertising on problem drinkers raises the most serious concern. These are the industry's best customers. The heaviest-consuming 10 percent consume more than 50 percent of all beverage alcohol. It is extremely important for the industry that this group at least maintains its consumption level. This does not mean that evil men in the liquor industry *want* to produce alcoholics. What they *want* is to sell alcohol and to produce an impressive bottom line. Their best customers are heavy drinkers and people addicted to alcohol. It would be a disaster for the industry if all alcohol abusers became moderate drinkers.

Magazines compete for alcohol advertising dollars by stressing the number and percent of their readers who drink heavily. Consider the observation of Robert McDowell, Anheuser-Busch group marketing manager. In an article entitled "How We Did It," published in *Marketing Times,* he explained the beer company's strategy for staying on top: "We created a new media strategy to achieve a share of voice dominance within the industry and increased advertising expenditures fourfold with greater sports programming to reach the heavy beer drinker"

(Jacobson, Atkins, and Hacker 1983, P.32). As Robert Hammond, Director of the Alcohol Research Information Service, wryly notes, "if all 105 million drinkers of legal age consumed the official 'moderate' amount of alcohol, the industry would suffer a whopping 40 percent decrease in the sale of beer, wine, and distilled spirits, based on 1981 sales figures" (Jacobson, Atkins, and Hacker 1983 P. 25).

Youth and Alcohol

Americans grow up in a cultural environment where the transition from soda to alcohol is normal and expected and where alcohol is associated with good times, pleasure, and occupational and social success. Drinking alcohol marks a transition from youth to adulthood, so it is not surprising that many adolescents and teenagers are anxious to begin drinking.

Johnston, O'Malley, and Bachman's (1985) major study of high school students' drinking and drinking/driving practices surveyed students in seventy-five high schools in seven states. Students were asked to indicate how many days during the last month (excluding religious services) they drank any beer, wine, or liquor. The students reported that the frequency of their drinking increased throughout the high school years. By age fifteen the majority of both males and females drank on at least one occasion during a given month. More than one-quarter of male high school students age seventeen or older said that they drank on ten or more occasions in a given month. Two of five high school seniors reported that they had five or more drinks on a single occasion during the two weeks prior to the survey. A significant proportion of adolescent binge drinkers claimed that alcohol intoxication is a necessary part of their lives.

Young people are an important market for alcohol advertisers. Producers know that if they can recruit a young drinker they may have a lifetime customer. Therefore they advertise heavily in magazines appealing to young audiences (e.g., *National Lampoon, Ms, and Rolling Stone).* At least until very recently, many beer companies hired college students to serve as campus representatives, who arrange for beer at campus functions and sponsor youth events such as rock concerts and sports contests.

Television and Alcohol

Television programs (not to mention movies), which the average American watches for six hours per day, also project important messages about alcohol consumption. Dillon (1975) found that 80 percent of prime-time television shows contain alcohol events. One content analysis found that television programs portrayed drinking positively 60 percent of the time and negatively 40 percent of the time (McEwen and Hanneman 1974). A steady television watcher is exposed to a constant imagery of heavy drinking associated with sociability, success, power, sex, and coping. By way of contrast, he or she sees only an occasional public service announcement (PSA) on alcohol. In fact, McEwen and Hanneman (1974) found that not more than 3 percent of alcohol messages were PSAs and that they appeared at the rate of once every sixteen hours of viewing time.

More recently, Wallach, Breed, and Cruz (1987) carried out a content analysis of alcohol episodes that were shown on prime-time television. They found that while depictions of problem drinking are few,

the alcohol message is not neutral. The frequency of drinking acts and the high level of alcohol reflects a "wet" environment which exceeds that of the real world. Conversations are held over drinks, cocktail parties are the setting for action, and bars are commonly seen as background settings for talks and meetings. Alcohol is ubiquitous in television life. The strong suggestion conveyed to viewers is that alcohol is taken for granted, routine and necessary, that most people drink and that drinking is part of everyday life. The drinkers are frequently glamorous; for many viewers they are setting an example regarding lifestyle. (P. 37)

Problem Drinking

In 1978 the NIAAA estimated that, of all Americans who drank, 36 percent could be classified as "either being problem drinkers or having potential problems with alcohol" (10 percent and 26 percent respectively). This translated into approximately 9.3 million to 10 million people or about 7 percent of the American population over the age of eighteen. The same NIAAA report also suggested the possibility of an additional 3.3 million problem drinkers among fourteen-to-nineteen year olds.

Drinking problems span a continuum from minor and infrequent to uncontrolled drinking, associated with physical, psychological, and social problems. Some problem drinkers may be psychologically habituated to alcohol while others are physically addicted. For some people drinking problems are mostly physical, while for others they are mostly psychological or social. Almost all types of emotional, psychological, social, and family problems can be exacerbated by alcohol. Likewise, alcohol problems are exacerbated by other types of problems. Therefore, sorting drinkers into such categories as social, abusive, and alcoholic is necessarily subjective.[2] Nevertheless, in a 1982 Gallup survey one-third of persons interviewed said that alcohol had caused problems in their families.

Alcohol researchers now tend to regard alcoholism as a multidimensional problem with multiple causes; some abjure the term "alcoholic" altogether, preferring simply to speak of drinkers who suffer from lesser and greater physical, social, and psychological problems associated with alcohol. In any event, even those who find alcoholism a useful concept recognize that not all problem drinking is symptomatic of alcoholism but that alcoholism is always associated with physical, social, or psychological problems. Depending on how one defines alcoholism, 3–21 percent of all Americans will be afflicted at some point in their lives.[3] In his masterful analysis of alcohol abuse and alcoholism, Harvard psychiatrist George Vaillant (1983, P. 310) has written that

the course of alcoholism can be conceived broadly as comprising 3 linked stages. The first stage is heavy "social" drinking—frequent ingestion of 2 to 3 ounces of ethanol (3 to 5 drinks) a day for several years. This stage can continue asymptomatically for a lifetime; or because of a change in circumstances or peer group it can reverse to a more moderate pattern of drinking; or it can "progress" into a pattern of alcohol abuse (multiple medical, legal, social, and occupational complications), usually associated with frequent ingestion of more than 4 ounces of ethanol (8 or more drinks) a day. At some point in their lives, perhaps 10–15 percent of American men reach this second stage. Perhaps half of such alcohol abusers either return to asymptomatic (controlled) drinking or achieve stable abstinence. In a smaller number of such cases such alcohol abuse can persist intermittently for decades with minor morbidity and even become milder with time. Perhaps a quarter of all cases of alcohol abuse will lead to chronic alcohol dependence, withdrawal symptoms, and eventual need for detoxification. This last stage is reached by perhaps 3–5 percent of American adults, with men probably outnumbering women 3 or 4 to 1. This last stage is much less plastic than the earlier stages and most commonly ends in either abstinence or in social incapacity or death.

Health and Social Problems

Alcohol abuse is involved in a quarter of all admissions to general hospitals. Approximately thirty thousand Americans a year die of cirrhosis of the liver, a disease prevalent among alcoholics. In addition, heavy abusive drinking is involved in a high percentage of both violent crime and suicide (Ford et al. 1979; Collins 1981). It is frequently associated with spouse and child abuse (Hamilton and Collins 1981), although causality is impossible to establish. While drunk driving deaths have been given the most attention in recent years, an equivalent number of deaths occur in other types of alcohol-related accidents—for example, drownings, fires, and falls.

Alcohol abuse is not synonymous with alcoholism. It includes situational binge drinking and drunkenness associated with dangerous and destructive activity. In other words, occasional or even light drinkers may become a danger to themselves and others if they go on heavy drinking sprees in contexts where injuries are likely to occur.

The Disease Model of Alcohol Problems

In the early years of our republic alcohol was defined as good, but drunks and inebriates were considered dissolute and immoral (see Aaron and Musto 1981). The temperance movement came to define alcohol itself as evil and poisonous; thus, it was ultimately declared an illegal substance during Prohibition (Lender and Martin 1982). Since World War II the disease model of alcoholism has achieved great prominence (see Gusfield 1963; Levine 1978) through the efforts of a sociopolitical "alcohol movement" (see Wiener 1981). The disease model posits alcohol as a neutral substance, having the potential for good and ill. According to this paradigm, some unfortunate members of society, for reasons for which they are not responsible, have a special vulnerability toward alcohol disease or addiction. Like victims of other diseases they should be afforded empathy and treatment.

The scientific basis for this view is traceable to the work of E. M. Jellinek, who headed Yale University's Center of Alcohol Studies (later moved to Rutgers) during the 1950s. Jellinek theorized that alcoholism was a disease with a symptomatic progression of phases leading eventually from psychological to physical addiction. Jellinek, like Alcoholics Anonymous, argued that once addicted the alcoholic could not temper his drinking—that he had ceased to be able to exercise control over alcohol. Increasingly, alcoholics and people with alcohol problems have come to be defined as sick and in need of treatment. A great deal of research has demonstrated a genetic predisposition to alcoholism, eroding still further the idea of moral responsibility. A vast alcohol treatment network has developed around such institutions as the NIAAA, the National Council on Alcoholism, and Alcoholics Anonymous.

The power of the disease model of alcoholism is evidenced by the fact that the Rehabilitation Act of 1973, proscribing discrimination against the handicapped, has come to be interpreted to include alcohol abusers.

The trend in business and in government has been to treat alcohol-abusing employees as sick and ill; employee assistance programs for alcohol problems have become common in private and public employment settings (Beyer and Trice 1978). With the availability of federal funds and the mandatory health insurance coverage of alcoholism, alcoholism treatment programs have greatly expanded since the 1970s. Much of the growth is accounted for by private programs which, driven by a need to fill beds, have broadened the definition of people in need of treatment for alcohol and alcohol-related problems (Weisner and Room 1984).

Alcohol Treatment

It hardly comes as a surprise to learn that a majority of people arrested for drunk driving can plausibly be labeled alcoholics, alcohol abusers, or problem drinkers. Light drinkers are not likely to exceed prohibited BAC levels, at least not very often. While drunk drivers have been a boon for alcohol treatment programs, they have proved to be a difficult group to treat (Dunham and Mauss 1987). Coerced into treatment by the criminal court, they often have little motivation to change their drinking or drinking/driving behavior.

This is not the place for a lengthy review of alcohol treatment programs. Nevertheless, it is important to recognize that since the founding of NIAAA a huge alcohol treatment establishment and new professions devoted to the treatment of alcohol problems have developed (Wiener 1981). Unfortunately, while research and experimentation continue, there have been no breakthroughs in the search for a cure for alcoholism (Office of Technology Assessment 1983). No particular treatment has emerged as superior. As a 1976 editorial in the *Annals of Internal Medicine* stated, "the treatment of alcoholism has not improved in any important way in 25 years . . . only a minority of patients who enter treatment are helped to long-term recovery" (see also Polich, Armor, and Braiker 1980; Office of Technology Assessment 1983; Vaillant 1983).

Alcohol and the Law

Even the criminal law has been affected by changing conceptions of alcohol abuse (see Hall 1944). In 1966 two federal appeals court decisions (*Driver v. Hinnant*, 356 F.2d 761 [4th Cir. 1966], and *Easter v. District of Columbia*, 361 F.2d 50 [D.C. Cir. 1966]) recognized alcohol as a disease. In passing the 1968 Alcoholic Rehabilitation Act (P.L.

90-574), the first federal law dealing specifically with the treatment of alcoholism, Congress declared that "the handling of chronic alcoholics within the system of criminal justice perpetuates and aggravates the broad problem of alcoholism, whereas treating it as a health problem permits early detection and prevention of alcoholism, and effective treatment and rehabilitation, relieves police and other law enforcement agencies of an inappropriate burden that impedes their important work, and better serves the interests of the public." In 1970 this initiative was substantially expanded, with the enactment of the Comprehensive Alcohol Abuse and Alcoholism Prevention, Treatment, and Rehabilitation Act of 1970 (P.L. 91-616) and the establishment of the NIAAA.

The criminal law reform movement during the late 1960s and 1970s led to the decriminalization of public drunkenness in many states (see *Harvard Law Review* 1981);[4] the number of arrests dropped from more than two million annually to about one million. In the states that adopted the decriminalization model, public inebriates were taken to detoxification centers rather than to jails, and no prosecution ensued.[5]

Increasingly, alcohol problems have been offered as a defense to criminal charges.[6] Many prominent people, including, recently, Michael Deaver, former aide to President Reagan, have pleaded for leniency or even exoneration from criminal responsibility on the ground that their offenses were caused by drinking problems over which they lack control. While the criminal law does not recognize an alcoholism defense, many judges may consider alcohol problems a mitigating factor in sentencing.

Drugs Other than Alcohol

It is indicative of the extent to which alcohol abuse dominates our thinking about traffic safety that attention to the role of other drugs is usually ignored when discussing the drunk driving problem. It is as if the national preoccupation with waging wars against heroin, marijuana, cocaine, crack, amphetamines, barbiturates, hallucinogens, and other drugs, licit and illicit, is suspended when attention turns to traffic safety.

It hardly needs emphasizing that the United States is a drug-oriented society.[7] Millions of Americans are regular users of illicit drugs, and millions more are regular abusers of licit drugs. Infrequent and casual drug use is a regular part of the lives of additional millions. We know that drug abuse is a major problem in the workplace. Large numbers of people go to work under the influence of drugs or, even worse, use drugs while at work. This inevitably means that large numbers of people drive their vehicles while they are under the influence of drugs other than alcohol. Indeed, a not insignificant proportion of people who are arrested for drunk driving are, when appropriate test procedures are employed, found to be multidrug users who are operating under the influence of licit and illicit drugs *in addition to alcohol.*

There is no good reason, then, to isolate the alcohol abuse problem from the drug abuse problem. Alcohol is one of many drugs that cause, exacerbate, or accompany social problems of many kinds. Abuse of other drugs raises many of the same problems as does abuse of alcohol, often even more dramatically.

The American Ambivalence toward Alcohol

Americans are ambivalent on the subject of alcohol, as Lender and Martin (1982), P. 191) point out in their perceptive history of drinking in American:

American ambivalence toward the subject is undeniable. Perhaps 30 percent of the nation's citizens do not drink at all, yet others tolerate considerable latitude in drinking behavior. "Geting loaded" at a college fraternity party, for example, more often than not is simply shrugged off as an instance of adolescent conduct. Hard-drinking, even to the point of drunkenness, is still accepted as the sign of "being a real man" in some social circles. In other cases, drinkers who see nothing wrong with their own imbibing have doubts about it in others. Adults who routinely attend cocktail parties express deep concern over drinking among their teenage (or younger) children, ... Americans still place a severe social stigma on alcoholism. Thus, there is no clear sense of what the public really thinks or wants in regard to alcoholism prevention and control.

Americans are also ambivalent about drunk driving, and their ambivalence is reflected both in their laws and in their strategies of social control. This ambivalence is understandable, given the nature of the crime. In one respect drunk driving is a regulatory traffic offense, one of many forms of careless and irresponsible driving, while in another respect it is a criminal offense equivalent to other reckless behavior that threatens harm. Furthermore, there is no sharp dividing line, at least in the public mind, between criminal drunk driving and noncriminal drinking/driving. To the extent that drunk driving is perceived to include any drinking/driving, the public reaction is likely to be mild. Nevertheless, the public reaction to wanton episodes of drunk driving is likely to be marked by intense anger and strong condemnation.

Conclusion

America is an alcohol-rich society. While a significant minority of Americans are abstainers or light drinkers, alcoholic beverages play an omnipresent and salient role in American social life. The transition from soda to beer, wine, and spirits marks a significant transition from childhood to adulthood in American life.

There may be as many as ten million alcoholics and prealcoholics in American society, although the term "alcoholic" is extremely elastic and imprecise. Nevertheless, Americans suffer from a great many alcohol problems, of which drunk driving is only one. Moreover, even Americans who are not alcoholics or regular alcohol abusers may drink destructively or dangerously on infrequent occasions. When they do so, they may be even greater drunk driving risks than are long-term heavy-drinking alcohol abusers.

Americans are ambivalent toward alcohol. The temperance movement has vanished from the landscape. Even abstainers do not campaign to prohibit the drug altogether. Drunkenness, if not an admirable feature of personal and social life, tends to be accepted as a normal human weakness and treated leniently, if not humorously. People with severe alcohol problems are increasingly considered to be sick rather than bad. These trends and features of American life explain why there is a great deal of drinking/driving and drunk driving. Pressure to punish drunk drivers more harshly conflicts with the widespread view of alcohol abuse as a disease. Nevertheless, there are many residues of the old view. For example, the Veteran's Administration considers "primary alcoholism" (that which is not a manifestation of an acquired psychiatric disorder) to constitute "willful misconduct," making the alcoholic ineligible for certain benefits available to veterans with physical or mental disabilities. In upholding this policy , the Supreme Court noted: "We are unable to conclude that Congress failed to act in accordance [with the Rehabilitation Act] . . . given what the District of Columbia Circuit accurately characterized as 'a substantial body of medical literature that even contest the proposition that alcoholism is a disease, much less that it is a disease for which the victim bears no responsibility'" (Traynor v. Turnage, 99 L. Ed. 2d 618 [1988]).

2

Highway Safety as a Social Problem

Eliminating drunk driving and other forms of irresponsible vehicular behavior are not ends in themselves. The ultimate goal is to reduce human injury (and, to a lesser extent, to reduce property damage). If automobile collisions and crashes did not produce serious injuries, they would not constitute a major social problem. It is important to keep in mind that drunk driving is a type of irresponsible behavior that occurs in the context of a transportation system that experiences staggering property and human losses. Even if there were no drunk drivers, traffic safety would still be a social problem and traffic casualties would still be a human tragedy. This chapter canvasses the role of the automobile in American life, reviews the facts on traffic casualties, and examines the social control strategies that aim to limit the carnage.

The Automobile in American Life

Except in unusual settings such as New York City, driving is a necessity for full economic and social participation in American society. The suburbanization of America after World War II assumed ubiquitous car ownership.[1] The societal expectation is that practically everyone can and will own and drive a car. There are approximately 157 million licensed drivers in the United States, 174 million registered vehicles, and several million miles of roadways. Americans drive an estimated *1.8 trillion* miles per year (National Safety Council 1985). America is a nation on wheels. Its economy, social organization, and culture are heavily influenced (if not dominated) by the automobile and the highway transportation system.[2]

The automobile, motorcycle, pickup truck, and recreational vehicle are status symbols as well as means of transportation. Through the vehicles they own and the way they drive, Americans tell themselves and others who they are. Driving can be a pastime, even a sport. It is also a rite de passage, marking transition from adolescense to adulthood (see Lewis and Goldstein 1983). The speed and horsepower of the

15

automobile, which are far greater than are necessary for operational purposes, must resonate with certain instinctual hungers for power and control.

We tend to take the smooth operation of the highway transportation system for granted. Traffic moves according to well-known conventions and rules. We travel fifty-five miles an hour or more on busy highways only a short distance in front, behind, and alongside other vehicles, confident that our cars will function properly and that our fellow road users will act responsibly and according to the rules. Few of us pause to consider the extraordinary interpersonal trust on which the system depends. Participation in the highway transportation system actually creates unique interpersonal dependencies by linking together people of all adult ages and demographic groups. Responsible participation in the highway transportation system should be considered a major obligation of citizenship. Unfortunately, it is seldom viewed in this way.

The Magnitude of Driver and Vehicle Failure

All is not well in our autotopia. The highway transportation system exacts enormous societal costs. By far the most important is the physical injuries and property losses resulting from crashes and collisions. Since the first recorded automobile death in 1899, approximately 2.5 million Americans have died in vehicular accidents, far more than in all twentieth-century wars. Given the complexity, magnitude, potential dangers, and relentless occurrence of crashes and casualties, it is a tribute to our capacity for repressing unpleasant truths that we continue to think of automobile injuries as aberrational and perceive driving to be safe compared with other (actually safer) modes of transportation, such as airplanes.

In 1984, according to the 1985 edition of *Accident Facts*, an annual report prepared by the NSC, every twelve minutes an American died in a motor vehicle ("mechanically or electrically powered transport vehicles, including trucks, tractors, taxicabs, buses, motorcycles, motor scooters, and motor bikes") or in a collision with a motor vehicle. All told, there were 46,200 motor vehicle fatalities during the year, a figure roughly equivalent to the total American combat deaths in Vietnam from 1964 to 1973.

Although the number of fatalities is the popularly accepted indicator of motor vehicle casualties, that statistic hardly indicates the full magnitude of the carnage. The NSC estimates that in 1984 there were 18.8

million vehicular accidents ("any accident involving a motor vehicle in transport . . . that results in death, injury, or property damage"), involving approximately 33 million vehicles; 1.7 million people are estimated to have sustained "disabling injuries" (death, some degree of permanent impairment, or injuries preventing the victim from effectively performing his regular duties or activities for a full day beyond the day of the injury). The estimated cost of all accidents exceeded $47 billion.

In addition to being a leading cause of death for people under the age of thirty-seven, motor vehicle crashes and collisions constitute a leading cause of head, facial, and spinal injuries and of a host of other disfiguring and incapacitating injuries (Insurance Institute for Highway Safety 1982).[3] In 1960 Daniel Patrick Moynihan observed that motor vehicle accidents are "the nation's most serious public health problem"; with the possible exception of AIDS, that assessment remains true today.

Who is Killed? Where? When?

Our picture of the classic fatal or highly injurious motor vehicle accident is that of two passenger cars colliding head-on. However, only 16 percent of vehicular fatalities fall into this category. NHTSA'S Fatal Accident Reporting System (FARS) reveals that more than half of all fatalities result from single-vehicle crashes. Approximately 15 percent of all fatalities are pedestrians; 10 percent are motorcyclists (see fig. 2.1).

Vehicular deaths are not randomly distributed across all age and demographic groups. In 1984, as in every year since World War II, persons between the ages of fifteen and twenty-four had the highest traffic fatality rate, 60 percent greater than the rates for those aged twenty-five to forty-four. The death rate for the oldest drivers (aged seventy-five plus) is also disproportionately high. The fatality rate for men is roughly twice that for women.

Rates of fatal motor vehicle accidents are highest in the southern and south-central states. Whether fatality rates are calculated in terms of deaths per hundred thousand population, per ten thousand registered vehicles, or per one hundred million miles of driving (estimated from gasoline tax receipts), New Mexico and South Carolina head the list; New Jersey, Rhode Island, and Massachusetts have the lowest casualty rates.

Two-thirds of fatal motor vehicle accidents occur in rural areas. The largest urban areas have the lowest death rates, not surprising in light of the greater number of people who do not drive, the availability of public transportation, the slower pace of traffic, and the shorter distances between home and drinking establishments and between crash sites and emergency medical services. Most fatal accidents occur on secondary or tertiary roads, not on high-speed interstates which often dominate public perceptions of what constitutes dangerous traffic. In both urban and rural locales, the vehicle fatality rate is approximately four times higher at night than during the day, although the absolute numbers of night-time and daytime fatalities are almost equal. Saturday is the peak day for fatal motoring accidents; July and August are the peak months.

Trends in Highway Fatalities

The total number of traffic fatalities was approximately the same in 1984 as in 1964 (see fig. 2.2). During those twenty years, however, there was a good deal of oscillation. Fatalities peaked at 56,278 in 1972. Then they declined sharply to 45,853 in 1976. From that point, they steadily climbed to 53,534 in 1979. Thereafter, the trend was

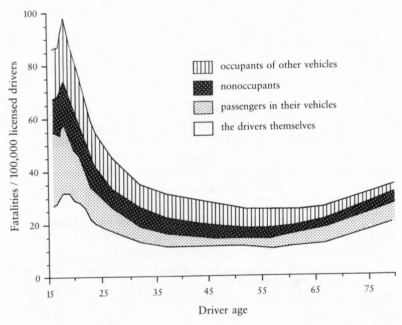

Figure 2.1. Fatalities associated with crashes of drivers of various ages, 1978. Source: Insurance Institute for Highway Safety.

again downward to 46,200 in 1984 and 45,700 in 1985.[4] Of course, over the twenty-year period 1964–84 the driving population increased considerably. Thus, the *rate* of traffic fatalities shows an impressive downward trend, as it has throughout the century. The rate of fatalities per one hundred million vehicle miles declined from 5.63 in 1964 to 2.68 in 1984. Likewise, the fatal motor vehicle accident rate per one hundred thousand people fell from 25.0 in 1964 to 19.6 in 1984, and the rate per ten thousand registered vehicles declined from 5.46 to 2.65. While traffic casualties constitute a *very serious* health problem, we may take comfort that the problem is not getting worse. Furthermore, unlike the rates for violent crime, American rates of traffic casualties are average for Western societies with high levels of vehicle ownership.

Many factors probably contribute to the decline in fatalities since 1972—for example, the aging of the population, the fifty-five-mile-per-hour speed limit,[5] improved emergency medical care, greater seat belt usage, the introduction of air bags, implementation of vehicle safety standards,[6] and drunk driving countermeasures. We must be wary of simplistic explanations. There is no satisfactory way to sort out all these factors. Therefore, we cannot determine whether a particular year's decrease is attributable to drunk driving countermeasures or to any other policy or program. It is also not possible to determine whether the decrease in fatalities reflects a decline in all traffic accidents. It is a sad commentary on the nation's commitment to highway safety that, until recently, there has been little effort to collect statistics on nonfatal vehicular accidents.[7] Quite possibly, fatal accident trends do not parallel nonfatal accident trends, since the former are uniquely affected by improved emergency medical care, seat belt usage, and vehicle design.

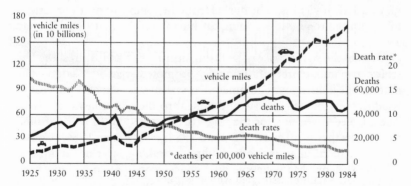

Figure 2.2. Travel, deaths, and death rates.

Social Control of Traffic

Reducing traffic casualites is an enormous challenge. The public tends to associate social control of traffic with improving drivers' skills and changing the attitudes and behavior of careless and irresponsible drivers. This is surely an important—but not the only or necessarily the most efficient—social control strategy. Thus, casualties can be reduced by (1) preventing crashes or (2) preventing injuries sustained in crashes. Crashes can be prevented by safer driving, better-designed vehicles, and safer roads. Injuries can be prevented or reduced in severity by more crashworthy vehicles, more crashworthy roads (i.e., roads with impact-absorbing crash barriers rather than trees and poles), and better emergency medical services.

Safer Cars

While recognizing human error in vehicular crashes, the safer-cars paradigm emphasizes crash and injury prevention. As early as the 1930s and 1940s various physicians and safety specialists argued that serious and fatal vehicle injuries were caused by a second collision, that between the vehicle occupant and the vehicle interior. Accident studies showed that most fatalities resulted from punctures and cuts caused by fixed steering columns and sharp objects on the dashboard. On collision, vehicle occupants were hurled against these dangerous surfaces with great force. Various features of the automobile contributed to the destructiveness of this second collision; for example, seats that detached from the vehicle floor moved forward with the seat's occupant and added to the force of the collision with the windshield and dashboard. Doors with weak locking mechanisms permitted many accident victims to be hurled from their autos to death or serious injury on the road (see Haddon, Suchman, and Klein 1964; Eastman 1984).

Despite the significance of such engineering design features, the Detroit car manufacturers traditionally promoted style over safety. The automobile industry was dominated by stylists who strived each year to produce new models that would appeal to the consumer's fantasies. The engineers working for the"Big Three" were told to work around the designs they were given (Eastman 1984; Halberstam 1986). Consequently, American automobiles had poor braking, steering, and transmission systems. Many people died in accidents that could have been avoided if vehicles had been designed to maximize maneuverability and safety.

The market apparently did not create an effective demand for safety innovations because drivers (1) tend to underestimate the likelihood of an accident and (2) are underinformed about the effectiveness of various safety features.[8] The manufacturers were inhibited from voluntarily introducing safety features because (1) it is difficult to do such innovating piecemeal and (2) advertising and marketing were based on the image of driving as liberating and exciting, not as dangerous and warranting concern.

Although various senators and congressmen, particularly Representative Kenneth Roberts (D.-Ala.), began calling for federal automobile safety regulation during the mid-1950s,[9] it was not until the mid-1960s that Senators Abraham Ribicoff and Gaylord Nelson and others were able to mobilize congressional action. Even these efforts would likely not have borne fruit (see Eastman 1984) had it not been for the appearance of Ralph Nader's (1964) pathbreaking book *Unsafe at Any Speed* and, perhaps more important, the revelation that General Motors had hired detectives to investigate Nader's private life in order to discredit him.

Nader's book showed how poor engineering in the Corvair resulted in large numbers of accidents and how General Motors had tried to suppress the truth about the car's safety defects. Nader's book and one by Jeffrey O'Connell and Arthur Myers (1966) blasted the automobile manufacturers for their rejection of automobile safety. These consumer advocates found a responsive public in the mid-1960s, and automobile safety moved to the top of the social problems agenda. Detroit's automobile magnates were summoned before Congress, and, when they admitted spending only a little more than $1 million a year for safety research in an industry that generated billions of dollars in profits, they were sharply criticized. As then Assistant Secretary of Labor (now Senator) Daniel Patrick Moynihan (1966, P. 15) said after listening to the manufacturing executives defend their resistance to demands for greater industry emphasis on safety, "there is a resistance to reasonableness in this field that is at once baffling and revealing. It was soon enough evident that the executives and engineers in the industry simply would not comprehend the ideas of designing their machines so that the injuries that result from accidents would be minimized."

The hearings led to passage of two historic safety laws in 1966.[10] They established two agencies, the National Traffic Safety Agency and the National Highway Safety Bureau, later merged to become the NHTSA. Congress delegated NHTSA authority to promulgate highway and automobile safety standards. Dr. William Haddon, a leading crusader for automobile safety, served as head of the agency from September 1967 until February 1969. The federal legislation also required the states to establish highway safety programs approved by the secretary of transportation, who was delegated authority to issue uniform guidelines in such safety-related areas as driver's education, traffic control, vehicle registration, and vehicle inspection.

NHTSA required the manufacturers to meet various safety standards, provided grants for research, and stimulated the auto safety movement. Cars slowly became safer, although battles continued.[11] During the 1970s a major controversy between safety advocates and the manufacturers swirled around seat belts and air bags.[12] The manufacturers had bitterly resisted the idea of standard seat belts as far back as the 1950s. After losing that battle, they fought the buzzer-interlock system and then the proposal to fit all vehicles with passive restraints (either seat belts or air bags that operate without voluntary efforts of the drivers and passengers). This controversy has dragged on for more than a decade and is not yet fully resolved.

In 1972 NHTSA adopted an amendment to Standard 208, which required installation of "complete passive protection" on automobiles manufactured after August 15, 1975. The rule was modified and delayed a number of times. In 1981, however, the Reagan administration turned against air bags,[13] and one year later it rescinded Standard 208. Several insurance companies (led by Aetna) challenged this action. In 1983 the U.S. Supreme Court found the rescission arbitrary and capricious and ordered NHTSA to reconsider.[14]

In July 1984 NHTSA issued a new rule requiring phased introduction of automatic restraints, beginning in 1986 (later delayed to 1989); however, the rule would be rescinded if two-thirds of the nation's population were covered by mandatory seat belt laws. Several insurance companies immediately challenged this new rule on the ground (among others) that it was arbitrary and capricious. The District of Columbia Circuit Court of Appeals in 1986 held that the case was not ripe for adjudication because "on the record before us, it appears singularly unlikely that the passive restraint standard will be rescinded by 1989".[15] The court so concluded because none of the existing state mandatory seat belt laws conformed to the standards the Secretary had promulgated. In fact, some states deliberately drafted their seat belt laws to be nonconforming so that they would not contribute to rescission of the passive restraint requirement.[16] The ultimate resolution of this single decision will probably affect more lives than all of the driver-oriented strategies now being implemented and proposed.

Social Control of Drivers

The sociologist Morris Janowitz (1976) once wrote that the most revolutionary aspect of the French Revolution was the arming of the masses. In a sense it was also revolutionary for a modern society to permit all its citizens to own and operate a several-ton vehicle capable of speeds up to and exceeding 100 miles per hour. Universal automobile ownership provides every member of the society with an instrument capable of causing injury or death. Just as the highway transportation system necessarily generates mass interpersonal trust, it also generates pervasive interpersonal threat.

Fortunately, in the mass operation of automobiles, personal as well as social controls are operative. Drivers obviously have strong self-interest in driving safely. If traffic rules are perceived to be associated with safety, they will be followed by most drivers most of the time. Furthermore, most people will follow traffic rules simply because they are rules and because the motivation to do otherwise is small.

Nevertheless, drivers violate traffic laws because they (1) do not know the rules, (2) are not capable of following the rules, (3) inadvertently fail to follow the rules, or (4) consciously choose to disobey rules.[17] We may assume that most drivers know most of the important traffic rules, although they may be uncertain about such matters as the number of car lengths that must be kept between vehicles or the precise number of alcoholic drinks necessary to reach the prohibited BAC level.

We can be less confident about the physical and mental capacity of all drivers to follow the rules at all times. There are millions of drivers who suffer from one type of disability or another (including alcoholism and drug addition) and millions more who are elderly and infirm. There is no viable medical or psychological screening system to identify unskilled and unreliable drivers who should be removed from the transportation system; nor is it clear how they could be successfully removed even if they were identified.

Immature and irresponsible drivers may be an even greater danger than infirm drivers. Some turn mundane driving into a fateful test of skill and luck, deliberately taking all sorts of risks—for example, engaging in real or imagined races or passing on blind curves. A small proportion of drivers are antisocial persons who have a defiant attitude toward traffic rules. Perhaps they wish to demonstrate to both themselves and others their daring and bravado, or perhaps they are angry, alienated, depressed, or mentally ill. Whatever the reason, they are not committed, even in principle, to the highway safety system and needless to say, do not feel a sense of obligation to fellow road users (see Goldstein and Susmilch 1982). Many members of this group may be involved in other forms of criminality and deviant behavior.

As most of us know from personal experience, even knowledgeable, capable, and mature drivers commit driving infractions on occasion. Over the course of years of daily driving, there are occasions when we fail to see other cars, pedestrians, signs, or lights and times when we drive too fast, corner too sharply, pass improperly, and drive too close to other vehicles. Minor crashes and collisions are such a common part of our lives that we speak of them as "accidents," indicating lack of fault or responsibility. One of the difficulties of enforcing traffic laws— and of properly prosecuting serious traffic offenders—is our inability to make distinctions between no- or low-fault "accidents" and high-fault reckless endangerments.

Social Control Strategies

Social control strategies for influencing driver behavior include education and exhortation, licensing, and policing. Exhortations to drive safely and responsibly are as old as the motorcar itself. The driver education movement dates back to the 1930s. It has been a favorite program of the automobile manufacturers and of Congress and NHTSA. Many states have encouraged teenagers to enroll in these courses by rewarding successful completion with an opportunity to obtain a license at an earlier age. Unfortunately, several researchers have found that the driver's education courses, when coupled with earlier licensure, produce more rather than fewer highway casualties (Robertson and Zador 1978; Insurance Institute for Highway Safety 1987b).

Other social control strategies rely on policing. Most states have special police forces (highway patrols or state police) assigned primarily to traffic duties. And within major metropolitan police agencies there is typically a traffic division. In many communities, when police are not answering calls they engage in traffic patrol as a fallback activity (Gardiner 1969).

The police strive to achieve social control of traffic in several ways. First, they actually control or direct traffic when, for example, they are stationed at busy intersections. Second, they stop, investigate, issue summonses to and arrest drivers whom they observe violating traffic laws. This constitutes a truly massive effort. It is estimated that the police write approximately sixty million traffic summonses annually (Economos and Steelman 1983). I have not seen any figures for traffic-related arrests, but, considering that annual drunk driving arrests number almost two million, the total number must be staggering. Third, the police exercise social control through deterrence. They consciously aim to create the impression of ubiquitous police surveillance, which will motivate drivers to follow the traffic rules. Sometimes this strategy is even implemented through the use of dummy or decoy (driverless) police cars or threatening warning signs. Roadblocks have become an increasingly popular enforcement strategy.

If the police issue a traffic citation or make an arrest, it is up to the courts to adjudicate the case. The legal status of traffic law has been a lively issue for legal scholars. There are those who point to its close connection with the criminal law and who therefore emphasize the obligation to provide traffic defendants with full criminal procedure protections. Other commentators emphasize the essentially regulatory aspect of traffic rules and advocate treating traffic cases (except for the most serious) through administrative mechanisms (see Force 1979). American practice is mixed. Some jurisdictions use administrative traffic courts to process traffic cases; others utilize the lowest courts of general jurisdiction.

The usual sanction meted out in traffic cases is a small fine, although in serious cases, such as drunk or reckless driving, a jail term can be imposed. In theory, the small fine will motivate drivers to operate more carefully in the future and will deter the general public from violating traffic laws. In addition to being fined, in moderate and serious traffic cases the violator is assigned "points" by the state department of motor vehicles. If the driver accumulates enough points within a certain period of time, the department can suspend or revoke his or her license.

In theory, license suspension and revocation are serious sanctions; the driver whose license is suspended or revoked is removed from the highways and prevented from violating the law again. Hundreds of thousands of licenses are suspended and revoked each year. In practice, license suspensions and revocations are often ignored. These violations only come to light if the police, for some reason, stop the driver and check the status of his license through the centralized motor vehicles records system. Even if the violation comes to light, there is no assurance that the violator will be prosecuted and, if prosecuted, punished. A California study (Finklestein and McGuire 1971) some years ago found that "only 21% of the [drunk] drivers apprehended during the period of their suspension were convicted of driving while suspended. This is due to the officer failing to cite the driver for this violation, the Department of Motor Vehicles not making the record available to the court, or the court not taking its action. This failure to control and identify problem drinkers reflects the inadequacies of drivers records and lack of enforcement of the one license/one record concept" (Tarrants 1984).

Safer Roads

If all blind turns, poor or nonexistent lighting, undivided traffic, trees, poles, and other roadside obstacles could be eliminated, there would be far fewer crashes of all sorts, particularly deadly crashes (see Fitzpatrick et al. 1975). On all highways built with federal funds federal standards pertaining to such matters as width of lanes, guardrails, lighting, shoulders, and markings are applicable. These roads typically divide traffic moving in opposite directions and eliminate all potentially deadly fixtures from the sides of the highway. No wonder these highways are far safer than secondary and tertiary roads, which are disproportionately the site of serious and fatal accidents. That no interest groups or constituencies have emerged to advocate the reconstruction of local roads reinforces the point that the dominant tendency in the American approach to social problems is to search for guilty parties, in the case of traffic casualties either irresponsible drivers or greedy, callous manufacturers.

Conclusion

Traffic safety is a major challenge in a modern society organized around universal motor vehicle ownership. Nevertheless, forty thousand to fifty thousand traffic casualties per year have not triggered a great deal of national concern, at least when compared with the concern shown for problems regarded as "serious", such as "crime." For decades there seemed to be collective repression of the human toll being exacted by our transportation system. Even now, the chances of involvement in a serious traffic crash tend to be vastly underestimated while the chances of being a violent crime victim are vastly exaggerated.[18] No doubt there is much greater unconscious fear of the gruesome stranger assaulting us or breaking into our homes than of fellow road users plowing into our cars. The attempt by citizens' action groups to redefine drunk driving as a serious offense and drunk drivers as serious criminals encounters resistance stemming from a deeply rooted social psychology of risk.

In the next chapter we will examine the overlap between the drunk driving problem and the traffic safety problem, but it is well to remember that the matter of traffic casualties is one of the nation's most serious public health problems—and that it would be so even if there was no drunk driving. The recent and passionate effort to make war on drunk drivers reflects our society's basic approach to social problems: criminalize wrongdoing and mount an intensive law enforcement effort to identify and punish wrongdoers. Environmental and technological strategies such as road reconstruction and air bags attract far less popular attention and support than do moral crusades; yet, in the final analysis, their payoff might be greater.

3

Drunk Driving and Traffic Casualties

Since drunk driving has become a prominent American social problem, the measure of its importance has been the number and percentage of traffic fatalities and casualties attributable to drunk drivers. The higher these statistics, the more important the problem. Producing a summary statistic that states that intoxication causes X percent of all traffic accidents or fatalities is a highly complex undertaking, requiring many questionable assumptions. There has been a great deal of loose talk and exaggeration. But to criticize loose and exaggerated claims is not to deny that drunk driving is a very serious problem. This chapter first explains how drunk driving's role in traffic crashes has been exaggerated. It then discusses the methodological difficulties of attributing some portion of traffic casualties to drunk driving. Finally, it discusses the most promising efforts to estimate the magnitude of this social problem.

Exaggerating the Role of Drunk Driving as a Cause of Traffic Casualties

The U.S. Department of Transportation's 1968 report *Alcohol and Highway Safety* is a seminal document in the emergence of drunk driving as an American social problem. It gave high visibility and, perhaps more important, a federal imprimatur to concern with the drunk driving problem. Its conclusions have been recounted, often incorrectly (see Zylman 1974), in countless publications and speeches, sometimes without reference to the original study. Richard Zylman (1974) has shown that the data on which the report was based are questionable and that the report's use of those data is dubious.

Chapter II of the report was devoted to "Alcohol in Crashes and Violations." The staff did not carry out its own research but attempted to summarize the research literature. Because all studies were based on small, geographically narrow samples, the staff's strategy was to lump them all together. Its principal conclusion was succinctly stated:

"When information from crashes of all types in which drivers are fatally injured is grouped together, it becomes apparent that almost half of the drivers were found to have blood alcohol concentrations of 0.10 or greater."[1]

The references cite the drivers in four studies: (1) 145 drivers in Baltimore, Maryland, 1951–56; (2) 485 drivers in Dade County, Florida, 1956–65; (3) 820 drivers in New Jersey, 1961–63; and (4) 2,794 drivers in California, 1965–66. I have not seen the last three of these studies and fear that they have long since disappeared from repositories available even to diligent researchers. We do not know anything about these studies, especially about how the samples were drawn. Were *all* fatally injured drivers tested or just a subsample disproportionately likely to be drunk?[2] The Baltimore study was reported in the *Journal of Forensic Science* (Freimuth, Watts, and Fisher 1958). While the report claims that this study presents data on the number of fatally injured drivers with BAC greater than 0.10, the published study actually presents no such statistic—or even any data from which such a statistic could be calculated.

The report's conclusion speaks only of "drivers"—and more precisely should have spoken of *dead* drivers. There was no sound justification for applying the ratio of drunk dead drivers to all dead drivers to fatally injured passengers, pedacyclists, and pedestrians.[3] Certainly, drunk pedestrians who died in collisions with sober drivers should not be counted as fatalities attributable to drunk driving. Nevertheless, once the 1968 report was published, anti–drunk driving advocates, journalists, and commentators almost universally reported that drunk drivers were responsible for the deaths of twenty-five thousand people (or more!) a year. It was hardly ever pointed out that the *majority* of persons killed by drunk drivers were the drunk drivers themselves and that a high proportion of vehicle passengers killed in alcohol-related crashes were the drunk drivers' drinking companion. In any event, since the total number of traffic fatalities steadily decreased from the early 1970s, 50 percent of total traffic fatalities was substantially less than twenty-five thousand.

In his book, *The Culture of Public Problems* (1981), the sociologist Joseph Gusfield, building on the work of alcohol researcher Richard Zylman, showed how the magnitude of the drunk driving problem has been consistently exaggerated, research studies distorted, and press releases turned into "facts"—in short, how a social problem was created. He linked the social construction of the drunk driving problem to negative societal attitudes toward alcohol abuse.

Zylman's and Gusfield's analyses are both very useful. Policy-making can benefit if policymakers appreciate the tenuousness of social facts and are thereby more willing to reexamine their assumptions and consider new ways of conceiving and tackling old problems. Nevertheless, it would be wrong to take from these studies the conclusion that drunk driving is not really a serious problem. It is commonly the case in the United States that a particular social problem is real and significant even though its magnitude has been exaggerated by those seeking to promote its position on the social problems agenda.

Epistemological and Methodological Problems in Estimating the Magnitude of the Drunk Driving Problem

Epistemological Problems: The Meaning of "Cause"

What are we looking for when we inquire into the cause(s) of traffic casualties? What assumptions do we bring with us when we ask this question? What hypotheses are foremost in our minds, and which ones have we ignored or ruled out? Are we interested in the make, model, year, condition, and mileage of crash involved motor vehicles? Do we want a complete mechanic's report on the brakes, steering, and engine? Have similar models of cars been involved in a disproportionate number of such accidents? Have other serious accidents occurred at the same place or in places with similar turns, curves, lights, markings, signs, or speed limits? Should we settle for anything less thorough than the kind of investigation carried out for airplane crashes? In practice, motor vehicle accidents are not subject to questions such as these. The prevailing paradigm explaining motor vehicle crashes focuses on driver culpability, and driver culpability has come to be associated with alcohol.

While most of us recognize that traffic accidents may involve factors relating to weather, roads, vehicles, and traffic controls, our instinct is to search for a single at-fault driver. For example, under "causes of accidents," *Accident Facts,* an annual summary of accidental deaths and injuries published by the NSC, observes that "in most accidents, factors are present relating to the driver, the vehicle, and the road, and it is the interaction of these factors which often sets up the series of events which culminates in the mishap." Yet *Accident Facts* presents only data on "the principal kinds of improper driving which were factors in accidents." "Speed too fast" is the leading culprit, followed by "failed to yield," "passed stop sign," and "followed too closely."

Most motor vehicle laws proscribe "first-order" driver failures—those involving the violation of specific traffic rules. It is an offense—or, more accurately, "an infraction"—to cross the double yellow line, to fail to halt at a stop sign or red light, or to fail to yield a right-of-way. For good measure, there is the catchall offense of "reckless driving."[4]

It is possible to seek a deeper explanation for a crash by examining second-order driver failures: why did the driver fail to stop, or why did he exceed the speed limit? What sort of answer are we looking for? The driver may claim that he did not see the sign or was not thinking about his speed. But we still may not be satisfied and still may feel the need to press further, consciously or subconsciously searching for an explanation such as one of the following: (1) the driver was distracted by a blasting radio or adoring companion; (2) the driver was determined to get home as quickly as possible; (3) the driver was emotionally distraught; or (4) the driver was intoxicated.

Under our prevailing traffic accident paradigm, we tend to feel that we have arrived at a satisfactory explanation when we discover that the driver was intoxicated or "drinking." In fact, the first question that we ask when we hear that a fatal accident has occured is, Was the driver drunk? In the public mind, fatal traffic accidents have come to be associated with drunks, the same way that street crime has come to be associated with minority youth. However, while the latter is often criticized as an inaccurate stereotype, the former has become more and more of a politically and socially legitimated dogma. Thus it seems almost heretical to point out that the majority of traffic fatalities and the vast majority of nonfatal crashes are attributable to something other than intoxication. There is practically no scholarly or political interest in non-alcohol-related reasons for traffic crashes. Even the possible role of illicit drugs in traffic crashes has been ignored, despite the massive attention that illicit drugs receive in other contexts. In other words, we have only two explanations for the massive number of traffic casualties that occur in the United States: "alcohol" and "other." "Other" stimulates little, if any, social or political interest.

It is important to question standard assumptions about alcohol's role in traffic crashes. If a crash-involved driver had been *drinking* prior to the accident, should we assume that he was *intoxicated* or that he *caused the accident?* Even if the driver *was intoxicated* and *caused the accident,* there may be no causal connection between the intoxication and the crash.

Why do we feel satisfied that we have arrived at a final explanation when we discover that one of the drivers in a traffic crash was intoxicated? We could press on. *Why* was the driver intoxicated? Did he not take driving seriously enough? Did his friends urge, beseech, and goad him toward inebriation? Did a tavern owner ply him with drinks? Had he just lost his job, broken up with his girlfriend, or suffered the loss of a close friend or relative? Is he a chronic alcoholic, a psychotic, or a confirmed criminal? Pressing still further we might ask, Why did the driver *drive* under the influence? Was he too intoxicated to know he was driving? Did he not know he was intoxicated? Despite his awareness of being intoxicated, did he believe he could drive safely? Was he suicidal? Our prevailing paradigm takes no account of the reasons for second-order driver failures.[5]

The prevailing paradigm also ignores questions about the environmental circumstances that allow, facilitate, or encourage second-order failure, particularly driving under the influence of drugs or alcohol. Are bars and restaurants inaccessible by public transportation? Is drinking—and even drinking/driving—promoted by advertising and promotional efforts? Clearly, an explanation that satisfies a police officer or a court should not necessarily satisfy a psychiatrist, sociologist, or highway safety specialist.

Moreover, by concentrating so intently on the cause of the crash, have we not overlooked something just as (if not more) significant, the cause of the *injury?* If traffic crashes caused no injuries or property damage, they would be of no more societal concern than electric bumper cars colliding with one another at the amusement park. Injury and death generally result from a second collision, that between the driver or passenger and his vehicle's interior. Might we say that poor packaging of the driver caused the injury or death? Might we attribute the injury to the driver's failure to buckle his seat belt? Might we even say that the ambulance's tardiness or the emergency room's incompetence caused the fatality? There is no right answer to these questions. What we will accept as a cause depends on our ideologies, preconceptions, paradigms, and policy options.

Methodological Problems

In trying to estimate the role of alcohol in traffic accidents, we would ideally like to know the role of alcohol intoxication in *all* traffic accidents, from the most trivial to those that are fatal. There is no reason to assume that alcohol plays the same role in traffic accidents of all seriousness levels. For example, fatal accidents are likely to differ from other accidents in many ways. They are more likely to involve driving at night, males, and single-vehicle crashes—in short, they are more likely to involve drunk drivers. Fender benders might well be associated with a different constellation of variables.

Unfortunately, we lack reliable data on nonfatal crashes. It seems incredible that, until very recently, there has been no governmental effort to collect data on nonfatal traffic accidents. The National Accident Sampling System (NASS), which was launched in 1979, may someday produce reliable data on a representative sample of all accidents *reported to the police*. However, even these data will not be representative, because there is wide variation in the types of accidents that are reported to the police in different states and localities. The coding of accident data by so many police officers around the country will necessarily involve a great deal of subjectivity. Most important for our inquiry here, since drivers involved in nonfatal accidents are seldom tested for BAC, the NASS data will not provide an opportunity for accurately estimating the role of alcohol in each traffic accident category.

NASS does offer estimates of alcohol involvement in accidents, but the data are unreliable for several reasons. First, the sample consists of accidents reported by police, and police reporting practices are notoriously diverse. Second, the category "serious" accidents is not clearly defined. Third, data on alcohol involvement is based on police statements as well as on chemical tests. For what it is worth, NASS's 1979–80 report found that about 11 percent of all accidents in 1979–80 *involved alcohol*. This proportion increased as the severity of the accident increased; 17.4 percent of all injury-producing accidents and 28.6 percent of serious injury accidents involved alcohol.

Practically all drunk-driving researchers have focused on fatal accidents (but see Borkenstein et al. 1974) because of the problems of obtaining adequate data on nonfatal accidents. Fatal traffic accident data are also of greatest public concern and political significance. Prior to the implementation of FARS in 1975, there was no federal effort to gather data on fatal traffic crashes. The NSC was the only organization involved in counting fatalities, and it relied on local police reports. However, the NSC's annual report, *Accident Facts,* did not rely on police reports in estimating that 50 percent of all traffic fatalities were alcohol related; it drew this statistic from the same inadequate studies that the 1968 report *Alcohol and Highway Safety* relied on. Consequently, the statistic remained unchanged from year to year.

FARS, operated and maintained by NHTSA's National Center For Statistics and Analysis, has clearly been a major step forward in our nation's ability to measure and analyze fatal traffic accidents. Nevertheless, a careful look at the 1984 FARS report demonstrates the difficulty of establishing or estimating the percentage of alcohol-related accidents and the number of drunk driving fatalities. FARS data are gathered on accidents that (1) occurred on a roadway customarily open to the public, (2) resulted in the death of a person within thirty days of the accident and, (3) were not the result of natural disasters such as earthquakes, floods, or torrential rains. FARS staff do not collect fatal accident data themselves; they supply forms to be filled in by state analysts working from local police reports.

The FARS report for 1984 points out that alcohol-related data on fatally injured drivers is presented because "surviving drivers are not routinely tested for alcohol in most states." In fact, even dead drivers are not routinely tested in some states; nationwide, only 63 percent of *fatally injured drivers* were tested for alcohol in 1984. Rather than attempt to treat the 63 percent as representative of all dead drivers, FARS's 1984 report presents data from fifteen "good reporting states," each of which conducted chemical blood tests for alcohol on approximately 85 percent of fatally injured drivers.[6] The FARS report treats the tested 85 percent as representative of the entire population of fatally injured drivers, although there is no convincing reason to do so. For this sample of fatally injured drivers, BAC was 0.01–0.05 for 5.2 percent, 0.06–0.09 for 5.5 percent, and 0.10 or more for 43.3 percent.

What can we conclude from the FARS data? In 1984 there were 44,241 traffic fatalities; 36,271 were vehicle occupants, and 7,970 were nonoccupants. Of the occupants, 25,582 were drivers and 10,689 were passengers. The majority of occupants (17,805) died in single-vehicle crashes, but FARS does not break down single-vehicle fatalities by drivers and passengers.

The FARS report does not attempt to estimate the number of people likely to have been killed by drunk drivers. It simply presents BAC levels for driver and pedestrian fatalities. This modesty is well advised; it cannot confidently be determined what percentage of all traffic fatalities are attributable to drunk drivers, and to attempt to do so would require many additional assumptions and quesses.

The Problem of Assigning Fault

FARS does not attempt to estimate the number or portion of fatalities *caused by intoxication.* To do so would require resolution of some enormously difficult practical and philosophical problems, especially in assigning fault and determining intoxication.

A police officer receives a message that a fatal crash has occurred on Route 1. Arriving at the scene, she finds that a crowd has gathered. Two badly damaged cars are blocking traffic. Several obviously injured people are sitting or lying beside the wreck. A few are sobbing hysterically, likely in shock. A gathering crowd must be kept back. The injured must be immediately cared for and removed to a hospital. The road must be cleared of debris so that traffic flow can resume.

The police officer did not witness the crash. Should she assume that one driver was at fault and that the other was faultless? It is possible that neither driver was at fault (a car might have malfunctioned or the road might have been slippery) or that both drivers were at fault (either equally or unequally).

Determining who was solely or predominantly at fault is no easy task. Even sorting out drivers and passengers may be difficult. The crash victims may be too badly injured or too distraught to be interviewed. They may refuse to answer questions. They may answer deceptively, fearing criminal or civil liability. There may be no witnesses. If there are witnesses, they may be unwilling to talk about what they saw. If they do give information, it may be inaccurate.

The police officer might or might not issue a traffic ticket charging one or both drivers with a traffic law violation. In a surprisingly high percentage of vehicle crashes, no tickets are issued. In any event, a traffic code conviction is not equivalent to proof of causation. It is one thing to say that a driver was speeding; it is another to conclude that he caused the accident. Even if the officer did not issue a ticket, she may express a judgment about fault when filling out NHTSA's accident forms.

If we are unwilling to accept the subjective judgments of police officers concerning driver responsibility for fatal crashes, what alternatives exist? In the final analysis, only a court, after hearing extensive testimony, some of it from experts, is empowered to determine authoritatively who was at fault in a traffic crash. Even then, can we be sure that a court has decided correctly? A legal understanding of an accident may differ from a highway safety researcher's understanding. For one thing, the court's decision depends on the law of torts. Some jurisdictions force the judge (or jury) to label one driver at fault even if the other driver was also at fault, albeit slightly less so. Other states, following the doctrine of comparative negligence, allow the judge or jury to find both parties at fault to some extent.[7] This is a good example of how paradigms create reality. In a traditional tort law jurisdiction, a driver might be held an innocent victim of a crash caused by someone else, while in a comparative negligence state the same individual might be held 49 percent responsible for the crash. Statistics developed in one jurisdiction would provide a view of the world very different from that provided by statistics developed in the other jurisdiction.

Research can hardly await judicial resolutions, which may take years. More important, very few crashes produce judicial fault determinations, because most disputes about liability for injuries sustained in traffic crashes are settled out of court. Should we be willing to assign fault to a party whose insurance company paid out something (anything) on claims arising from the accident, on the ground that this is an implicit admission of responsibility? Would drivers in states with no-fault automobile insurance laws (see Chapter 10) be labeled responsible or not responsible for their crashes?

The Problem of Determining Intoxication

When the emergency is over, the officer will fill out a stack of forms explaining what happened. A box with the notation "alcohol related" will be either checked or left blank, depending on the officer's percep-tions and impressions. At least until very recently when FARS launched its major effort to obtain BAC results on drivers involved in fatal acci-dents, it was by tabulating the check marks beside the boxes marked "alcohol related" that a precise-sounding statistic on the number and percentage of alcohol-related deaths was computed. Yet, there is a great deal of subjectivity in the police officers' judgments. A police officer might be mistaken in judging whether one of the drivers had been drinking at all. Several studies have shown that police officers are quite inaccurate in identifying drunk drivers even under nonemergency con-ditions (Johnson 1984). They are more likely to underestimate than to overestimate the presence of alcohol.[8] In any event, "drinking" does not mean "intoxicated," much less "impaired." Time and again, ana-lysts and activists concerned with drunk driving take police judgments averring the presence of alcohol to mean "drunk."

The best policy obviously would be to give each driver, alive or dead, a chemical test for alcohol. While not infallible, these tests eliminate the subjectivity of human observation; but they substitute an imperfect correlate of intoxication (see Chapter 5). Unfortunately (or, perhaps, fortunately), drivers cannot be involuntarily subjected to BAC tests unless there is probable cause to believe they were intoxicated at the time of the crash. The crash alone does not provide probable cause.[9] Furthermore, even if there is probable cause, a driver might refuse to take the test, fearing (quite rightly) that the evidence could be used against him in a serious criminal prosecution. While the Supreme Court has held that where probable cause exists blood can be extracted against the arrestee's will (*Schmerber v. California*, 384 U.S. 757 [1966]), most police officers and medical personnel resist the idea of holding the defendant down to get a blood sample, even when it is feasible to get the driver to a medical setting in time for blood to be extracted involuntarily.

Because it has not proved possible to obtain chemical tests from more than a minority of *surviving drivers* involved in fatal accidents, researchers have settled for chemical tests performed on dead drivers.

Nevertheless, it has not proved possible to obtain tests on all dead drivers. Some fatally injured drivers are not delivered to medical settings in time for a test to be given. Even when corpses are delivered in a timely fashion, some harried medical personnel may see no reason to test for alcohol when the possibility of intoxication seems remote, or may not cooperate, or may inadvertently fail to conduct the required tests (see Perrine 1975). In any event, dead drivers may not be representative of all drivers involved in fatal crashes.

What BAC level establishes a crash or fatality as alcohol-related? Should we say that if any driver tests positive for *any* alcohol, the accident should be labeled "alcohol-related?" This hardly seems appropriate, since one or two drinks consumed hours before the crash probably played no causal role (Borkenstein et al. 1974). Nevertheless, some studies define "alcohol-related" in this way.

What BAC level should qualify a driver as drunk? Ten years ago most states considered that a BAC of 0.15 or greater created a presumption of intoxication. Today a BAC of 0.10 conclusively establishes driving under the influence (DUI) in most states. However, it is not necessarily appropriate for a researcher to adopt this standard as proof of alcohol causation of traffic crashes. For the purpose of setting safe driving standards and regulating the highways, it may be justifiable to demand that all drivers conform to safety standards embodying generalizations about speed and intoxication levels likely to prove dangerous. Nevertheless, it would not be proper for researchers to assume alcohol causation for every crash that involves a person who exceeds these standards, any more than it would be proper for us to assume that every speeding driver caused the crash in which he was involved. In other words, some accident-involved drivers with a BAC level in excess of 0.10 cause crashes for reasons having nothing to do with their alcohol consumption. The opposite is also true; some drivers cause crashes because they were under the influence of alcohol although their BACs were below 0.10.

The Problem of Causal Inference

If, for example, at-fault drivers are intoxicated in 40 percent of all fatal accidents, could we conclude that 40 percent of all such fatal accidents are caused by drunk driving? In the absence of information on the percentage of all drivers who are intoxicated, the answer is no. Suppose 60 percent of all at-fault drivers are drunk but that 90 percent of all drivers on the same roads also are drunk. We would have to conclude that drunk drivers are *underrepresented* in traffic fatalities; far from being a *cause* of fatal accidents under these assumed facts, drunk driving would appear to have a suppressor effect on fatal accidents. Thus, to draw causal inferences properly it is necessary to have good data on the BAC levels of drivers who are on the same roads at the same time as crash-involved drivers (see Borkenstein et al. 1974).

Promising Strategies for Estimating the Role of Alcohol in Traffic Crashes

Discriminant Analysis

Dr. James C. Fell of NHTSA's research staff and Dr. Terry Klein of Sigmast, Inc., have recently utilized discriminant analysis to estimate the percentage of traffic fatalities that *involve alcohol*. This method is more promising than any earlier efforts.

Starting with fatal accidents in which the drivers' BAC is known, Fell and Klein search for those characteristics of the drivers and their accidents that best predict the drivers' BAC levels. These independent variables are entered into discriminant functions, which for any fatal accident driver predict the probability that he or she had (1) BAC = 0.00, (2) BAC = 0.01–.09, (3) BAC = 0.10 or greater. They sampled all 1982 fatal accident drivers in FARS's fifteen "good reporting states" who had a known BAC. The independent variables included sex, age, hour, day and time of the accident, type of road, driving record, severity of injuries, and driver restraint use. They developed separate discriminant functions for automobiles, motorcycles, light trucks and vans, medium and heavy trucks, and special vehicles. The researchers then validated their models by applying their discriminant functions to predict the BAC levels of FARS 1984 fatal accident drivers having known BACs. The predictions were exceptionally accurate, within 1 percent of actual BACs. The next step was to use discriminant analysis to predict BAC levels of drivers having unknown BACs.

When the Fell and Klein model was applied to all driver fatalities for 1982, 1983, and 1984, the results shown in table 3.1 emerged. These data show that approximately 30 percent of all drivers involved in fatal crashes have a BAC greater than the legal limit of 0.10. Some of these

Table 3.1. All Drivers Involved in Fatal Crashes

Alcohol Level	% Drivers with BAC		
	1982	1983	1984
.00	61	62	64
.01–.09	9	8	9
>.10	30	29	28

"drunk drivers" caused their own deaths, some caused the deaths of others, and some caused no deaths. This statistic certainly gives strong indication that alcohol is a significant factor in a large proportion of fatal accidents. Nevertheless, even Fell and Klein's findings do not tell us what percent of all traffic deaths are attributable to drunk drivers.

The Grand Rapids Study

By far the most impressive experimental study of the causal role of alcohol in traffic crashes was carried out by Professor Robert Borkenstein and his colleagues at the University of Indiana during the early 1960s. This study continues to be cited as the definitive statement on the relationship between BAC level and accident probability (Borkenstein et al. 1974).

Borkenstein and his colleagues obtained BAC and other information on a large sample of accident-involved Grand Rapids drivers, at the scenes of their accidents. They compared this group of accident-involved drivers with a control group of non-accident-involved drivers drawn at random from drivers passing the sites of a large sample of accidents that had occurred over the previous three years. The principal research question was whether the accident drivers and the control drivers differed in terms of either BAC or sociodemographic characteristics.

Ultimately Borkenstein obtained BACs for almost six thousand accident-involved drivers and for approximately seventy-five hundred control drivers. The rate of BAC refusal for both groups was extremely low. Sixteen percent of the accident-involved drivers but only 11 percent of the control drivers tested positive for any alcohol. Six and three-tenths percent of the accident-involved drivers but less than 1 percent of the control drivers had BACs equal to or greater than 0.10. This demonstrates persuasively that drinking drivers are significantly overrepresented among accident-involved drivers. Moreover, drivers at each higher BAC level are even more disproportionately represented among the accident-involved group. Thus Borkenstein et al. (1974 P. 16) carefully concluded that "blood alcohol concentrations (BACs) over .04% are definitely associated with an increased accident rate. The probability of accident involvement increases rapidly at BACs above .15% (see fig. 3.1). When drivers with BACs over .08% have accidents, they tend to have more single vehicle accidents, more severe in terms of injury and damage accidents, and more expensive accidents than sober drivers. BACs of .04% and below apparently are not inconsistent with traffic safety."

Borkenstein et al.'s study persuasively demonstrates that *drunk driv-*

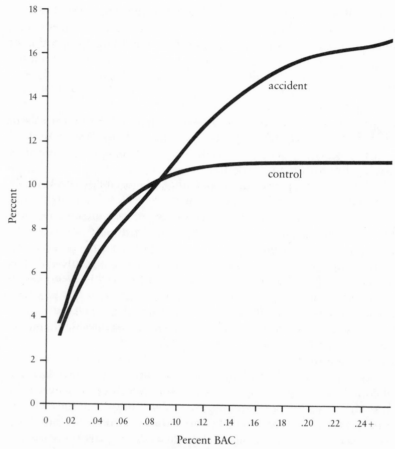

Figure 3.1. Cumulative percent at or below specific BACs for accident and control groups. Source: Borkenstein et al. [1964] 1974.

ers have a greater probability of becoming involved in an accident. It does not prove that alcohol *causes* accidents, because something other than alcohol (psychopathology or traumatic life events) might cause both drinking and crashing. Moreover, the presence of alcohol obviously is not invariably associated with an accident. The Grand Rapids study also does not purport to show what percentage of drivers at different BAC levels are likely to crash. It is important to emphasize that approximately 90 percent of the Grand Rapids accident-involved drivers tested *negative for any alcohol.* Clearly, while significant alcohol consumption does increase the probability of an accident, intoxication is not the cause of the majority of traffic accidents, especially minor ones.

Conclusion

Historically, public opinion and public policy on drunk driving have been shaped more by perceptions and imagery than by facts. For example, the U.S. Department of Transportation's 1968 *Alcohol and Highway Safety* report's claim that 50 percent of all traffic fatalities— that is, twenty-five thousand deaths—are attributable to "the use of alcohol by drivers and pedestrians" established drunk driving as a national problem, paved the way for the expenditure of public funds, and stimulated the anti–drunk driving movement. Even though traffic fatalities have decreased during the ensuing decades, these same statistics (or even larger numbers) have been recited again and again to prove the significance of drunk driving and to justify claims on resources and political attention.[10] It seems an iron rule of American political life that a social problem has to be projected in large enough—even exaggerated—terms before it can command a place on the social problems agenda. The larger the drunk driving problem is perceived to be, the more resources and attention can be claimed to combat it. The larger the problem, the more justifiable (indeed necessary) are serious punishments and intrusive police tactics.

My intent in this chapter has been to demonstrate (1) the complexity of estimating the percentage of traffic casualties that can be attributed to drunk driving and, therefore, (2) the difficulty of estimating the extent of drunk driving's contribution to traffic accidents. In estimating the percentage of traffic casualties caused by drunk drivers, we know a great deal less than we think we know. Estimates can only give us an idea of the *range* within which the true percentage falls. As we shall see, the same point might be made about most empirical issues relevant to drunk driving and drunk drivers. Policy analysis and policy-making must proceed with the best possible available information, but the best information is sometimes far from complete. This should heighten our sensitivity to the critical role of values and judgment in policy analysis and should cause us to be modest about the validity of our policy choices.

Even though we cannot accurately estimate the number of innocent people whose deaths have been caused by drunk drivers, there is no doubt that the number is large, certainly many thousands. Fell and Klein have shown convincingly that approximately 30 percent of drivers in fatal accidents have BACs exceeding the legal limit. The majority of fatalities are drunk drivers themselves, and the majority of these latter die in single-vehicle crashes. Thus, the category of wanton drunk driving deaths includes behavior akin to both suicide and homicide. Moreover, of the passengers who die, a significant percentage are the drinking companions of drunk drivers. In addition, perhaps 10 percent of the pedestrians who die in traffic accidents have high BACs. They are not part of the drunk driving problem, but they are part of the alcohol problem.

The brilliantly conceived Borkenstein et al. study found that approximately 7 percent of all Grand Rapids accidents involved drivers with BACs equal to or greater than 0.10. Clearly, drunk driving is not the predominant cause of run-of-the-mill accidents. Nevertheless, the driver whose BAC exceeds 0.08 significantly increases his probability of becoming involved in an accident. Unfortunately, we cannot say what that probability is. However, the more serious the accident, the greater the probability that alcohol is involved.

4

Patterns of Offending

Very little of the vast research on drunk driving has focused on characteristics of drunk drivers and on their patterns of offending. One researcher has aptly summarized the situation as follows: "lacking systematic in-depth research on the attributes and characteristics of drinking drivers, the literature offers only an incomplete mosaic of fragmented, often incomparable studies that vaguely suggest, and do not identify, high risk groups of these drivers" (Simpson 1985, P. 36). Another has observed: "We have produced a body of research that is shallow, not deep; tendentious, not objective; fragmented, not co-ordinated; dictated by fashions and trends and often of little scientific validity" (Haight 1985, P. 14).

Despite the paucity of data, this chapter attempts to dispel some myths about drunk drivers and to take stock of what is known. It should be emphasized that increasing our knowledge about drunk drivers must be a high priority if more effective policy initiatives are to be designed and implemented.

The Myth of Universal Offending

There are many myths about drunk driving. One of the most common is that it is a crime that practically everyone commits. Perhaps all that is meant by such an assertion is that on some occasion over a lifetime a high percentage of Americans have driven a vehicle after having imbibed enough beverage alcohol to perceive some effects. If so, the claim is not controversial or very interesting. It does not even seem to be a claim about drunk driving.

Even if a high percentage of people on a small number of occasions over the course of a lifetime have driven while intoxicated, this would not make drunk driving a crime that everyone commits, at least if the assertion implies that drunk driving is a regular or customary behavior. A person who once drives drunk should not be labeled a drunk driver and should not be assumed to be sympathetic to drunk drivers, any

42

more than a person who once steals a magazine should be labeled a thief who sympathizes with shoplifters and robbers.

Most Americans' drinking practices make them unlikely to drive drunk, at least on a regular basis. The 1983 U.S. Department of Health and Human Services' report *Alcohol and Health* showed that 79 percent of the population have drinking habits that make them unlikely to drive under the influence of alcohol on a regular basis. Three of four Americans either do not drink alcohol at all or drink in such moderation that they would rarely, if ever, be on the road at illegal BACs. A second category, perhaps amounting to 15 percent of all drivers, comprises heavy social drinkers who sometimes may be on the road at illegal BACs. Ten percent of all drivers are problem drinkers, whose drinking patterns are likely to bring them frequently into conflict with the DWI laws.[1]

The main reason for the exaggerated belief in drunk driving's pervasiveness is the loose habit of equating all drinking/driving with drunk driving. While practically everyone who drinks and drives necessarily engages in drinking/driving, drunk driving is qualitatively different, involving more than the mere combination of drinking and driving; it involves degraded and impaired driving capacities, the severe deterioration of judgment and control over the vehicle, and an endangering of one's own life and the lives of passengers, other road users, and pedestrians. It is essential to maintain the distinction between *drunk* driving and *drinking*/driving. The more blurred the distinction, the greater the number of "normal" and "nondangerous" drinking/driving episodes will be labeled criminal, thereby undermining the effort to identify and isolate drunk driving as a major problem.

Frequency of Offending

There are no available estimates of either the total amount of drunk driving (number of offenses per year or annual rate per hundred thousand population) or the number of offenders; the "dark figure" is unknown and probably unknowable. A victims survey is not feasible; while drunk driving is not a victimless crime, it usually does not produce victims, unless one considers those motorists, cyclists, and pedestrians who have knowingly or unknowingly been put at risk.

A few sample surveys have sought to determine the amount of drunk driving by asking people whether they drive drunk (see, e.g., Gallup 1977). However, one of the oddities of DWI is that it is difficult for a respondent to know whether he has committed the offense. Since the definition of the crime is vague or technical (driving with BAC above 0.10), most people cannot be sure whether any particular driving episode violated the law. Respondents' judgments about the propriety or legality of their own behavior will vary enormously. Some people may hold themselves to very high standards of responsible driving, others to low standards.

For example, in response to Gallup's (1977) question, "Have you ever driven when you thought you had too much to drink to drive safely?" 37 percent of respondents answered affirmatively. Notice, however, that the question seems to require the respondent to search his entire past life for a drinking/driving episode and, if one is recalled, to remember what he thought at the time it occurred. Even if a respondent could accurately accomplish this feat, what can we infer? Maybe the respondent's judgment at the time was poor. Perhaps, having consumed a dozen beers, he did not appreciate any risk—or, having consumed two beers, he had been unwarrantedly concerned.

Many people who at some point in their lives have driven while intoxicated will not even remember the incident (as they would, for example, a burglary), either because they were too drunk or because it was so uneventful. Others who may admit to having (at least once) driven either while drunk or after having had too much to drink would have passed a field sobriety or chemical BAC test. Despite all the publicity that drunk driving has generated during the past several years, I find hardly any acquaintances or students who know either the legal standard for drunk driving or how many drinks it takes to reach the prohibited BAC level. When I ask classes of law students how many drinks it takes to produce an illegal BAC, the majority say two or three, which is about half the actual number.

Recently the Roper organization, at the request of the insurance industry's All-Industry Research Advisory Council (1985), asked 1,491 randomly chosen adults over the age of eighteen: "In the past year have you driven after drinking alcohol?" Only 37 percent of the respondents answered affirmatively. Affirmative responses were positively correlated with males, higher education, higher income,[2] and residence in the north-central region. Respondents eighteen to thirty-four years old were more likely to answer affirmatively than were older respondents.

To my mind, this survey, like its predecessors, is fundamentally flawed. Moreover, like many other surveys, it seems designed to exaggerate the drunk driving problem. Roper's question asks about "drinking" driving, not about *drunk* driving. It does not define "after" or "drinking." Incredibly, it gives the respondent no indication of either the amount of alcohol or the immediacy of driving that would call for an affirmative response. How should a person respond who recalls years ago having driven home hours after having imbibed a single glass of beer or wine at lunch? Hasn't this person "driven after drinking alcohol"? Moreover, since the survey question does not ask about frequency of drinking/driving, it is not possible to draw any inferences about *rates* of offending. A better question would be, How many times during the past month have you driven within an hour of having imbibed one, two, three, four, five, or more alcoholic drinks (which could be coded as intoxication/ no intoxication, depending on the respondent's height and weight)? However, the accuracy of the survey would still depend on respondents' abilities and willingness to report accurately.

Another way to obtain estimates of the amount of drunk driving, without relying on respondents' recall and truthfulness, is through roadside breath testing at roadblocks that stop either all or a random sample of road users and determine their BAC levels through drivers' voluntary submission to a breath test and an interview (see Palmer and Tix 1985). In theory, roadside surveys could produce very accurate data on the percentages of drinking drivers (of different ages, sexes, income levels, etc.) at different times of the day and night. Unfortunately, roadside surveys are expensive to mount and difficult to implement; many have failed to obtain much sociodemographic information.

A properly designed roadside survey should include all types of drivers, from all types of communities, at all times of the day and night. It is likely that the frequency of drunk driving varies from place to place, depending on religion, ethnicity, drinking practices, demography, age mix of the population, and percentage of population living in urban areas.

In designing a roadside survey, it would be important not to distort the results by choosing roadways with disproportionate numbers of particular kinds of drivers (e.g., college students, blue-collar workers, or churchgoers) or by choosing times of the day or week when a disproportionate number of drunk drivers are or are not on the road. For reasons of expense and logistics, no study could achieve a truly random sample. Many roadside surveys have not even tried to do so, apparently having been designed to determine the frequency of drunk driving on weekend nights when drinking/driving is most prevalent (see Palmer and Tix 1985).[3] It seems as though many research efforts have been designed in order to produce the highest possible estimate of drunk driving. This would not be surprising, since the researchers who conduct such studies usually have a stake in the magnitude of the problem.

Needless to say, it is vital for roadside surveys to obtain near universal cooperation. We can be practically certain that the percentage of those who refuse to give a breath sample will be greater among those who are drunk than among those who willingly cooperate. Thus, roadside surveys must understate the amount of drunk driving, although by how much is not clear. The results are worthless if large numbers of drivers refuse either to stop or to submit to the voluntary BAC testing. When drivers are promised anonymity and immunity from prosecution (see Valverius 1982), rates of cooperation in excess of 90 percent have sometimes been achieved.

The small number of well-executed roadside surveys reported in the literature constitute a valuable source of information on drunk driving; the most famous such survey is Professor Robert Borkenstein et al.'s (1974) "Grand Rapids Study" in which drivers were tested at all times of the day and night at sites in the Grand Rapids area where accidents had occurred during the previous three years. The results showed that only 0.75 percent of all drivers who were tested had a BAC level above 0.10; another 2.47 percent had a BAC of 0.05–0.09 percent. Ten percent of all drivers tested positive for the presence of any alcohol.

A nationwide (eighteen-state sample) roadside survey was carried out in 1973 by the University of Michigan's Highway Safety Research Institute (see Wolfe 1974); it stopped 3,698 late-night weekend drivers, those most likely to be intoxicated, at 185 sites and obtained just over 90 percent cooperation. The researchers found that 3.2 percent of all drivers tested between 10:00 P.M. and midnight had a BAC at or above 0.10 and that 6.3 percent had a BAC of 0.05–0.09. From 2:00 A.M. to 3:00 A.M., 11.1 percent of the drivers tested above BAC 0.10, 13.5 percent at 0.05–0.09 (Wolfe 1974).

Prior to implementing the ASAPs, nineteen of the designated communities conducted nighttime random roadside breath test surveys. Five and two-tenths percent of the drivers had a BAC above 0.10 (Voas 1981). From 1970 to 1974, twenty-eight of the thirty-five ASAPs conducted various roadside surveys. When these results were combined with the University of Michigan's results, 6 percent of weekend and nighttime (after 10:00 P.M.) weekday drivers were found to have a BAC at or above 0.10 (Goldstein and Susmilch 1982).

A 1985 Minnesota roadside survey (Palmer and Tix 1985) found that, of 838 drivers on the road between 8:00 P.M. and 3:00 A.M., 82.3 percent tested negative for any alcohol, 6.0 percent tested at 0.05–0.09 (a lesser included DWI offense in some states), and only 2.4 percent tested above the legal limit of 0.10. These results have to be viewed cautiously, since almost 25 percent of the drivers who were stopped refused to cooperate.

Recently the Insurance Institute for Highway Safety reported the results of a replication of the 1973 national roadside survey.[4] Three thousand one hundred drivers were stopped on Friday and Saturday nights between the hours of 11:00 P.M. and 3:00 A.M.; 91.9 percent provided a breath sample. The percentage of 1986 drivers with illegal BACs was much lower than that in 1973. Only 3.1 percent of those drivers who provided a breath sample had a BAC of 0.10 or greater. In the 1986 survey the refusal rate was 9.9 percent, compared with 13.7 percent in 1973. Since the probability of illegal BACs is likely to be higher among the refuseniks, it seems safe to conclude (1) that in the 1986 survey the actual percentage of drivers having a BAC at or above 0.10 was higher than 3.1 percent and (2) that the differences between the 1973 and 1986 surveys are at least somewhat accounted for by the greater percentage of refuseniks in 1973.

These roadside surveys provide rough estimates of the amount of DWI offending that occurs on any given day (or, more accurately, during late-night weekend hours). During the peak offending period, Fridays and Saturdays 10:00 P.M.–3:00 A.M., perhaps 3–4 percent of the drivers on roads all around the United States are legally drunk. An unknown percentage are driving under the influence of licit and illicit drugs and cannot be identified by roadside BAC test procedures.

Who Is the Drunk Driver?

If all facts were known, DWI offenders could be sorted along a continuum according to their rates of offending. Unfortunately, we know neither the rate of offending for high- and low-rate offenders nor whether chronic, occasional or infrequent drunk drivers are the most dangerous.

The sociodemographic characteristics of American drunk drivers have not yet been adequately researched. Nevertheless, bits of insight can be gleaned from police statistics, studies of drunk drivers in treatment programs, roadside surveys, and data from FARS.

There is a good deal of confusion about the age distribution of drunk drivers. One major source of confusion arises from the construction of age categories. There is no standard or consistent definition of "young drivers." Some studies compare drivers age sixteen to twenty-four with drivers age twenty-five to forty-four and with drivers age forty-five and above. Each age category includes a different number of years, and the youngest age category extends from new teenage drivers to adults in their mid twenties.

The UCRs are one source for data on the age distribution of drunk drivers, although police statistics cannot be taken as representing true rates of offending.[5] According to the UCR, in 1984 teenagers had lower-than-average rates of drinking/driving arrests, despite their high vulnerability to police attention, inferior driving skills, lesser drinking experience, and overrepresentation among weekend drivers. Perrine's (1974) study of Vermont drivers on the road at the same times and places as previously fatally injured drivers found that 9 percent of drivers *under age twenty* "had been drinking," compared with 14 percent of drivers older than age twenty. A similar study in Huntsville, California (Farris, Malone, and Lilliefors 1977), found that 8 percent of under-twenty-year-old drivers had been drinking, compared with 12 percent of drivers older than twenty years. The University of Michigan's Highway Safety Research Institute's 1973 roadside breath-testing study found that during 10:00 P.M.–3:00 A.M. 88.4 percent of the sixteen-to-seventeen year olds and 81.5 percent of the eighteen-to-twenty year olds registered BAC scores at the lowest level, 0.01 or less. Only 8.2 percent and 11.2 percent of the sixteen-to-seventeen and eighteen-to-twenty year olds, respectively, had BACs above 0.05 (Wolfe 1974, P. 48). While fewer young drivers drink, those who do are more dangerous drivers and are significantly overrepresented among traffic fatalities (see Wagenaar 1983, chap. 2).[6]

Drunk driving is an overwhelmingly male activity; almost 90 percent of arrestees are male. Unlike most crimes, drunk driving is not an urban phenomenon. Indeed, among fatally injured drivers, a higher proportion of those who died on country roads had a BAC above 0.15 than did those who died on city roads. Drunk drivers diverge from the typical pattern of minority overrepresentation; whites constituted 89.8 percent of those arrested in 1984. This is the highest percent of white offenders for any crime reported in the UCR. Perhaps the race-specific rates of arrest for DWI can partly be explained by the lower level of car ownership among minorities and by the lower rate of driving in urban areas where racial minorities disproportionately reside. In part it no doubt reflects the lower priority given to drunk driving by large-city police officials. While it is often said that drunk drivers are "white-collar" offenders, most studies (e.g., Wolfe 1975) that have attempted to identify social class have found the lower socioeconomic groups to be disproportionately represented.

Social Drinkers, Problem Drinkers, and Alcoholics

The most important unanswered research question about drunk drivers has to do with their drinking habits: we would like to know what portion of drunk driving is accounted for by alcoholics, alcohol abusers, binge drinkers, and social drinkers. Since alcoholics and alcohol abusers are much more frequently intoxicated than light and moderate drinkers, they will more often drive under the influence.

Nevertheless, since light and moderate drinkers are far more numerous, they may account for a substantial number of drunken episodes (Moore and Gerstein 1981). Drunk driving would still be a social problem even if there were no alcoholics and alcohol abusers.

We know practically nothing about the alcohol habits of the most dangerous drunk drivers. Chronic alcoholics may not be the most dangerous drunk drivers. Heavy drinkers develop a tolerance for alcohol, as well as compensatory mechanisms. Hurst (1973) has shown that at all BAC levels infrequent drinkers have a higher crash probability. This makes sense. Those who are less accustomed to alcohol's effects on driving will be less able to cope with those effects. Since, by definition, light drinkers only very infrequently drive while drunk, it is reasonable to assume that some extraordinary circumstances and life events account for these episodes. Filkins et al. (1970) examined the driving records of 1,247 hospitalized alcoholics who were known to be drivers; only 17 percent had had a DWI charge or "more than one driving conviction" during *the previous six years*. Thus it seems likely that not all alcoholics drive drunk, and, of those who do, it may be only a minority who drive dangerously enough to attract police attention. It is also important to remember that the most dangerous drunk drivers are those who seem to have completely lost all control or all concern about risk.

Researchers have used a variety of screening instruments (e.g., the Michigan Alcohol Screening Test [MAST] and the Mortimer-Filkins Test) to sort drunk drivers into categories of alcohol abusers and social drinkers. Ehrlich and Selzer (1967), Waller (1967), Selzer (1969, 1971), and Yoder and Moore (1973) all have concluded that more than 50 percent of the DWI arrestees in their respective samples were alcohol abusers or alcoholics. ASAP evaluators categorized half of arrestees as problem drinkers, one-third as social drinkers, the remainder fell in between. In Yoder and Moore's (1973) study, 26 percent of the first offenders and 48 percent of the repeat offenders gave affirmative answers to the question, "Have you ever thought you might have a drinking problem?" Owing to the plasticity of the categories, there is undoubtedly room to quarrel with the criteria for labeling people "alcoholics" and "alcohol abusers," but there seems little doubt that a high percentage of people arrested for drunk driving are heavy drinkers. Indeed, it takes heavy drinking to reach the 0.10 BAC level—and very heavy drinking to reach the much higher levels attained by many arrestees. We still do not know, however, how often the different types of drinkers are likely to drive while drunk or whether different types of drinkers are likely to be different types of drunk drivers.

Recidivism and Other Prior Criminal Record

The UCR does not tell us how many individuals account for the 1.8 million arrests. Apparently, in a given year very few offenders are arrested more than once for drunk driving. According to NHTSA's *Review of the State of Knowledge* (1978), 93 percent of arrestees have never been previously arrested for DWI. Likewise, FARS data show that approximately 7 percent of fatal injury drivers who tested positive for BAC had had a recorded DWI conviction during the preceding three years. Like all first-offender statistics, this one must be handled with care. The likelihood of being arrested for drunk driving is low, and DWI defendants often plead guilty to lesser traffic offenses. Since most studies utilize motor vehicle records to test for recidivism, previous drunk driving arrests and convictions are often not revealed. Certainly we should not assume that a first-time arrestee is a first offender.

A recent Minnesota study (Crime Control Institute 1986) provides a more detailed picture. Minnesota has had an administrative per se law since 1982. This means that any drunk driver who tests above the legal limit or who refuses to take a BAC test will have his license automatically suspended. Because few apprehended drunk drivers are able to avoid the administrative revocation, the number of identified drinking drivers with prior revocations will be quite complete. The Minnesota study of drivers involved in fatal accidents found that 7 percent had been convicted of DWI during the preceding three years. Of the *drinking drivers* involved in fatal accidents, 13 percent had had a DWI conviction during the preceding three years; 25 percent had had a license revocation during the preceding *eight* years. Goldstein and Susmilch (1982) found that 31 percent of drunk drivers in Madison, Wisconsin, who caused serious injuries had accumulated "a significant number of convictions for traffic violations." These recidivism statistics do not point to a large high-rate-of-offending population, but that may be the result of low rates of apprehension.

The popular image of the drunk driver is of a white, middle-class, law-abiding fellow whose drunk driving is aberrational and inadvertent. This image may not be accurate. Data from the state of Massachusetts, for example, show that of a statewide sample of thirteen hundred DUI defendants, 32.6 percent (of males) had previously been arraigned for non-drunk-driving criminal offenses, that 8.8 percent had previously been arraigned only for drunk driving, and that 20.1 percent had previously been arraigned for both drunk driving and another criminal offense; only 38.7 percent had never before been arraigned (i.e., no prior involvement with the criminal justice system).[7] These

results are quite surprising; and if they are generalizable to other jurisdictions, our image of the drunk driver would need refocusing.
However, very recent Massachusetts data showing DWI recidivism
more in line with findings in other studies suggest that the first study
needs to be reanalyzed (Taylor 1987).

The Psychology and Social Psychology of Drunk Drivers

Unlike most other offenses, drunk driving carries a risk of significant
injury to the offender and often to his friends and family members.
Nevertheless, a great deal of drunk driving occurs. Why? How do
drunk drivers deny or rationalize their behavior to themselves and
others?

Unfortunately, there is little, if any, research on this question. The
role of personality traits, recent stresses, and life changes has simply not
been sufficiently studied (Richman 1984). Any explanation of why
people drive under the influence should begin by noting the enormously
different offense rates of men and women. From an early age, women
drink less than men; four times as many eighteen-to-twenty-year-old
men as women (20 percent vs. 5 percent) can be classified as heavy
drinkers (U.S. Department of Health and Human Services 1983). Alcohol consumption has a different social meaning for men and women.
Some male social groups accord prestige to hard drinking; a "real man"
can consume large quantities of alcohol and hold his liquor. It would be
a painful loss of face for men, especially young men, to admit to their
drinking buddies that they are not competent to drive. For men, heavy
drinking usually occurs in groups; for women, it more often occurs
when they are alone. Furthermore, men drive a great deal more than
women. They account for two-thirds of all driver's licenses and for 90
percent of all driver fatalities.

Several studies have shown that the typical drunk driver is on his way
to or from a tavern or restaurant. Yoder and Moore (1973) found that
52 percent of all DWI arrestees had been drinking in a bar or pool hall
prior to arrest (see also O'Donnell 1985). Palmer and Tix (1985) found
that drivers whose trips began at a bar or restaurant had an average
BAC nearly four times greater than those whose trips began at the next
most frequent location, a friend's or relative's house.

Tavern drinking plays a major role in male social life, and in the
United States tavern drinking practically assures drinking/driving and
drunk driving. A society that permits and promotes so many drinking
establishments inaccessible by foot or public transportation necessarily
produces a great deal of drinking/driving. Gusfield, Rasmussen, and
Kotarba (1984) found that regulars in several San Diego taverns and

bars hardly ever referred to their competency to drive or to the state's tough drunk driving laws. Apparently, regular participation in bar culture requires the drinker to maintain a posture of competency, to hold his liquor, and to take care of his transportation (therefore, to drink and drive). To challenge that competency is to challenge an individual's status as a bar regular and as a real man. Such challenges are rarely made. Bar regulars believe that they are competent drinkers, and drinking companions support each other's claims. Undoubtedly, their view of themselves as competent is reinforced by many previously uneventful drinking/driving experiences.

While the alcoholic's drunk driving does not seem difficult to account for or to understand, the social drinker's behavior is more problematic. How does a social drinker end up drunk behind the wheel? This is neither social drinking nor social driving. Is it a highly aberrational behavior for the individual, perhaps triggered by a traumatic life event?

Whether most drunk driving arrestees (and, by inference, drunk drivers) can accurately be characterized as alcoholics or the near equivalent, alcoholics have more traffic accidents and more traffic violations (Selzer et al. 1967). FARS estimates that 43 percent of drivers in fatal accidents had a BAC greater than 0.10. These levels are very unlikely to be achieved by light or moderate drinkers, even when they are on a binge. This suggests that the most dangerous drunk drivers are either very heavy drinkers or moderate drinkers on a binge.

Within the world of alcohol abuse research there has long been debate between those who view alcohol abuse as symptomatic of severe psychological problems and those who see psychological problems as symptomatic of severe alcohol abuse. The same debate reverberates through drunk driving and traffic accident research (see Tillman and Hobbs 1949). For example, in Yoder and Moore's (1973) sample of DWI arrestees, "a problem or event was given as a reason for drinking by 17%" (see also Selzer, Rogers, and Kern 1968).

A few researchers have sought to demonstrate that people involved in serious traffic accidents are consciously or unconsciously bent on suicide or are at least extremely depressed, paranoically aggressive, or otherwise psychologically disturbed (Selzer et al. 1967; Tabachnik 1973).

While the link between suicide and alcohol-related traffic death has not been much studied, it is a hypothesis that bears consideration (see Selzer and Payne 1962; Selzer et al. 1967; Selzer and Barton 1977). Sixty percent of all alcohol-related traffic fatalities are single-vehicle fatalities. Many of these occur on clear roads on clear nights. How many of these are conscious or unconscious suicides (see Tabachnik 1973)? It is well to recall that alcohol is present in about one-third of U.S. suicides (Gerstein 1981); it has been estimated that alcoholics commit suicide from six to fifteen times more frequently than the general population (U.S. Department of Health and Human Services 1983). Therefore it seems plausible that some suicidal persons drink themselves into stupors and then crash their vehicles into abutments or other vehicles. This might be a rational form of suicide for persons desiring not to have their deaths revealed as suicides.

Conclusion

Drunk driving is a common offense, although not as common as is often asserted. The large majority of Americans have drinking habits that make them highly unlikely to be frequent drunk drivers. The whole effort to identify, condemn, and control drunk driving is made difficult by the tendency to equate drinking/driving with drunk driving.

Drunk driving follows both some patterns that are the same as those of most serious American crimes and some patterns that are different. Like other offenses, drunk driving is overwhelmingly committed by men and is most frequently committed on weekends. Like many serious crimes, drunk driving involves irresponsible and antisocial behavior under the influence of alcohol. However, unlike most other serious crimes, drunk driving occurs more often in rural counties than in major metropolitan areas. It is committed overwhelmingly by white males and spans a wider range of the socioeconomic continuum. There is neither a single explanation for drunk driving nor a single type of drunk driver. The majority of arrested DWI offenders do not have previous arrests for DWI or other serious offenses. We are not dealing with a criminal underclass, although a minority of DWI offenders have arrests and convictions for non-drunk-driving offenses. A substantial portion of drunk driving offenses is committed by a minority of heavy drinkers and alcohol abusers.

Determining the precise amount of drunk driving and the precise identity of drunk drivers is not possible. The behavior we are dealing with varies from region to region, from state to state, and from county to county. It also varies from one year to the next—and probably, to some extent, from month to month. In the final analysis, drunk driving, like other crimes, is a local phenomenon, and each community's own varied patterns of drunk driving need to be examined and analyzed (see, e.g., Goldstein and Susmilch 1982) if the most appropriate countermeasures are to be deployed.

Young people do not disproportionately engage in drunk driving, but they are more dangerous drivers, whether drunk or sober. The statistics do not reveal a high percentage of recidivist drunk drivers, but this may be an artifact of lax enforcement and plea bargaining. Alcohol abusers are more likely than social drinkers to drive drunk, but it is not clear what type of drunk drivers are the most dangerous.

II

Criminal Law and Procedure

Crime is a legal construct. A crime is whatever the criminal law, comprised of legislation and judicial interpretation, defines it to be. To fully understand the phenomenon of drunk driving, it is essential to understand what the law means by "drunk driving." In the four chapters comprising Part II we will see that the criminal law defining drunk driving and its enforcement is surprisingly complex. Chapters 5–7 explore the jurisprudence of drunk driving. We will see that drunk driving law raises serious jurisprudential concerns which have been ignored by the courts and legal commentators, perhaps because DWI has traditionally been regarded as a traffic offense, not as a "real crime."

Chapter 5 focuses on the threshold of criminal liability. Why is drunk driving formulated as a specific offense rather than subsumed under the traffic laws? Why is drunk driving defined as a criminal offense rather than as an administrative infraction? Chapter 6 focuses on the formulation of DWI as a criminal offense. There is much cause for confusion; even the elements of the offense are unclear. The jurisprudence of DWI is still in its infancy; many important issues have not been addressed, much less resolved. Some of the issues become increasingly significant as penalties for DWI escalate. Chapter 7 focuses on aggravated forms of drunk driving, on drunk driving committed by recidivists, and on drunk driving resulting in injury and death. The law of drunk driving has not done well in distinguishing the most culpable and dangerous incidents of drunk driving from run-of-the-mill incidents; the basic grading formula is very crude. Furthermore, efforts to grade drunk driving homicides have been particularly incoherent.

Chapter 8 turns to several issues of criminal procedure that arise in the enforcement of the drunk driving laws. In this chapter as in the three chapters on substantive drunk driving law that precede it, we will see traditional doctrines and values of criminal procedure stretched to their limits to make the apprehension and punishment of drunk drivers more efficient and automatic.

5

The Crime of Drunk Driving

Why There Is a Crime of Drunk Driving

It might seem odd to enquire why there should be a crime of drunk driving. Drunk driving is obviously a serious social problem caused by irresponsible and antisocial behavior. It has been an offense in most jurisdictions almost since the advent of the motorcar.[1] The question is useful, however, because the search for a satisfactory answer both demonstrates what an unusual offense drunk driving is and forces us to consider various models for stigmatizing, punishing, and controlling this behavior. From a policy standpoint it makes a difference whether run-of-the-mill drunk driving incidents are handled in traffic court, where few criminal procedures are required, or as criminal offenses in criminal court, where the full panoply of criminal procedural rights apply.

Drunk Driving and Traffic Law

The traffic law specifies (1) a panoply of traffic infractions (e.g., speeding, crossing the center line, tailgating, failure to signal, and reckless driving), the violation of which is presumably dangerous, and (2) the penalties for their violation. Except for intoxication, what caused a driver to violate one of these traffic laws is legally irrelevant. Offenses are not formulated so as to proscribe failing to stop at a traffic signal "owing to sleepiness or inattention." It is enough that the driver failed to stop. Except for the condition of alcohol impairment, traffic law does not attempt to punish a driver who *might not* stop because of a physiological, psychological, or emotional impairment.

Why is DWI singled out for special treatment, as a traffic law defined in terms of impairment rather than in terms of driving? Why aren't drunk drivers punished for actually violating specific traffic law provisions rather than for the probability of violating them? Are drunk drivers who speed or fail to abide by traffic signals any more dangerous or culpable than sleepy, angry, or distracted drivers who speed or fail to abide by traffic signals?

Professor Robert Force (1979) has argued for the abolition of drunk driving as a separate and distinct offense and for the prosecution of drunk drivers for the traffic offenses that they commit, although he would want the punishments enhanced because of the aggravating factor of alcohol. This proposal would leave drunk drivers who do not violate any traffic rules free from criminal santions.

One argument for singling out drunk driving for special treatment—and for rejecting Professor Force's proposal—must be that drunk driving presents a type of wrongdoing more culpable and/or more dangerous than mere violation of the traffic laws. Drunk drivers, it might be argued, act in a particularly antisocial way by voluntarily putting themselves in a condition in which their driving skills are blunted and (what is worse) in which their perceptions of and attitudes toward risks are distorted. While sleepy and distracted drivers may also be responsible for their impaired driving abilities, we are more likely to excuse their behaviors as inadvertent. Moreover, while the sleepy or distracted driver may have impaired reaction times, coordination, and general alertness, he is less likely than the intoxicated driver to misperceive, ignore, or court risks.

This argument for treating the intoxicated driver as more culpable and dangerous is plausible—but it involves several assumptions and generalizations. Not all intoxicated drivers are deliberate risk takers; some, in fact, may strive mightily to avoid risks. All drunk drivers are not more culpable owing to their impaired driving abilities than are all sleepy or distracted drivers; some sleepy or distracted drivers could easily be blamed for their impairments. Some drunk drivers could claim lesser culpability because their intoxication occurred inadvertently or as a result of alcohol addiction.

One mundane explanation for the special treatment of drunk driving is that it is not as subtle to identify or as difficult to prove as is, for example, distracted driving. Once apprehended and confronted by a police officer, the distracted driver will no longer be distracted; the intoxicated driver, despite his best efforts, may be unable to pass for sober. Intoxication can be measured by chemical testing, whereas distractedness cannot be. The availability of the BAC test makes possible much of the law defining and enforcing drunk driving. While the relative ease of detection gives us a means to criminalize drunk driving, however, it does not fully explain the motivation for doing so.

Two additional factors help explain the special treatment of DWI. The first involves the dual standard of competence to which drivers are held: (1) an absolute standard for licensing, set fairly low to facilitate mobility and permit widespread access, and (2) a relative standard that, perhaps compensatorily, requires each individual driver to operate at or near his own capacity. Thus, as Professor Philip Cook notes, a person blind in one eye can be licensed to drive but a person only nearsighted in one eye will be ticketed for driving without corrective lenses.

For this reason, we would be unpersuaded by the attempt to defend a driver's intoxication on the ground that he was still able to drive more competently than an inexperienced or elderly driver.

The underlying duty to drive as safely as one can is violated in a particularly egregious way by self-induced impairment. Even though we can exert a good deal of control over our exhaustion, distraction, and irritation when driving, variations in alertness, attention, and mood are inherent in human functioning. Intoxication, by contrast, seems deliberately to inject an artificial and gratuitous handicap.

Another reason for the special treatment of intoxication is the aggravated nature of the risk it creates. Unlike driving without glasses or brakes, intoxication not only effects the driver's motor and perceptual skills but his ability to judge and his willingness to take risks. The combination of reduced skills and distorted judgment is a serious compound danger nicely illustrated by an example from the New York State Driver's Manual:

> You have just stopped at a stop sign. You see another vehicle approaching the intersection from a distance that requires you to make a quick decision: is it safe to go through the intersection now, or should you wait?
>
> Under the influence of alcohol, you are more likely to make a bad decision and take a chance. And because your reaction time is slower, you might not get through the intersection as efficiently as you would when sober. If the bad driving and the poor reaction lead you into trouble, the influence of alcohol also gives you the loss of a chance to get out of it. (P. 65)

In the final analysis, the strongest rationale for singling out intoxicated driving for special statutory treatment is that intoxicated driving is more dangerous, by an order of magnitude, than other forms of impaired driving. It is not enough simply to punish the drunk driver for a particular rule infraction; he should be punished for creating a significant risk of injury or death to fellow road users. Indeed, according to this rationale, it is not even necessary that an intoxicated driver violate any rule of the road; simply operating a vehicle while intoxicated creates a serious risk of injury to other road users. The drunk driver is defined in the law as something like a ticking bomb.

The ticking-bomb analogy is imperfect, however; drunk drivers do not inevitably, or even frequently, explode. While alcohol-intoxicated drivers as a group pose a greater risk to fellow road users than do nonintoxicated drivers, the vast majority of intoxicated driving episodes do not result in collisions or injuries. Other contributing variables—such as weather; road conditions; the behavior of other drivers, pedacyclists, and pedestrians; and the driver's own personality, intent, attitude, and emotion—determine whether and to what degree drunk driving results in harm. Furthermore, not all drunk drivers are equally dangerous. The most dangerous are those who are very intoxicated and those who violate many traffic laws in the course of their offending. In Chapter 6 we will ask whether the law of drunk driving should be reformulated to punish aggravated drunk driving more severely than run-of-the-mill drunk driving.

Drunk Driving as an Inchoate Offense

Like the law of criminal attempts and conspiracy, drunk driving is an inchoate offense; its commission is not dependent on the occurrence of any harm. A person is guilty of drunk driving regardless of whether he injures anyone or even puts anyone at risk. As in criminal attempts, the harm resulting from DWI may require additional acts by the offender. In this respect, the offense of drunk driving is much like illegal possession of a handgun. A particular handgun possessor may not pose a specific risk, but the legislature has chosen not to wait until a lethal threat materializes. Similarly, mobilizing the criminal justice system against the drunk driver before any harm or specific risks develop or driving violations occur is a preventive or prophylactive strategy: why wait until harm occurs before subjecting dangerous drivers to social control?

Clearly, society wants to *prevent* dangerous driving. The existence of the drunk driving laws reflects a judgment that the traffic laws that proscribe various forms of dangerous driving bring the criminal law into the picture too late. The prohibition against drunk driving is an effort to prohibit conduct that *might lead* to dangerous driving. Under this preemptive strategy, it does not matter whether the drinking driver is actually driving dangerously at the time he is stopped.[2] In fact, if he is driving dangerously, there is no need for the preemptive law; the driver can be arrested for reckless driving or for specific traffic code violations. The special value of the preemptive law is that it proscribes behavior before its dangerousness becomes manifest.

Unlike criminal weapons possession, the offense of DWI requires a test to determine whether the suspect is violating the law. The test should establish whether, owing to alcohol, the suspect is a potentially dangerous driver. The traditional test for identifying drunk drivers was called a "field sobriety test." If a driver could not touch his nose or count backward from ten or walk a straight line, he had crossed the forbidden threshold of alcohol intoxication. The field sobriety test is open to two criticisms: (1) it is not sufficiently closely correlated with dangerous driving, and (2) interpreting the results is fraught with subjectivity and potential for abuse.

Over time the drunk driving laws have become even more preemptive. The law now punishes a driver for operating a vehicle while his BAC exceeds a certain level—this regardless of whether the driver could pass a field sobriety test, much less whether he is driving competently. In effect, the law makes it an offense to drive while possessing a physiological characteristic that correlates with the inability to pass a test that itself correlates in turn with unsafe driving.

Defining drunk driving as a criminal offense means that the police can take preemptive action—that is, action *before* a traffic calamity occurs. In theory, the same logic and strategy could be deployed against sleepy, distracted, or depressed driving, but these forms of potentially dangerous driving are less detectable, less provable, and less amenable to legislative formulation and court adjudication. They also do not call forth the negative stereotypes associated with drunk driving.

Drunk Driving as an Irrebutable Presumption of Recklessness

While preemptive punishment of DWI may be justified, the question remains why it should be treated differently than other forms of reckless conduct in which the substantial and unjustifiable nature of the risk has to be proved in each case.

The advent of the Model Penal Code during the 1960s introduced a new offense into the criminal code: reckless endangerment. It is defined by the code (sec. 211.2) as follows: "A person commits a misdemeanor if he recklessly engages in conduct which places or may place any other person in danger of death or serious bodily injury." Under the Model Penal Code (sec. 2.02), a person acts recklessly when "with respect to a material element of an offense . . . he consciously disregards a substantial and unjustifiable risk that the material element exists." There is no doubt that under the code many incidents of drunk driving could be prosecuted as reckless endangerment. But the code does not presume that any general type of wrongdoing always and invariably constitutes reckless endangerment. By contrast, the offense of drunk driving rests on a conclusive presumption that all instances of DWI and driving with

BAC greater than 0.10 are reckless—that is, significantly endanger other road users. Conclusive presumptions about whole categories of persons, activities, and behaviors, even if formulated as substantive offenses, are incompatible with a criminal jurisprudence that emphasizes individual culpability.

A different model of drunk driving would require the prosecutor to demonstrate that each drunk-driving defendant recklessly endangered other road users. If recklessness is apparent from the defendant's actions, it should not be difficult for prosecutors to prove. Moreover, making recklessness an explicit element of drunk driving would at least leave open the possibility of acquittal in appropriate circumstances. In most cases the drunk driver consciously has disregarded a substantial and unjustifiable risk of harming other road users, but there might be unusual cases when a defendant's behavior could not be so characterized. Perhaps the defendant, feeling intoxicated shortly after getting into his vehible, pulled onto the shoulder and went to sleep at the wheel or drove extremely cautiously without violating any traffic laws.

Intoxication as a "Defense" to Drunk Driving

If drunk driving were recognized as a crime of recklessness, and if recklessness requires conscious assumption of risk, it might be thought that some defendants would be acquitted on the ground that their drunkenness rendered them unconscious of whatever risks they took. If such an argument were accepted, it would stand the whole jurisprudence of dangerous drinking on its head; instead of drunkenness *establishing* culpability, it would negate culpability.

The effect of intoxication on criminal responsibility has greatly troubled the architects of modern American criminal jurisprudence Hall 1944; (Wald 1974; LaFave and Scott 1985; Robinson 1985). Since so much crime is associated with intoxication, it would be a substantial blow to law enforcement and social control to recognize intoxication as a defense. On the other hand, a jurisprudence that believes in mens rea has trouble disregarding evidence that the defendant did not act purposefully, knowingly, or recklessly.[3]

The drafters of the Model Penal Code simply made a practical (if unprincipled) compromise. They allowed for intoxication to be raised as a defense to offenses requiring proof of purposeful or knowing conduct but not to offenses requiring the lesser standards of culpability, recklessness, and negligence.[4] The Model Penal Code compromise has been widely followed, at least to the extent that no states are more liberal in defining intoxication as a defense; and some are more conservative.[5] Since, under the code, drunk driving, if it requires a mental state at all, does not require a mental state more culpable than that of recklessness, intoxication cannot be raised as a defense.

While this might not be an unjust result if the defendant was negligent or reckless in becoming intoxicated, under the Model Penal Code formulation the defendant would be precluded from arguing that his drunkenness was inadvertent and without fault. Although this may be a general problem in Anglo-American criminal jurisprudence, it is especially salient in the drunk driving context, where drunken behavior is the essence of the offense and where culpability tends to be assumed rather than required as an element of proof in individual cases.

Criminal versus Administrative Models

Since there is such an awkward fit between drunk driving and criminal law, it is worth considering whether routine occurrences should be treated as administrative violations rather than as minor crimes. This approach would not be unprecedented. While most states define DWI as a misdemeanor triable in criminal court, some states, such as Wisconsin, define a first DWI offense as a traffic violation without the possibility of a jail term.[6]

When drunk driving is defined as an administrative infraction, the following consequences result: First, the police have even greater leeway in conducting investigations. They can conduct breath tests whenever a stop is made, just as they now can check for a valid driver's license, vehicle registration, and proof of insurance. Drivers with prohibited BACs can immediately be removed from the road, their licenses immediately suspended, and their vehicles impounded. Due process would only demand an administrative hearing. There would be no right to a jury trial, assigned counsel, or a proof-beyond-a-reasonable-doubt standard of proof. None of the jurisprudential tensions (discussed in Chapter 6) that flow from defining drunk driving as a crime would arise. This administrative model might be a more efficient way to deal with the mass processing of almost two million cases a year than would the criminal procedures which most states now employ.

In opposition to this administrative model, it might be argued that DWI is so dangerous and culpable that its formulation as a mere administrative infraction would deprecate the seriousness of the wrongdoing and perhaps weaken the deterrent effect of the law. This hardly seems likely. There is no reason why administrative sanctions cannot be "serious." While it is true that incarceration cannot be imposed for violation of an administrative regulation, licenses can be revoked or suspended, vehicles can be impounded or forfeited, and heavy fines can be imposed. Since incarceration traditionally has not been a major factor in the anti–drunk driving arsenal, significant sanctioning options would not be lost.

The administrative model would not mean decriminalization of aggravated drunk driving or of drunk driving resulting in injury or death. A criminal offense could, for example, be formulated to punish a person who drives with BAC greater than 0.15 or 0.20. Egregious cases of highly dangerous drunk driving could be criminally prosecuted under reckless-endangerment statutes, and, if injury had resulted, a prosecution could be brought under aggravated-assault statutes or under special statutes criminalizing dangerous (or drunken) driving that causes injury. In the case of death, the homicide laws could be employed as they are now.

Suffice it to say at this point that, while drunk driving is undoubtedly dangerous behavior, more than concern about dangerousness drives the law on this subject. Drunk driving is also an offense against morality, decorum, and good citizenship. To understand why there is a special body of law aimed at the drunk driver, the offense must be seen in the context of societal attitudes toward alcohol and alcohol abuse (see Gusfield 1981). Historically, drunkenness was viewed as a moral failing. Driving while drunk continues to evoke the image of a social miscreant.

Conclusion

Drunk driving is an offense with one foot in the traffic code and one foot in the criminal code. It fits very uneasily into the law of crimes. If it were defined as an administrative infraction rather than as a criminal offense, many jurisprudential problems could be avoided. There would be less reason to worry about the basic fairness of the per se laws and about an essentially inchoate offense that punishes a condition that is thought to correlate closely with dangerous driving. If drunk driving is defined as a crime—and as one with increasingly severe sanctions—there is reason to be concerned about that continuous avoidance and watering down of traditional criminal law standards that seeks to make the offense easier and quicker to prove.

6

Defining and Grading Drunk Driving

In this chapter we examine the elements of the two drunk driving offenses, the traditional DWI or DUI offense and the newer per se crime—that is, driving with a BAC greater than 0.10. We will see that what might first appear as a simple, straightforward definition of prohibited conduct is riddled with unresolved ambiguities and even constitutional tensions.

The Elements of DWI

The elements of criminal offenses must be clearly stated so that citizens will know precisely what conduct is prohibited and be able to govern themselves accordingly. Furthermore, precisely defined crimes are a check against abuse of police and prosecutorial authority.[1] Law enforcement officials cannot arrest anyone whose conduct they find offensive. They can arrest and charge only those persons whom they have probable cause to believe have committed defined offenses. It is hornbook criminal law that criminal offenses are defined in terms of an actus reus (criminal act) and a mens rea (criminal mind). The prosecution must prove both to establish guilt.

Actus Reus of Drunk Driving

The least problematic aspect of DWI is *driving*.[2] Driving would seem to be an unambiguous term. Yet, like every other aspect of the jurisprudence of drunk driving, there is more here than meets the eye. Courts have wrestled with such questions as whether leaving a tavern, entering a car, and turning on the ignition constitutes "driving." Likewise, there have been many cases ruling on whether a person slumped behind the wheel of a car on the side of the road is "driving," some courts resolving the issue according to whether the motor is on or off (for a full discussion, see 7A Am Jur 2d 481–484). While answers to such questions are not obvious, these questions need not detain us long. There are uncertainties about the boundaries of all criminal laws, but, once an answer is

65

provided, it provides guidance in subsequent cases. Unfortunately, a more profound problem plagues the second aspect of the actus reus of drunk driving: *intoxicated*.

What does it mean to be under the influence of alcohol or intoxicated? Are we concerned with a physiological or psychological state, impairment of certain mental and physical capabilities or distortion of judgment and willingness to take risks? How much of a change, impairment, or distortion is required? Any alcohol ingestion produces biological and psychological effects, even if they are so slight that neither the drinker nor the observer can discern them. The very act of imbibing alcohol, independent of intoxication, can trigger a change of mood, reduction of inhibitions, and desire to take risks.[3]

The criminal law does not prohibit all drinking/driving. Driving following light or moderate consumption is permissible; driving after excessive, irresponsible, abusive drinking is unacceptable. But these adjectives are difficult to corral; what is "normal" and "moderate" drinking for one person may be abnormal and excessive for another. Given differences in individual size, shape, age, maturity, experience with alcohol, and drinking contexts, how can this legal prohibition be formulated as a neutral, objective standard amenable to routine, predictable, uniform enforcement?

"Intoxication" does not have a scientific definition. It is a social judgment like "pretty" or "good." It means different things to different individuals and subgroups. This is not to deny a high degree of consensus about extreme examples of intoxication; we can all recognize the drunken stereotype. In the real world, however, most drinkers, even heavy drinkers, do not conform to such caricatures.

Thus, there exists a serious, unavoidable linguistic imprecision in the legal definition of DUI or DWI.[4] Unfortunately, courts typically glide over the problem, ingenuously assuming that judges and juries know it when they see it. Of course, the trier of fact does not witness the allegedly intoxicated condition but only hears about it, usually from a police officer. Consider the following language from an important New York Court of Appeals drunk driving case that rejected a void-for-vagueness challenge to the DWI law:[5] "Although the legislature did not include a definition of intoxication in the statute, it does not follow that the term is without a definite or ascertainable meaning. . . . The standard for determining intoxication is constant; that is, whether the individual's consumption rendered him incapable of employing the physical or mental abilities needed to, for instance, form a specific intent, understand the nature and effect of a contract, or to testify truthfully and accurately" (*People v. Cruz*, 399 N.E. 2d 513 [1979]).

This is a clearly inadequate explanation of what "intoxication" means for purposes of the crime of drunk driving. First, one might wonder what relation the minimal standard for understanding a contract or testifying at a trial has to the minimal standard for operating a motor vehicle. Second, the court's formulation merely restates the question; what minimal degree of sobriety is necessary to understand the nature and effect of a contract? Third, is this a standard that the average police officer or juror can properly discern and apply? The New York court elaborated further: "In sum, intoxication is a . . . degree of impairment which is rendered when the driver has voluntarily consumed alcohol to the extent that he is incapable of employing the physical and mental abilities which he is expected to possess in order to operate a vehicle as a reasonable and prudent driver." [6]

This portion of the court's explanation is somewhat more satisfying. It focuses on intoxication-caused *impairment,* although the court offers no assistance in discerning what are "the physical and mental abilities which . . . [a driver] is expected to possess in order to operate a vehicle as a reasonable and prudent driver." Indeed, it is not clear whether the court has an objective or subjective standard in mind. Is an impaired condition not prohibited as long as the driver can perform at some minimally acceptable level, or is impairment prohibited if it reduces the driver's usual level of judgment and performance by a certain percentage?

Some courts seem to view the intoxication necessary to prove drunk driving as the impairment of driving skills below a threshold level of safety. This is what we might consider an "objective" standard. Other courts define the requisite intoxication as "intoxication in the slightest degree"—that is, when the individual's mental, psychological, or physical capacities are degraded in the slightest degree, regardless of whether the individual can still drive above the safety threshold. This is what we might consider the "relative" standard. The following "explanation" from a legal encyclopedia (7A *American Jurisprudence 2d,* sec. 301 [1980]) evidences the jurisprudential confusion:

With regard to the offense of driving while under the influence of intoxicating liquor, it has been held in several jurisdictions that even the slightest degree of intoxication is sufficient to support a conviction, and that intoxication need not be of such a degree that it interferes with the proper operation of a motor vehicle. Other courts have held that to be under the influence of intoxicating liquor within the meaning of such a statute, an accused must have been rendered incapable of operating a motor vehicle in a manner in which an ordinary prudent and cautious person in full possession of his faculties, using reasonable care, would operate a similar machine under like conditions. Another holding is that one is under the influence of intoxicating liquor within the meaning of such a statute where it appears that it is less safe for such a person to operate a motor vehicle than it would be if he were not so affected. Loss of normal control of body and mind has also been held to be a proper test to determine whether or not one is under the influence of liquor within the meaning of these statutes.

Admittedly, this is not the only instance of an undefined standard in our jurisprudence. Tort law, for example, holds us to the standard of a reasonable person without specifying how a reasonable person acts in particular situations. Criminal law normally puts special emphasis on notice and specificity, but there are exceptions. A few criminal laws are defined in terms of negligence (or even in terms of what appears to be strict liability), but they have been sharply criticized. For example, H. L. A. Hart (1968), the great English legal philosopher, objected to the use of a negligence standard in criminal law, both on the ground that it could ensnare the hapless rather than the wicked and because the standard is so subjective that different judges and juries could interpret it differently.

The Problem of Vagueness

The citizenry is ordered not to drive while intoxicated or, in some states, not to do so under the influence of alcohol, but it is not told what these standards mean. To be on the safe side, a person could refrain from any alcoholic beverages before driving, but clearly that is not what the law means or intends; nor is it realistic, given the range of situations in which people are likely to imbibe some alcohol before driving. Vague and ambiguous criminal laws are very much disfavored in our jurisprudence. Indeed, they may be unconstitutional under the void-for-vagueness doctrine of the due process clause.

The U.S. Supreme Court has repeatedly expressed its concern about vague or broadly defined laws, which in effect, make the police law definers as well as law enforcers. In *Lewis v. City of New Orleans* (415 U.S.130 [1974]), for example, the Court struck down a New Orleans ordinance prohibiting the use of "obscene or opprobrious language." In his concurring opinion, Justice Lewis Powell explained that "This ordinance . . . confers on police a virtually unrestrained power to arrest and charge persons with a violation. Many arrests are made in "one-on-one" situations where the only witnesses are the arresting officer and the person charged. All that is required for conviction is that the court accept the testimony of the officer" (P. 135).

The same concerns could be applied to DWI and DUI. Police officers, prosecutors, judges, and juries are drawn from a society comprised of people with vastly different drinking habits. At least 30 percent of the American adult population are alcohol abstainers; another third claim to drink no more than a few drinks per month. The heaviest-drinking third consumes 95 percent of all beverage alcohol. The heaviest drinking 10 percent accounts for 50 percent of total consumption (Moore and Gerstein 1981). People whose drinking habits differ so widely must have very different ideas about what it means to be "under the influence," "intoxicated," or "impaired" and will judge others' behavior accordingly.

Furthermore, when it comes to judging the degree of intoxication or impairment of an accused drunk driver, neither judge nor jury will be examining firsthand evidence. The "facts" are typically the police officer's subjective evaluation of the defendant's condition and behavior. In many jurisdictions the police officer is entitled to testify as an expert on the subject of intoxication, basing his opinion on the defendant's glassy eyes, slurred speech, alcoholic breath, and inability to pass a police-administered field sobriety test (walking a line, touching the nose, or performing addition and subtraction).[7] At a trial, cases necessarily degenerate into a swearing contest between the police officer and the defendant. The oddity of this type of adjudication is illustrated by a recent opinion of the Wyoming Supreme Court (*Crum v. City of Rock Springs*, 652 P. 2d 27 [1982]), in which the court reversed a DWI conviction on grounds of insufficient evidence:

Evidence of a blood test is not required to prove that a person was under the influence of intoxicating liquor. Here the arresting officer presented the only testimony concerning the appellant's appearance and behavior. The officer testified that appellant's face was flushed, that his speech was slurred, that he was having some trouble maintaining his balance without leaning up against the car, and that he could not perform the field sobriety tests "too well."

The testimony by the policeman that the appellant did not do "too well" on the sobriety test is not enough by itself to allow a trier of fact to draw a reasonable inference of intoxication. We would be adopting a rule permitting an inference of intoxication to be drawn from a decision to test for intoxication. . . .

A person could fail to do "too well" on a sobriety test for a number of reasons having nothing to do with intoxicating liquor.

The court's discussion illuminates both the vagueness of the standard and the subjectivity of the police officer's evaluation of the driver's performance on the field sobriety test.

The lack of objective guidelines to determine whether a driver was "intoxicated" or "under the influence of alcohol" has led to continuous efforts to define the offense more specifically and scientifically. With the advent of breath-testing methods during the early 1940s, statutes began to treat certain BAC levels as presumptive evidence of DUI. In many states, for example, a driver whose BAC exceeded 0.15 was presumed to be intoxicated; a driver whose BAC was 0.05–0.15 was presumed to be impaired (the lesser offense), while a driver whose BAC was less than 0.05 was presumed to be innocent. Today the DWI and DUI statutes remain on the books in all jurisdictions, but they are supplemented by per se laws that criminalize driving when one has a BAC above 0.10. However, when no BAC test is available (e.g., when the defendant has refused to take the test), the defendant must be prosecuted, if at all, under the traditional DWI and DUI formulations.

Per se Laws and the Problem of Notice

According to a January 1985 NHTSA survey (U.S. Department of Transportation 1985), all but eight states have adopted per se laws that make it an offense for one to operate a motor vehicle when one has a BAC greater than 0.10. These per se laws do not require the prosecution to prove that the defendant was intoxicated, impaired, or unable to operate a vehicle safely; the prosecutor only has to prove that the defendant was driving with a BAC above the prohibited standard. The imperfect fit between BAC and actual performance gives rise, as we will see, to a serious notice problem.

As we noted in Chapter 5, the per se laws are a further step removed from addressing actual risk creation than are the traditional DWI and DUI laws. While the latter require some evidence of impairment in ability to drive, the former do not. They assume such impairment because of the correlation between BAC and impaired driving ability. It is important to emphasize that a correlation is only a statistical probability; it points to a general relationship, but it will not hold true in every case.

BAC 0.10 Standard

The majority of drunk driving convictions today are obtained under the per se laws with the assistance of a BAC test. BAC, measured in terms of the weight of the quantity of alcohol in a given volume of blood, expresses the ratio of weight to volume (or breath), in terms of a percentage. Thus, in practice, "drunk" driving usually means driving when one has a BAC above 0.10. If the law were to reduce the prohibited threshold to 0.05, there would be vastly more "crime"; likewise, if the BAC threshold were elevated to 0.15, there would be vastly less "crime." There could be no clearer example of the point made at the outset of this chapter: crime is first and foremost a legal construct.

If the designated 0.10 BAC level is so critical for defining the most common offense in America, one might well ask, why this level and not some other? In truth, there is nothing magical about the 0.10 BAC standard.[8] According to a study by the American Medical Association Committee on Medicolegal Problems (1970), at BAC 0.10 approximately half of the population will show signs of intoxication. This means that half of the population will not show such signs and might well pass a field sobriety test—and therefore avoid conviction under the DWI or DUI laws.

While the BAC 0.10 standard might seem arbitrary or unfair, it is reasonable to set a general standard for highway safety that does not necessarily track the competencies of every driver. Prophylactic safety standards are more common in administrative law, but they have now secured a beachhead in criminal law as well. We have become accustomed to traffic laws that make speeding an infraction or violation, even though a particular speeding driver may not pose a danger (and even though professional race drivers may consistently be better drivers at speeds above the lawful limit than are 90 percent of non–professional drivers at legal speeds.

Lately there has been pressure to reduce the chemical threshold for DWI. The citizens anti–drunk driving groups' efforts may someday succeed in lowering the prohibited BAC to 0.08 or even to 0.05 (see DiMaio and Garriott 1985).[9] While this redefinition of drunk driving would criminalize more alcohol-affected drunk driving, it might damage the effort to reduce dangerous driving—and dangerous drinking/driving in particular.

If the DWI laws were seen as criminalizing only serious, irresponsible, and aberrational drinking/driving, they might well be able to mobilize citizen sentiment in their support. However, if the prohibited BAC level was lowered and the behavior of more moderate drinkers was swept into the criminal law net, citizen support would diminish. Moreover, the criminal justice system would be unable to deliver swift and serious punishment to a much larger number of drunk driving defendants. If the drunk driving laws attack low level drinking, they will likely suffer the same fate as Prohibition. Furthermore, Professor Robert Borkenstein et al.'s (1974) classic Grand Rapids study found that BACs below 0.04 "were not inconsistent with safe driving"; the probability of a crash began to increase dramatically at 0.08.[10] With the prohibited BAC fixed at 0.10, drivers with lower BACs who appear to be impaired can be prosecuted for DWI.[11]

BAC Testing Technology

The per se laws essentially make a machine test determinative of guilt (see Nichols 1983), just as radar evidence has come to establish conclusive proof of speeding. The reliance on a machine in the drunk driving context is more anomalous because the offense is not a traffic infraction but a misdemeanor or, in the case of a recidivist, a felony. There is a substantial scientific and legal literature on BAC testing (see Nichols 1983). In the United States the most common form of BAC testing is a breath test, which is conducted (usually at the station) by requesting the arrested driver to blow deeply into one of several types of machines; since the late 1940s the most popular has been the Breathalyzer (see Borkenstein 1960), but many other machines are in use, including the Intoxilyzer. The state of Washington's Court of Appeals (355 P. 2d 806 [1960]) has described the operation of the Breathalyzer as follows:

The breathalyzer is a machine designed to measure the amount of alcohol in the alveolar breath and is based upon the principle that the ratio between the amount of alcohol in the blood and the amount in the alveolar breath from the lungs is a constant 2100 to 1. In other words, the machine analyzes a sample of breath to determine the alcoholic content of the blood. . . .

To operate the machine, the subject blows into the machine through a mouthpiece until he has emptied his lungs in one breath. The machine is so designed that it traps only the last 52.5 cubic centimeters of air that has been blown into it. This air is then forced, by weight of a piston, through a test ampoule containing a solution of sulphuric acid and potassium dichromate. This test solution has a yellow hue to it. As the test sample bubbles through the test solution, the sulphuric acid extracts the alcohol, if any, therefrom, and the potassium dichromate then changes the alcohol to acetic acid, thereby causing the solution to lose some of its original yellow color. The greater the alcoholic content of the breath sample, the greater will be the loss of color of the test solution. By causing a light to pass through the test ampoule and through a standard ampoule containing the same solution as the test ampoule (but through which no breath sample has passed), the amount of the change in color can be measured by photoelectric cells which are connected to a galvanometer. By balancing the galvanometer, a reading can be obtained from a gauge which has been calibrated in terms of the percentage of alcohol in the blood. (P. 809)

The Breathalyzer operator need only start the machine, insert the ampoule, run a purge and blank reading utilizing an atomizer bulb or a pump, and read the defendant's score off the display. One can hardly imagine a more cut-and-dried criminal case. The operator must be certified as competent to operate the machine. At trial, before introducing a BAC score, the state must lay a foundation by showing that the machine was cared for and operated according to standard procedures. Nevertheless, a small number of criminal defendants who have the resources to mount an extensive defense continue to raise questions about breath-testing technology.[12]

The breath-testing machines assume a constant ratio of alcohol in the breath to alcohol in the blood.[13] This is based on the modal ratio in a large population; there is variation among individuals (Jones 1978). Recently the Nebraska Supreme Court overturned a drunk driving conviction on the ground that if the defendant's actual alcoholic breath : blood ratio was lower than 2,100 : 1, the amount of alcohol in his blood would have been below the prohibited level (*State v. Burling*, 224 Neb 725, 400 N.W. 2d 872 [1987]). Thus, the court announced its willingness to give defendants the benefit of the doubt in all prosecutions based on breath-testing machinery. If utilizing the alcoholic breath : blood ratio most favorable to a defendant produces a non-prohibited BAC, the prosecutor's case will fail.

There are other criticisms of the breath-testing technology. For example, every machine has its own small error factor. Some researchers claim that BAC can vary with air temperature, humidity, breathing pattern, and body temperature (Hlstala 1985). The machine test can be distorted if the subject has vomit or other foreign matter in his mouth when he blows into the machine. The chemicals could be defective, or the machine could be improperly calibrated. During the early 1980s it was revealed that several Smith and Wesson Breathalyzer models provided distorted BAC results when operated in the presence of radio frequency interference, thus registering inaccurate scores when operated in the presence of a police radio; many convictions were reversed before these models were adapted to correct the problem (see *Durand v. City of Woosocket*, 82-4808 [Super. Ct. R.I. 1982]; Kelly and Tarantino 1983). However, none of these limitations or qualifications regarding the accuracy of breath-testing procedures has led to rejection of the machinery, much less to rejection of the per se laws.

In recent years, defense lawyers have asserted the state's obligation to preserve the breath ampoule so that it can be submitted for independent testing if the defendant wishes. State courts ruled both ways on the question (compare, e.g., *Municipality of Anchorage v. Serrano*, 649 P. 2d 256 [1982] and *People v. Hitch* [California], 1974 with *State v. Shutt*, 363 A. 2d 406 [1976], and *State v. Cantu*, 569 P. 2d 298 [1977], before the U.S. Supreme Court held that due process provides no such right (*California v. Trombetta*, 467 U.S. 479 [1984]. Subsequently some state supreme courts, on state constitutional grounds, have reaffirmed the state's obligation to save the used ampoules or to provide the defendant a second test to fortify confidence in the accuracy of the procedure.

The Problem of Notice

While it may be more precise to define DWI in terms of BAC rather than in terms of intoxication, it also provides drinkers with less notice of what the law prohibits. Drinkers can monitor their own sensations, behavior, and speech for the telltale signs of intoxication, but they cannot be expected to carry around their own breath- or blood-testing devices. This would not be a problem if BAC always corresponded closely with the outward symptoms of intoxication, but it does not. There are heavy drinkers who have no mental or physical indication of intoxication when their BAC reaches 0.10. Some drinkers who believe that the effects of their drinking have dissipated to a safe level may not feel drunk even though their BAC is illegally high.

Courts rejecting notice challenges have held that defendants should be able to discern when they are intoxicated. A 0.10 BAC requires a "significant quantity" of alcohol, and "any person with common sense will know when consumption is approaching a meaningful amount. At that point he proceeds at his own risk" (*State v. Muhlenberg*, 347 N.W.2d 914 [Wis. App. 1984]). Those concerned with problems of vagueness and notice in the criminal law will be no more satisfied with this formulation than with the DWI or DUI formulations. If individuals differ significantly on whether a person is "intoxicated" or "under the influence," they will hardly agree on when drinking "is approaching a meaningful amount."

A more realistic response to the notice argument would emphasize that drivers have constructive notice of their potential criminal liability. It could be argued that it would be reasonable to require people who drink alcohol to carry and consult readily available pocket conversion tables that indicate how many drinks it takes to bring them above the legal limit. Unfortunately, however, these tables are neither consistent nor reliable. Because there is variation in the amount of drinking necessary to bring a person in a given weight range over the proscribed BAC level, estimates are necessarily rough averages. The choice of averages is essentially political; there is strong motivation for the table constructors to underestimate the number of drinks it takes to produce an unlawful BAC. Indeed, *overestimation* would provide a plausible reliance defense for a defendant who reached the prohibited level despite having relied on the table's guidance (*Wisconsin v. Hinz*, 121 Wis. 2d 282, 360 N.W.2d 56 [1984]).[14]

The Mens Rea of Drunk Driving

Subjective culpability is the cornerstone of modern Anglo-American criminal jurisprudence. Normally, to establish guilt it must be demonstrated that a defendant engaged in proscribed behavior intentionally, knowingly, or recklessly. Some criminal laws require proof only of negligence (i.e., the defendant should have been aware), but these are considered exceptional and are not usually employed in the definition of serious crimes.

The criminal law also includes a small number of strict-liability offenses, those that do not require any particular mens rea or even negligence. Guilt is predicated merely on having committed the prohibited act or conduct. Such laws, however, are rare and controversial (compare Wasserstrom 1960 with Hart 1968). Traffic offenses might be thought of as an entire genre of strict-liability offenses because they typically affix responsibility and impose punishment regardless of whether the violator intended, knew, or had reason to know that he was violating a particular provision of the traffic law. Nevertheless, they are not really exceptions, because they are not true crimes but a species of less serious administrative "infractions" or "violations." They do not impose stigma or severe punishment.

Since the early twentieth century there has been a tendency to define drunk driving differently from other traffic offenses and to brand its perpetrators as criminals. In most states a first drunk driving conviction is a misdemeanor, and a second conviction within a rather lengthy time period (e.g., in New York, ten years; in Pennsylvania, seven years) is a felony. First offenders face mandatory jail terms in many states, and recidivists face felony sentences. Strict liability is clearly inappropriate for an offense this serious.

Although it is the most commonly prosecuted offense in our criminal courts, there is, remarkably, little case law on what mens rea, if any, is required for proof of drunk driving: must the driver intend, know, or even have reason to know that he is impaired or chemically intoxicated when he takes the wheel? Courts gloss over the issue. Most of them, like the Wyoming Supreme Court (*Crum v. City of Rock Springs*, 652 P. 2d 27 [1982], seem to assume that drunk driving is a strict-liability offense:[15] "the elements of the offense are that the accused was (1) driving or in actual physical control of the vehicle; and (2) under the influence of an intoxicating liquor to a degree that renders him incapable of safely driving a motor vehicle, and (3) within the City of Rock Springs at the time of the driving."

It might be thought that failure to require the prosecution to prove a guilty mind is not a serious problem because recklessness or at least negligence is inherent in the commission of the offense. Hasn't a drunk driver always consciously disregarded the risk that he would become intoxicated and drive? Alternatively, hasn't a drunk driver always acted unreasonably (i.e., negligently) for a person in his situation? The answer to both questions is, not necessarily. Perhaps the defendant did not know that the substance he drank was alcoholic; perhaps he had explicitly and reasonably (though mistakenly) assured himself that it was not. Perhaps the defendant was unaware that he had consumed so much alcohol, either becuase his glass had been refilled without his knowing it or because he had inadvertently miscounted. Perhaps the defendant realized he might get drunk and took reasonable steps to ensure that he would not be driving. While such situations may not arise often, the law of drunk driving refuses to acknowledge them. This is not acceptable when the offense has come to be defined as a misdemeanor and even a felony and when penalties include mandatory incarceration.

Lesser-included Offenses

In addition to statutes prohibiting drinking (or even carrying open bottles of) alcoholic beverages in motor vehicles,[16] some states, such as New York, have a lesser-included traffic infraction (violation) called "driving while ability impaired" (DWAI); BAC 0.08–0.10 is prima facie evidence of impairment.[17] In New York State DWAI carries lesser maximum penalties than DWI, a $250 fine and/or fifteen days in jail, compared with a maximum $5,000 fine and/or one year in jail. A second DWAI conviction is punishable by a $300 fine and/or thirty days in jail.

DWAI was created to close a loophole—that is, allowing DWI defendants to plead down to non-alcohol-related offenses such as reckless driving or speeding. Anti–drunk driving advocates charged that plea bargaining meant that a recidivist drunk driver would appear to be a first offender—and therefore that prosecutors and judges, unaware of his previous drunk driving, might let the defendant plea bargain again. Thus, DWAI was meant to structure plea bargaining. First-time drinking/driving offenders would be permitted to plead to this lesser offense, which would count as a DUI conviction if the defendant were arrested again.

DWAI can also be justified as a prophylactic measure. It could be argued that if drivers know that they can be charged with a traffic violation if they are intoxicated to the slightest degree, they will have an even greater incentive not to drink alcohol before driving. Thus, the argument concludes, fewer people will drink at all, and fewer will drink to levels of intoxication proscribed by DWI statutes. While this argument is logical, the positive contributions of DWAI are offset by the negative impact of DWAI on the norm against *drunk* driving.

DWAI to the slightest degree could be used to convict a large percentage of drivers who are driving safely and under control. Professor Borkenstein et al.'s (1974) Grand Rapids study showed that drivers with low BAC levels (i.e., 0.04 or less) were no more likely to have a collision than were drivers with no alcohol in their blood. Moreover, if the use of DWAI in effect reduces the drunk driving threshold, enforcement will suffer to the extent that the citizenry comes to regard drunk driving as normal and acceptable rather than deviant.

While there is a certain logic in having a lesser-included drunk driving offense that would assist in the administration of justice, the existence of DWAI confuses the substantive law of drunk driving. In New York State DWAI can be charged either if an arrested driver's ability to operate a vehicle is diminished by alcohol "even in the slightest degree" (apparently a purely subjective standard for responsible driving) or if the arrestee's BAC is 0.08–0.10. Thus, the net of criminal liability is cast over a greater proportion of drinking/driving behavior.[18]

The availability of three substantive drunk driving offenses (two misdemeanors and an infraction) gives substantial discretion to prosecutors, judges, and juries. The definitions of DWI and DWAI substantially overlap, as is evident in the following New York Court of Appeals explanation: "[DWAI is not vague;] the question in each case is whether, by voluntarily consuming alcohol, this particular defendant has actually impaired, to any extent, the physical and mental abilities which he is expected to possess in order to operate a vehicle as a reasonable and prudent driver.

[DWI requires] a greater degree of impairment which is reached when the driver has voluntarily consumed alcohol to the extent that he is incapable of employing the physical and mental abilities which he is expected to possess in order to operate a vehicle as a reasonable and prudent person" (*People v. Cruz,* 399 N.E. 2d 513 [1979]).

Conclusion

Drunk driving fits uncomfortably within general criminal law jurisprudence. Two types of formulations define drunk driving, the "intoxication" and "per se" standards. The traditional statute requires proof of DWI or DUI, a vague standard that puts a great deal of de facto power both in the hands of the police officer who makes the arrest and administers the field sobriety test and in the hands of the judge or jury which applies the vague standard. Moreover, the elements of the offense have not been clearly defined in most jurisdictions. Most courts treat drunk driving as a strict-liability offense, leaving no escape for defendants whose intoxication was inadvertent and even "reasonable."

The modern per se offense is even more questionable than traditional DWI and DUI. It is a prohphylactic-type criminal law that imposes strict liability regardless of subjective culpability or manifest dangerousness. A driver who was operating his vehicle flawlessly and who could pass a field sobriety test would still be guilty of drunk driving if a breath test showed his BAC to be 0.10 or greater.

7
Aggravated Forms of Drunk Driving

Like other offenders, drunk drivers present a continuum of culpability and risk. The drunk drivers who are the most culpable and dangerous warrant the strongest controls and severest punishments. This chapter examines the ways in which the law of drunk driving deals—or fails to deal—with serious offenders, recidivists, and drunk drivers who cause injury and death.

Aggravated DWI

Drunk drivers present a continuum of dangerousness, depending on age, personality, alcohol experience, skill, impairment, and actual conduct. There are drunk drivers who drive well below the speed limit, overcautiously hugging the shoulder of the road, and there are drunk drivers who weave wildly through traffic at high rates of speed. There are drunk drivers with BACs of 0.10, and there are those with BACs of 0.25 and higher. At a BAC of 0.10 some drivers can operate a vehicle with reasonable skill and judgment; at a BAC of 0.20, even heavy drinkers are highly impaired and pose a significant threat to other roadway users.

Drunk drivers also present a continuum of culpability. The most culpable are those who intentionally set out to become intoxicated, well aware that they will subsequently be driving, and who, conscious of their intoxication, intentionally take to the road. Indeed, some offenders intentionally become intoxicated while they are driving. Recidivists are also among the most culpable, because they continue to violate the law despite warnings and previous sanctions. At the other end of the continuum are people who inadvertently drink to excess, who are not conscious of being intoxicated, or who consume alcoholic beverages with no expectation of having to drive later.

Because the legal definition of drunk driving encompasses such a broad continuum of dangerousness and culpability, one might well ask whether a single offense category lumps together offenders who should properly be distinguished. Would it not make sense to carve out an aggravated form of DWI for the most culpable and dangerous offenders? Aggravated DWI could be defined as a criminal offense while ordinary DWI could be defined as a traffic law violation, thus addressing some of the problems discussed in Chapter 5. Interestingly enough, while many states have formulated lesser-included forms of DWI, none has formulated an aggravated form of the offense to cover offenders with exceptionally high BACs, those drinking while driving, and those driving recklessly.

The Scandanavians, to whom we often look for wisdom in this field, do define an aggravated form of drunk driving for BAC levels above 0.15. In Sweden a distinction is made between driving when not sober, punishable by a fine, and drunk driving (BAC above 0.15), which is punishable by imprisonment. It is surprising that a similar approach has not found favor in the United States, in light of our proclivity for grading criminal offenses (e.g., burglary by day and burglary by night, robbery and armed robbery, larceny and grand larceny, and, in capital punishment states, murder and aggravated murder; New York has seven grades of criminal drug sale and possession). It would certainly make sense to stigmatize and punish the most dangerous and culpable drunk drivers with a conviction for aggravated drunk driving.

American jurisdictions also use sentencing to make distinctions about the gravity of offenses. With only a few exceptions, sentencing law provides a range of penalties that can be imposed on those convicted of a particular offense. Thus, for example, if the maximum penalty for a first drunk driving offense is thirty days in jail plus a $1,000 fine and six-month license suspension, the most serious offenders can be sentenced to the maximum and the least serious to a suspended jail term, modest fine, and briefer license suspension.

Despite the flexibility of our sentencing law, there are good reasons to consider grading DWI according to ordinary and aggravated forms. The most important reason may be symbolic. Just as armed robbery and armed robbers are defined as more dangerous and culpable than garden-variety robbers, it would be proper to condemn and stigmatize all extremely impaired drivers, those who drink while driving as well as those who drive recklessly. Moreover, the appropriate sentencing range for aggravated DWI would be broader than for garden-variety drunk driving; sentencing maxima might include an extended, even mandatory, jail term, an elevated fine, license revocation, and perhaps vehicle forfeiture.

Recidivism: Misdemeanor/Felony Formula

American criminal jurisprudence generally treats recidivists more seriously than it does first offenders; most often the differentiation is made at the sentencing stage, but on occasion it is built into the definition of the crime itself.[1] Most jurisdictions treat a first DWI offense as a misdemeanor and a second conviction within a specified number of years (ten years in New York State) as a felony.

This legislative strategy for grading drunk driving offenders has the same strengths and weaknesses as the general practice of treating recidivists more harshly, as well as a few strengths and weaknesses of its own. Recidivist statutes correctly strive to impose more severe penalties on those offenders who have shown themselves to be undeterred by less severe sanctions. Thus, the criminal laws in many states provide that offenders with a certain number of prior (usually felony) convictions can be sentenced as "multiple," "dangerous," or "habitual" offenders.

A more serious problem is in deciding how much extra punishment prior conviction(s) warrants. This issue has generated a large and stimulating literature (von Hirsch 1985). I adhere to the view that prior record should be permitted to escalate a current sentence *modestly*. However, the current sentence should principally be based on the defendant's culpability and on the dangerousness evidenced by the offender's current crime.

One weakness of this general approach, however, is the difficulty of operationalizing the notion of "chronic" or "habitual" offender. It strikes some observers as perverse that habitual offender statutes have been applied against petty crooks with convictions for shoplifting, check kiting, and larceny or against persons with three assaults over the course of a twenty-year period.[2] Under scrutiny, it seems that society is unsure what it means by habitual or chronic offenders.

In the context of the drunk driving issue, we can feel confident that persistent recidivist drunk drivers are a greater threat to the community and are more resistant to ordinary punishments and deterrents than are occasional offenders. Moreover, the repeat drunk driver will have notice that drinking might lead to an episode of intoxicated driving, making his culpability clearer than that of the first offender. Nevertheless, it is not obvious how the class of dangerous recidivist offenders can be identified, a problem shared with other habitual offender schemes. New York State defines a second DWI conviction *within ten years* as a felony. This may be seriously overinclusive, sweeping up into its net many run-of-the-mill offenders who are neither especially active nor especially dangerous; the link between two apprehensions in ten years and "chronicity" seems quite attenuated. It might be countered that, given the small chance that a drunk driver will be apprehended, a person who is convicted twice for drunk driving may be safely presumed to be an active offender. Unfortunately, little is known about rates of DWI offending for different types of DWI offenders.

Reserving more severe punishment for repeat offenders also poses a special problem in the drunk driving context. Recidivist drunk drivers may be the offenders least able to control their drinking, and, arguably, they are less culpable than run-of-the-mill first offenders. Yet "drinking problems" are not a general excuse or mitigating factor in criminal cases; given the strong link between alcohol and crime, there is little likelihood that they could or would be so defined. Moreover, it would be confusing and contradictory to define a special recklessness offense based on driving a vehicle while intoxicated and then to mitigate the offense because the defendant's drinking problems were responsible for his intoxication.

If, perhaps unwisely, a state does provide draconian penalties for habitual offenders, do DWI convictions count as predicates for the purpose of triggering such statutes? Consider the case of a defendant charged with burglary who has two previous felony convictions, one for assault and battery and one for felony DWI. If the state has a habitual offender law triggered by a third felony conviction, is it proper to charge this defendant as a habitual offender? There would seem to be no reason not to do so, unless felony DWI is in some way different from other felony convictions. In making repeated DWI a felony the legislature determines that it is *not* a less serious crime than assault, larceny, burglary, or many other felonies.

The idea that some felonies are less equal than others has no basis in modern criminal codes. Any number of felonies might be criticized on one ground or another as not meeting the threshold of seriousness that, in someone's judgment, the term "felony" should imply. Nevertheless, most courts that have considered the matter have refused to consider felony DWI convictions when applying habitual offender–type statutes, on the ground that to do so would be to double bootstrap drunk driving: the offender is being treated as a felon because of a previous DWI misdemeanor conviction and as a habitual offender because of the felony DWI conviction. This position reflects either misplaced sympathy for DWI offenders or reluctance to apply habitual offender statutes. Repealing or redefining the habitual offender statutes would be a more appropriate resolution of these concerns.

Procedural Implications of Aggravated and Felony DWI

American constitutional criminal procedure distinguishes between minor and serious offenses. An indigent defendant charged with a petty offense is not constitutionally entitled to assigned counsel; nor is he entitled to a jury trial. Both rights are guaranteed to a defendant charged with a serious offense. The dividing line between a serious and a petty offense is different for these two rights.

For purposes of assigning counsel, a serious offense is any offense for which a jail term is a possibility (*Scott v. Illinois*, 440 U.S. 367 [1979]). Thus, if an offense carries a possibile one-day jail term, an indigent defendant is entitled to an assigned counsel. For purposes of the federal constitutional right to a jury trial, a serious offense is an offense punishable by more than six months incarceration (*Baldwin v. New York*, 399 U.S. 66 [1970]). Some states are more liberal in defining eligibility for jury trial.

These principles affect the law of drunk driving in several ways. If states wish to get tough with first-time DWI offenders, they will have to afford them assigned counsel (a potentially large expense for small rural counties). If they formulate an offense of aggravated DWI with a maximum incarceration of six months or more, they would have to extend the right of trial by jury. Indeed, a jury trial may be necessary even if the maximum jail term is less than six months, if a recent U.S. Court of Appeals decision prevails. In *Landry v. Hoepfner* (818 F.2d 1169 [1987]) the court held that, because DWI is "a serious crime" within the meaning of the Sixth Amendment, a DWI defendant is entitled to a jury trial *regardless of whether the offense is punishable by six months imprisonment. Landry* will be the governing law in all the states included in the U.S. Fifth Circuit Court district unless the decision is reversed by the U.S. Supreme Court. It remains to be seen whether other circuits will follow suit.

The law regarding felony DWI is somewhat more complex. The maximum penalty for felony DWI typically exceeds six months incarceration, and therefore a jury trial is required. However, a problem arises if the first offense was defined as a misdemeanor for which no jail time was possible—and, therefore, no assigned counsel was provided. A defendant faced with a felony DWI charge will argue that he cannot be sent to jail because no assigned counsel was available at the first phase of the misdemeanor/felony grading sequence. While some courts may have accepted this argument (see, e.g., *State v. Novak*, 107 Wis. 2d 31, 318 N.W. 2d 364 [1982]), the better view holds the other way; the crime for which the defendant must have counsel is the present one, not the prior one which serves as the aggravating factor. There is no "compound" offense, only a present offense enhanced by a past one.

Drunk Driving Resulting in Injury

Drunk drivers, even those with excessively high BACs or prior DWI offenses, rarely cause much public concern unless they are involved in a crash causing injury or death. Such events frequently are reported in the media and attract significant public attention. Intuitively we feel that a drunk driving episode that results in serious injury or death is worse than one that results in no tangible injury—and we feel that the perpetrator should be punished more harshly.

Once again, we have stumbled on a major issue in criminal law jurisprudence: why should wrongdoing resulting in injury be punished more seriously than wrongdoing that causes no harm? While the issue is too rich to canvass here, our criminal law does take resulting harm into account in grading and punishing (Schulhoffer 1974). For example, attempts are punished less severely than completed crimes, assaults less seriously than homicides. To take a specific example, the Model Penal Code treats the crime of reckless endangerment less seriously than it does reckless homicide. This could be justified on the ground that causing injury demonstrates greater dangerousness or greater culpability.

There are at least two general rationales for treating injury as aggravating a criminal offense: (1) a presumption of greater dangerousness and (2) the assumption of risk.[3] Both rationales seem particularly well supported in the DWI context. Drunk drivers who cause serious injuries are not merely a random sample of all drunk drivers. They constitute a higher-risk group. Drivers who cause serious injury or death are disproportionately likely to have been acting more dangerously than those who have not caused injury or death.

As discussed in Chapter 5, the very act of driving a vehicle while intoxicated often involves consciously reckless conduct. In many crash/injury situations a drunk driver did consciously disregard a general risk of injury or death by getting into his vehicle aware of his intoxication and impairment. When a defendant consciously has chosen to take such risks, it is entirely fair, and consistent with criminal law jurisprudence, to hold him responsible for the injuries he causes.[4]

Drunk Driving Resulting in Death

Of those who die in alcohol-related crashes, about 60 percent are the drunk drivers themselves. This leaves approximately eight thousand fatalities who are either passengers in drunk drivers' cars or "innocent" drivers, passengers, bicyclists, or pedestrians. How should the criminal law deal with these deaths? Should they all be treated alike, as a special homicide category? Should they be grouped into several different homicide categories? Should they be treated within existing homicide categories?

The advent of the motorcar caused special problems for the law of homicide. Automobile accidents quickly became a major cause of death, and in the vast majority of cases a driver could be blamed for carelessness and violation of traffic laws. Prosecutors first had to decide whether all or some portion of fatal traffic accidents warranted criminal prosecution and, if so, what the charge should be. Without a specific statute to cover traffic fatalities, prosecutors were likely to deploy general manslaughter statutes (*Nebraska Law Review* 1962), which required proof of recklessness or gross negligence.[5]

It is frequently said that the traditional homicide laws proved unsatisfactory (from a prosecutorial standpoint) in drunk driving fatality cases because juries would acquit (rather than convict of manslaughter) a solid citizen "who had had one too many." I know of no empirical data to support this claim and find it improbable in light of the substantial antialcohol sentiments of that period. Furthermore, it was probably not true that most drunk driving homicide defendants were "solid citizens." Perhaps folklore about jury nullification reflects the values of prosecutors and judges more than it does those of common citizens. Alternatively, it might reflect a general prosecutorial aversion to litigating cases when outcomes are uncertain (Albonetti 1987). In any event, given American reliance on plea bargaining, only a minority of drunk driving homicide prosecutions went to trial.

For whatever reasons, beginning in the 1920s states began to pass specific vehicular homicide statutes which carried less stigma and lesser penalties than did the general manslaughter statutes.[6] The following Nebraska statute was one of the first: "If any person operating a motor vehicle in violation of the provisions of this act shall by so doing seriously maim or disfigure any person, or cause the death of any person, or persons he shall, upon conviction thereof be fined not less than two hundred dollars nor more than five hundred dollars, or be imprisoned in the penitentiary for not less than one year nor more than ten years. (Neb. Laws c. 222 sec. 32 [1919]). Later, perhaps still dissatisfied with the uncertainties of homicide prosecutions arising from drunk driving episodes, Nebraska and other states passed more specific homicide statutes to cover drunk driving resulting in death.[7] Once again the penalties were reduced.

The availability of a new statute did not foreclose the possibility of prosecution under the older statutes. Thus, in time, a drunk driver responsible for another person's death could be charged with manslaughter by automobile, negligent homicide, reckless homicide, homicide by criminal negligence, negligent operation of a motor vehicle, and driving so as to endanger that results in death. The penalties for vehicular homicide were less than those for manslaughter; probation or a short jail term was a typical penalty for killer motorists, including killer drunk drivers. However, vehicular homicide laws did not prevent the prosecution from charging a higher level of homicide if the facts warranted it.

Current Charge Escalation for Drunk Driving Homicides

If, until recently, sentimentalism or unrealistic fears of jury nullification led to devaluation of drunk driving homicides, the current animus toward killer drunk drivers has produced some extraordinary efforts to ease the prosecutorial path to drunk driving homicide convictions and to upgrade those convictions, from vehicular manslaughter to manslaughter and even to murder.

Some statutes and court decisions even seem to extend the idea of strict liability to the homicide context. For example, a recent Florida statute states that

it is unlawful for any person, while in an intoxicated condition or under the influence of intoxicating liquor, model glue . . . or any [controlled substance] to such an extent as to deprive him of full possession of his normal faculties, to drive or operate over the highways, streets, or thoroughfares of Florida any automobile, truck, motorcycle or other vehicle.

. . . and if the death of any human being be caused by the operation of a motor vehicle by any person while intoxicated, such person shall be deemed guilty of manslaughter, and on conviction be punished as provided by existing law relating to manslaughter.

In other words, to obtain a manslaughter conviction under this statute the prosecution need prove only that (1) a death occurred, (2) the death resulted from the operation of the defendant's vehicle, and (3) the defendant was intoxicated. Neither proof of mens rea nor proof of relationship between the driver's intoxication and the victim's death is necessary. The Florida Supreme Court explained in *Baker v. State* (377 So. 2d. 17 [1979]) that the legislature meant this to be a strict-liability offense(!), a legislative judgment justified by the gravity of the drunk driving problem. The Florida court, like many others, found sufficient culpability in the defendant's decision to drink in the first place:

the negligence occurred at the time the driver, drunken to the extent named in the statute, entered the vehicle and proceeded to operate it, and that negligence attached at the time the collision occurred, resulting in the death for which the defendant was placed on trial. It was not necessary to show that there was additional negligence when the collision occurred and no error was committed on the part of the court when he referred in his charge to a "collision" and did not place upon the state the burden of establishing beyond a reasonable doubt that there was some further wrongdoing on the part of the defendant before conviction would be warranted.

If the negligence required for a manslaughter conviction is satisfied by the very act of getting drunk or entering the vehicle while intoxicated, there is hardly anything to litigate. All drivers involved in a fatal traffic crash who are found to be "intoxicated" will be guilty of manslaughter, regardless of their responsibility for getting drunk, their consciousness of getting into the vehicle, and their due care behind the wheel.

Florida is not alone in emasculating its homicide law in order to more easily snare and punish killer drunk drivers. Recently the Colorado Supreme Court (*People v. Rostad*, 669 P. 2d. 126 [1983]) had the opportunity to interpret a new homicide law that provides that "if a person operates or drives a motor vehicle while under the influence of any drug or intoxicant and such conduct is the proximate cause of the death of another, he commits vehicular homicide. This is a strict liability offense." What could this mean? Apparently that the prosecution does not have to prove that there is gross negligence—or any negligence—in getting drunk, getting behind the wheel, and driving; there is a presumption that negligence is proved by the driver's intoxicated state. The prosecution must prove only that the defendant was intoxicated and caused the victim's death. It is not clear whether his intoxication must be a part of the *conduct* causing death—or whether, as in Florida, it need not play a causal role.

Murder

Thirteen states, on at least a single occasion each, have used the doctrine of implied malice to uphold a murder conviction for a drunk driving death. Malice has been established by showing either intentional, wilful, and premeditated killing (usually first-degree murder) or wantonness, extreme recklessness, and depraved heart (usually second-degree murder). It was not hard for appellate courts to rule that certain drunk driving episodes met these criteria. Most of these cases were decided during the era of Prohibition (Grass 1984; 21 A.L.R.3d 150). During the 1970s there were less than a dozen reported appellate cases upholding murder convictions of drunk drivers. By the early 1980s only

Alabama and Tennessee continued to treat drunk driving killings as possible murders (*Cumberland Law Review* 1978; Grass 1984).

The anti–drunk driving crusade of the 1980s created renewed pressure to label drunk driving homicides as murders. Images of the killer drunk driver have come to symbolize the horrors of drunk driving. The assumption that a killer drunk driver deserves a lesser penalty than other homicidal offenders is anathema to groups such as MADD and RID. Under their prodding, and in an atmosphere of intense anti–drunk driving sentiment, prosecutors are filing murder charges against drunk drivers all around the country.[8] In my view, this trend should be questioned (see *Cumberland Law Review* 1978; *California Law Review* 1983; but see also Steinbock 1985). Historically murder has been reserved for the most serious forms of homicide. Under the common law murder required proof of malice; under the Model Penal Code (sec. 210.1) it requires proof of either an intent to kill or recklessness "manifesting extreme indifference to the value of human life" (i.e., extreme recklessness).

Some of the courts that have recently upheld murder convictions have employed analyses that would make every killing attributable to a drunk driver a murder. These courts have tended to analyze drunk driving homicides as a single offense rather than in terms of levels or categories of culpability or in terms of the individual circumstances of the offense. The California Supreme Court's language in *People v. Watson* (637 P.2d 279 [1981]), is illustrative:

The defendant had consumed enough alcohol to raise his alcohol content to a level which would support a finding that he was legally intoxicated. He had driven his car to the establishment where he had been drinking, and he must have known that he would drive later. It also may be presumed that the defendant was aware of the hazards of driving while intoxicated. As we stated in *Taylor v. Superior Court,* (598 P. 2d 854 [1979]): "One who willfully consumes alcoholic beverages to the point of intoxication knowing that he must thereafter operate a motor vehicle, thereby combining sharply impaired physical and mental faculties with a vehicle capable of great force and speed, reasonably may be held to exhibit a conscious disregard of safety of others." Defendant drove at highly excessive speeds through the city streets, an act presenting a great risk of harm or death.

The *Watson* court focused excessively on the act of getting drunk, at the expense of not considering the defendant's driving. Watson drove at a speed in excess of eighty miles per hour through village streets, nearly colliding with one vehicle and then crashing into a second vehicle and killing three people. His BAC level was 0.25. A proper analysis should have focused on the specific behavior leading up to the fatal collision. The court should have based its judgment on whether Watson's *specific behavior* was reckless and manifested gross indifference to human life. Did he act maliciously and wantonly? Did he consciously disregard the risk of a serious traffic accident? The prosecutor could easily have carried the burden of proving murder under that standard in Watson's case. The court's needlessly broad language paves the way for the murder convictions of all drunk drivers who cause death. This may satisfy interest groups' desire for an *emphatic symbolic* denunciation of drunk driving, but it rides roughshod over the jurisprudence of homicide.

The U.S. Fourth Circuit Court of Appeal's decision in *United States v. Fleming* (739 F. 2d 945 [1984]) demonstrates a better—albeit not totally satisfactory—effort; the court focused more on the particular homicide before it than on the whole category of drunk driving homicides. The defendant, David Fleming, was driving southbound along Virginia's George Washington Memorial Parkway at seventy to one hundred miles per hour in a forty-five-mile-per-hour zone. On several occasions, while being pursued by police officers, he crossed into the northbound lanes (of a divided highway) to pass southbound traffic. Ultimately he lost control of his vehicle, struck a curb on the northbound side of the road, and then struck a northbound car head-on, killing its driver. His BAC was an astronomical 0.315.

The federal statute, following the common law, defined murder as unlawful killing with malice aforethought. The prosecution argued that malice aforethought only required proof that the defendant's conduct demonstrated disregard for the lives and safety of others. The defendant argued that under that definition all drunk driving homicide would result in murder convictions. The U.S. Fourth Circuit Court of Appeals attempted to distinguish drunk driving that was grossly negligent (and thereby suitable for involuntary-manslaughter prosecution) from drunk driving that demonstrated (1) heartless disregard for life and safety and (2) extreme recklessness.

According to the *Fleming* court, the typical drunk driver makes an impaired attempt to drive normally; he is dangerous because, while trying to drive safely, he makes errors of judgment and execution. The malicious drunk drivers, such as Fleming and Watson, drive wantonly and wildly, seemingly unconcerned about their own and others' lives. Such defendants, according to the court, are proper candidates for murder prosecutions. In effect, the *Fleming* court constructed two modal types of drunk driving homicides. This is much better than constructing a single type but not as good as dispensing with "types" and treating each homicidal incident on the basis of its own facts.

Conclusion

This chapter has canvassed the criminal law's efforts to deal with the most serious, dangerous, and culpable drunk drivers. American jurisdictions have not defined an aggravated form of drunk driving which would specially stigmatize and punish the most egregious incidents of drunk driving. Thus, DWI encompasses a very broad range of offending and offenders. It would certainly be worth considering defining an offense of aggravated drunk driving that would cover (1) drivers with very high BACs, (2) drunk drivers who drive recklessly, and (3) drunk drivers who drink while driving.

The law has drawn a distinction between defendants convicted for the first time and defendants convicted two or more times within a time period as long as ten years. The latter are treated as felons and are eligible for prison terms of a year or more. One might ask whether this misdemeanor/felony grading scheme is too crude an attempt at drawing a line between run-of-the-mill and serious offenders.

When drunk driving results in injury or death, a whole array of criminal statutes is applicable. Historically, drunk driving killings have been treated as a lesser form of homicide, but now there is pressure to bring murder charges in such cases. A problem arises because of the judicial tendency to think of all drunk driving homicides as being of a single type or class of offense. The better strategy is to formulate charges according to the facts of each case, as prosecutors routinely do for other forms of homicide. The most wanton and reckless drunk drivers should be charged with murder; others should be charged with manslaughter. I see no reason for a special vehicular homicide offense, much less one narrowly tailored to convict drunk drivers.

8

Criminal Procedure and Drunk Driving

The legal history of drunk driving is marked by "a protracted struggle to define scientifically a standard for intoxication and to provide some objective evidentiary basis upon which to determine guilt or innocence" (King and Tipperman 1975). That history is also marked by persistent efforts to ease the path of enforcement and to foreclose opportunities for avoiding arrest and conviction. The result is a comprehensive web of substantive and procedural criminal and administrative laws that facilitates the arrest and conviction of drunk drivers. Jurisprudential and constitutional values, which have figured prominently in the evolution of criminal law and procedure, have been ignored or slighted in the case of drunk driving.

Criminal procedure tightens the web that substantive criminal law has spun around the drunk driver. Because of watered-down standards of probable cause, the police have wide latitude in making vehicle stops and investigating for intoxicated driving. Recently a majority of state supreme courts have given their approval to sobriety checkpoints at which the police stop all drivers, dispensing with probable cause altogether. After they are stopped, under the auspices of implied-consent laws, drivers must cooperate with the breath-testing procedures or face mandatory license forfeiture. Once the charge of drunk driving is filed, conviction is practically inevitable. The whole process has become increasingly automatic, a prime example of the mass processing of criminal cases that is characteristic of our criminal justice system.

In this chapter we will see how, in the name of more efficient enforcement, criminal procedures have been pushed to their constitutional limits and sometimes beyond. We will deal first with the probable-cause standard and with roadblocks, then turn our attention to right to counsel, implied-consent laws, and postarrest procedures.

Vehicle Stops and Investigations

Arrests for drunk driving are typically made when a police officer stops a car for violating a traffic law (or when the officer comes on the scene of an accident) and in the course of the stop finds probable cause to believe that the driver is intoxicated. In *Delaware v. Prouse* (440 U.S. 648 [1979]) the Supreme Court held that cars cannot be stopped at random in hope of turning up an unlicensed driver. However, full-fledged probable cause is not needed to justify a stop. The Court held that a stop is permissible if the police officer has an *articulable suspicion* that a traffic offense is being committed. Thus, if the police officer observes a vehicle drifting in and out of its lane, speeding, or lacking proper operating lights, he may stop the vehicle. The Maine Supreme Court's interpretation (*State v. Griffin*, 459 A.2d 1086 [1983]) of the proper standard provides a good example of the breadth of police discretion. To initiate an investigation short of a formal arrest, a law enforcement officer must act on the basis of specific and articulable facts that, taken together with rational inferences from those facts, reasonably warrant that intrusion. However, the basis for the investigatory stop need not amount to probable cause for an arrest, and, in fact, the observed conduct giving rise to the officer's suspicion of criminal activity may be "wholly lawful in itself."

These legal standards give the police enormous latitude in making vehicle stops. Given the number and complexity of traffic laws, articulable suspicions are ubiquitous. Furthermore, some courts have held that a traffic violation may not be necessary. For example, in *State v. Goetaski* (507 A. 2d 751 [1986]) a New Jersey state trooper on routine patrol observed the defendant at 4:00 A.M. slowly driving his vehicle, with the left-turn indicator flashing, on the northbound shoulder of a highway in a rural fifty-mile-per-hour zone. The trooper observed the vehicle for one-tenth of a mile and then stopped the driver. The court upheld the stop and subsequent conviction for DWI, stating that although "[T]he record is clear that no specific violation, such as swerving erratically or equipment defect, was observed by the officer, the trooper had a right to inquire whether something was wrong . . . I am more than satisfied that the hour of the night and the manner of the operation of the vehicle, and the operating on the shoulder of the road are more than sufficient to give a reasonable police officer a basis to stop and make appropriate inquiry."

Thus, a police officer striving to stay within the bounds of legality but willing to press his authority to the limits has enormous opportunity to make vehicle stops. Moreover, police officers who do not feel constrained to abide by legal standards can stop whatever vehicles they like, confident that they can always manufacture reasonable suspicion if necessary. Who could dispute a police officer's claim that a vehicle stop was justified by the vehicle's excessive speed, weaving, or erratic maneuvers?

Once the vehicle is stopped, the officer has authority to order the driver out of the vehicle and to subject him or her to a frisk for weapons (*Pennsylvania v. Mimms*, 434 U.S. 106 [1977]). The officer may observe the driver's demeanor and take note of his general condition and speech. If the officer has a further articulable suspicion that the driver is intoxicated, she may ask the driver to submit to a field sobriety test (including the horizontal gaze nystagmus [HGN]test) or to exhale into an Alco-sensor, a portable breath-testing device that provides a reasonably accurate reading of the driver's BAC level. If, in the officer's opinion, the driver fails the field sobriety test or scores above the prohibited limit on the Alco-sensor, the officer will have probable cause to arrest him for DWI. Some states have passed preliminary breath-testing (PBT) laws, which give the police authority to require a preliminary breath test from *any* driver lawfully stopped for a traffic violation or accident (see, e.g., New York Vehicle and Traffic Law, sec. 1193[a]). These laws, in my view, are of doubtful constitutionality under the Fourth Amendment because they constitute a search without probable cause or articulable suspicion.

Roadblocks

During the early 1980s, the anti–drunk driving movement and the Presidential Commission on Drunk Driving (1983) urged the implementation of sobriety checkpoints, which would stop all drivers on a given road and subject them to brief investigations for intoxication. If there was reason to suspect driver intoxication, the officer would press on with her investigation by ordering the driver to pull off the road to submit to a field sobriety or Alco-sensor test. By 1984 these roadblocks were operational in at least twenty-one states (National Transportation Safety Board 1984).

Roadblocks raise important questions about constitutional law and the proper role of the police (*Georgetown Law Journal* 1983; Jacobs and Strossen 1985). The Fourth Amendment protects the citizenry from unreasonable searches and seizures. Traditionally, a search without probable cause has been per se unreasonable (see, in general, LaFave and Israel 1985). For example, the police cannot stop and search everyone in a park for drugs, interrogate all motorists about terrorist activities, or search all homes in order to turn up evidence of crime.

Such dragnets, hallmarks of authoritarian regimes, are inconsistent with the legal and cultural values of American society.

During the past two decades, however, the Supreme Court and lower federal courts have carved out certain limited exceptions to the proscription against searches and seizures without probable cause and have upheld a few police practices according to a doctrine of "general reasonableness." The Supreme Court first recognized this exception in *Camara v. Municipal Court* (387 U.S. 523 [1967]), where the constitutionality of areawide building inspections in Baltimore, Maryland, was in question. Even though there was no probable cause to suspect violations at any particular premises, the Court found that these inspections were reasonable because they were not personal, had a long history of public acceptance, and served a primarily administrative purpose and because there was no other effective way to guarantee that the code regulations were being followed. Nevertheless, the Court required the building inspectors to obtain an "area-wide" search warrant from a court before embarking on their inspections.

During the next decade the Court upheld the use of permanent roadblocks at or near the country's borders to detect illegal aliens (*United States v. Martinez-Fuerte*, 428 U.S. 543 [1976]). These roadblocks, which stopped every (or every *n*th) motorist along the road to allow a brief search for illegal aliens, were clearly not supported by probable cause. The Court's rationale for upholding them, a mix of precedent and balancing, was similar to that in *Camara*. In subsequent years the Court also recognized a few other limited exceptions, particularly inspections of certain highly regulated industries, as in *Donovan v. Dewey* (452 U.S. 594 [1981]). In *Delaware v. Prouse* the Court refused to permit probable cause–less *random stops* to determine whether drivers had proper licenses and vehicle registrations. The Court's dictum, however, indicated that roadblocks used to achieve the same ends would be permissible: "this holding does not preclude the State of Delaware or other states from developing methods for spot checks that involve less intrusion or that do not involve the unconstrained exercise of [the police officer's] discretion. Questioning of all oncoming traffic at roadblock-type stops is one possible alternative" (440 U.S. 648 [1979], P. 663).

This was all the encouragement that some states needed. However, NHTSA added an economic incentive. It listed drunk driving roadblocks as one of several countermeasures that would qualify a state for supplemental highway safety funds.[1] The Presidential Commission on Drunk Driving added its blessing. Soon roadblocks began to appear across the United States.

These proliferating roadblocks were challenged under the Fourth

Amendment and its state-constitutional analogues. The majority of state courts approved the roadblocks (see, e.g., *State v. Deskins*, 673 P.2d 1174 [Kan. 1983]; *Little v. State*, 479 A.2d 903 [Md. 1984]; *People v. Scott*, 473 N.E.2d 1 [N.Y. 1984]; *State v. Martin*, 496 A. 2d 442 [Vt. 1985]; *City of Las Cruces v. Betancourt*, 735 P. 2d 1161 [N.M. 1987]), provided that they were implemented pursuant to departmental criteria and not according to the whim of individual line officers.[2] These courts purported to balance the necessity for and the intrusiveness of roadblocks against the interest in highway safety, as the Supreme Court had balanced analogous concerns in *Camara* and *Martinez-Fuerte*. Like the Supreme Court, most state courts concluded that the necessity outweighed the intrusion.

Courts reaching the opposite conclusion have emphasized roadblocks' incompatibility with traditional Fourth Amendment values and have questioned the claim that roadblocks are a more effective general deterrent to drunk driving than are traditional police strategies (see *State v. Bartley*, 466 N.E.2d 346 [Ill. 1984]; *State v. Smith*, 674 P. 2d 562 [Okla. 1984]; *Nelson v. Lane County*, 720 P. 2d 1291 [Ore. 1986]; *State v. Crom*, 383 N.W. 2d 461 [Neb. 1986]). (Research on the deterrent effects of various drunk driving strategies is discussed in Chapter 9.) If the burden of proof is on roadblock proponents, these courts are correct. There are presently no reliable data to support the claim that sobriety checkpoints have a significant marginal deterrent effect—or that whatever effect they do have could not be matched by committing equivalent resources to other enforcement strategies.

Like the administrative searches upheld in *Camara* and in *Martinez-Fuerte*, drunk driving roadblocks are a striking departure from the traditional balance between state power and individual autonomy. Motorists are detained and investigated without any reason to believe that they have violated any laws. Sobriety checkpoints do not target individuals reasonably suspected of having committed a crime. Rather, on the chance of turning up criminal law violators, police officers investigate all motorists who pass through the checkpoints. That this police practice appears "logical," "necessary," and "appropriate" reflects both the current salience of drunk driving as a social problem and the tendency to consider drunk driving in the context of traffic offenses in which fundamental rights and liberties do not seem to be threatened.

The departure from traditional restraints is actually far greater in the case of sobriety checkpoints than in that of building or border checks. Unlike the procedures upheld in *Camara* and *Martinez-Fuerte*, drunk driving roadblocks are not a form of administrative regulation but a strategy of criminal law enforcement. Not only is the threat to personal liberties greater than in administrative searches, but the justification is also far weaker: traditional enforcement techniques produce more arrests for drunk driving than for any other offense for which national data are collected, and crackdowns, which increase the resources available to the police, have invariably produced even more arrests. The roadblocks are, at best, a marginal supplement to the already massive anti–drunk driving effort.

Moreover, the acceptance of sobriety checkpoints on a wide scale might have profound implications for American policing, paving the way for other mass searches, sweeps, and dragnets.[3] Thus, it is well to bear in mind the Oklahoma Supreme Court's admonition in *State v. Smith* (674 P. 2d 562 [1984]): "The Court finds drunk [driving roadblocks] . . . draw dangerously close to what may be referred to as a police state. Here, the state agencies have ignored the presumption of innocence, assuming that criminal conduct must be occurring on the roads and highways, and have taken an "end justifies the means" approach . . . [A] basic tenet of American jurisprudence is that the government cannot assume criminal conduct in effectuating a stop. . . . Were the authorities allowed to maintain such activities . . . the next logical step would be to allow similar stops for searching out other types of criminal law offenders."

Right to Counsel

In some jurisdictions a drunk driver is formally arrested before being asked to take a breath test; elsewhere the suspect must be given an opportunity to take the breath test before being placed under arrest. Whenever the formal arrest occurs, however, once a driver is placed in custody, he must be given *Miranda* warnings, which inform him that he has a right to remain silent, that anything he says may be used against him in criminal proceedings, that he has a right to a lawyer, and that if he is indigent a lawyer will be appointed for him (*Berkemer v. McCarty*, 104 S. Ct. 3138 [1984]). He is simultaneously informed that he must submit to a breath test for alcohol and that if he refuses to submit he will automatically lose his license. In those states where a refusal is admissible at a criminal trial, the suspect must be so informed.

Most courts have held that there is no right to consult an attorney before deciding whether to take the Breathalyzer test.[4] *Miranda* does not apply because the police request for a BAC sample is not interrogation for *testimonial* evidence; the Sixth Amendment right to counsel does not attach because the election of whether to take a BAC test is not a *critical stage of the criminal proceeding* (see *Davis v. Pope*, 197 S. E.

2d 861 [Ga. 1973]; *Newman v. Hacker,* 530 S.W. 2d 376 [Ky. 1975]; *Dunn v. Petit,* 388 A. 2d 809 [R.I. 1978]). According to legal doctrine, no criminal proceeding exists until the defendant is charged.[5] Nevertheless, laymen might be surprised to learn that the decision about whether to take the breath test is *not* considered to be a critical stage of the criminal proceeding against the drunk driver, particularly since the test result constitutes practically the state's entire case.

A slightly different question arises if the defendant *asks to consult* with a lawyer before deciding whether to cooperate in the BAC test procedures. Even though refusal may not be unconstitutional, courts are clearly uneasy about permitting police officials to refuse such requests. Thus the New York Court of Appeals (*People v. Craft,* 28 N.Y. 2d 274 [1971], P. 279) held that "there is a vast difference between a failure to advise or warn a defendant of his rights . . . and a flat refusal . . . to afford him 'access to counsel' after he has requested the assistance of a lawyer." The court called denial of a direct request for counsel "so offensive as to taint the subsequent criminal trial" but reaffirmed its view that it is unnecessary to inform a defendant that he has a right to contact an attorney for consultation.

Implied-Consent Laws

The laws that require drunk-driving arrestees to provide a blood, urine, or breath sample on pain of license revocation are called "implied-consent" laws.[6] New York State passed the first such law in 1953. Every state subsequently passed a similar law.[7] They are referred to as "implied consent" because they are predicated on the fiction that, in applying for a license to drive, a person implicitly consents to cooperate in a BAC testing procedure if requested to do so by a police officer with probable cause to suspect DWI. Ironically, there is no real consent, and since the state conditions issuance of the license on compliance with the enforcement proceedings, nothing is implied. The state's authority to demand the test is specified in the vehicle and traffic law (see Lerblance 1978).

Some implied-consent laws (e.g., New York State's) give the defendant a choice of taking the chemical test or of refusing the test and accepting a license suspension. Others demand that the test be taken and state the penalties for refusal but say nothing about a choice. This silence may mean that, if the police have probable cause, they have the authority to administer the test forcibly, usually by extracting blood. The Supreme Court upheld this practice in *Schmerber v. California* (384 U.S. 757 [1966]). In reality, except in cases when the defendant happens to be in a medical setting because of an accident, the police will rarely exercise this option.

If the defendant refuses to submit to the BAC test, his license will be revoked. The defendant is entitled to an administrative hearing to determine certain limited issues (see *Bell v. Burson*, 402 U.S. 535 [1971]; *Mackey v. Montrym*, 443 U.S. 1 [1979]; *Illinois v. Batchelder*, 463 U.S. 1112 [1983]), such as whether the police officer had probable cause to demand the Breathalyzer test and whether the defendant actually refused. The hearing need not be held prior to the license revocation.

The threat of automatic revocation leads the majority of drunk drivers to cooperate in the testing procedures, thereby assuring the evidence that the state needs to prosecute defendants criminally under the per se laws. One suspects, however, that as criminal penalties for drunk driving increase, more defendants will refuse to incriminate themselves with a breath sample. Thus, states have begun to escalate the penalties for refusal. Some states permit the defendant's refusal to be entered as evidence against him at his criminal trial. Some states even make refusal an independent offense![8] Many states have recently passed administrative per se laws that make license suspension automatic and immediate as soon as the arrestee fails the BAC test (see National Transportation Safety Board 1984). Police may seize the defendant's driver's license at the station house. The defendant's only recourse is to request a subsequent hearing on the issue of whether he actually failed the test.

The Supreme Court has rejected a variety of challenges to implied-consent procedures. The Court has held that drivers are not entitled to a presuspension or prerevocation hearing (*Dixon v. Love*, 431 U.S. 105 [1977]; *Mackey v. Montrym*, 443 U.S. 1 [1979]). More important, perhaps, the Court has held that encouraging or coercing arrestees to take the blood, urine, or breath test does not violate the Fifth Amendment right against compelled self-incrimination because the amendment protects against being forced to provide incriminating *testimony*, not against being compelled to provide *physical evidence* such as urine, saliva, blood, or breath (*Schmerber v. California*, 384 U.S. 757 [1966]).

The Court faced a somewhat subtler issue in 1983, when a drunk-driving defendant in South Dakota challenged the state law that permitted the prosecution to enter into evidence presented at the criminal trial the defendant's refusal to submit to a chemical test for BAC. The refusal, it was argued, constituted compelled testimony. The Supreme Court disagreed (*South Dakota v. Neville*, 459 U.S. 553 [1983]). It held that the Fifth Amendment was not violated because the evidence, regardless of whether it could be characterized as testimonial, was not compelled. The Court explained that South Dakota was not compelling people arrested for drunk driving to refuse to take a BAC test. To the contrary, according to the Court, South Dakota was trying to compel people arrested for drunk driving to take the test and to provide physical (nontestimonial) evidence of BAC that could be used against them at a criminal trial. Thus, the results of the BAC have been held admissible because they are nontestimonial, while the refusal to take the test, although arguably testimonial, has been held not to be compelled.

Postarrest Proceedings

Once a defendant has been charged with DWI, the chance of escaping conviction is small. In this respect, not surprisingly, drunk driving parallels the processing of crimes generally. The overwhelming majority of DWI defendants, like most criminal defendants, plead guilty. Joseph Little's (1973) careful empirical study of the administration of justice in drunk driving cases found that 58.5 percent of apprehended DWI offenders were convicted as charged and that 89.2 percent were convicted of either the original or a lesser charge. In their study of drunk driving in Madison, Wisconsin, Goldstein and Susmilch (1982) found that 88 percent of DWI defendants were convicted of that charge; *there were no acquittals in an entire year's sample of cases*. The FBI's UCRs consistently report a DWI conviction rate of more than 90 percent.

It is a myth that American juries nullify the law by regularly acquitting guilty drunk drivers. For one thing, very few drunk driving cases involve jury trials. Under the Sixth Amendment the right to a jury trial only attaches if there is a possible sentence of more than six months in jail (*Baldwin v. New York*, 399 U.S. 66 [1970]). In states where a first DWI offense does not carry a maximum jail sentence of that length, there is no federal right to a jury trial.[9] When a jury trial is available to a DWI defendant, it is very rarely exercised. In general, jury trials are the exception rather than the rule in the administration of criminal justice, accounting for less than 5 percent of all criminal dispositions. The strongest disincentive for requesting a jury trial is the likelihood of a harsher sentence on conviction. There are also higher legal fees and the unpleasant experience of living for months or years with a pending criminal case.

The vast majority of drunk driving prosecutions are resolved by negotiated guilty pleas. In jurisdictions where plea bargaining is based on charge bargaining, drunk driving charges are typically reduced to lesser traffic offenses, unless there is a special lesser-included alcohol-related offense such as DWAI. A recent NHTSA-sponsored study shows that, even in states where there are mandatory rules against plea bargaining in drunk driving cases, charges in a high percentage of cases are nevertheless reduced. In jurisdictions where plea bargaining is carried on by sentence bargaining, drunk drivers typically plead guilty to obtain a sentence more lenient than the statutory maximum.[10]

The convicted DWI defendant is likely to be fined, have his license suspended or revoked, and perhaps be given a short jail term. The severity of the license suspension may be eased by a provisional or occupational license which permits the defendant to drive to work. The severity of the jail sentence may be reduced by weekend scheduling and by giving two days credit for a stint that begins just before midnight Friday and ends just after midnight on Saturday. A fine may, in fact, also be discounted if it is not collectable, which is a serious problem in many courts. On the other hand, a defendant's financial costs may be increased by treatment program costs, lawyers' fees, and insurance surcharges.

Conclusion

Law enforcement and the administration of justice in DWI cases are very routinized. One by one, impediments to the apprehension, investigation, arrest, and conviction of drunk drivers have been removed. While the police cannot stop drivers randomly to check for drunk driving, they can stop them on suspicion of violating any traffic law— or, at a properly established sobriety checkpoint, even when there is *no* suspicion. Once a driver is stopped, he can be subjected to a field sobriety test on the slightest suspicion of alcohol, or (under PBT laws) he can be required to submit to a preliminary breath test even when there is no suspicion. If probable cause surfaces from these investigations, the driver can be arrested. His cooperation in providing a breath sample for use in later criminal prosecution will be "encouraged" by threat of license suspension for refusal. If he passes the breath test, he will probably be released. If he fails the test, his license can be seized on the spot and he will be subject to DWI charges. All told, approximately 1.8 million Americans are arrested for DWI each year. Close to 90 percent are convicted.

Contrary to popular belief, very few drunk-driving defendants contest their guilt. In part this is because most of the sanctions can be applied against them administratively, regardless of whether they are convicted. Many states now limit plea bargaining in drunk driving cases. Neither prosecutors nor defense lawyers have many options. The "going rate" is well known and predictable. Occasionally a wealthy defendant may contest the charges and retain expert witnesses to impeach the breath-testing technology or its administration, but the number of such cases is insignificant. In processing drunk driving cases, the criminal justice system essentially functions as a guilt-stamping machine.

III

Institution Building in the Social Control of Drunk Driving

There are indications that the frequency of drunk driving has declined somewhat during the past ten years. The most persuasive evidence is the 1986 roadside survey conducted by the Mid-America Research Institute under the supervision of Arthur C. Wolfe, who was also the principal investigator of the 1973 national roadside survey. The survey stopped drivers between 11:00 P.M. and 3:00 A.M. in thirty-two localities around the country. The researchers found that the proportion of drivers with a BAC greater than 0.10 declined from 4.9 percent in 1973 to 3.1 percent in 1986 and that the percentage with BAC greater than 0.05 declined from 13.2 percent to 8.2 percent. If these results reflect reality, they demonstrate a real shift in drinking/driving behavior over the past fifteen years. Drivers are either drinking less or separating their drinking and driving more effectively. Interestingly, and somewhat surprisingly, the researchers found strong support for the first hypothesis. Drivers in 1986 indicated a striking overall decrease in alcohol consumption, 31.5 percent were abstainers in 1986 versus 17.5 percent in 1973. In part this reflects more women drivers in the 1986 sample, but the rest of the variance is difficult to explain, since no other studies with which I am familiar indicate that Americans are drinking less alcohol or abstaining in greater numbers. Most studies during the past several decades have found that approximately one-third of American adults are alcohol abstainers, so there may be something unusual about the 1973 sample of road users.

The Fell and Klein study, discussed in Chapter 3, estimated that in 1981 the proportion of driver fatalities who were drunk was 30 percent compared with 28 percent in 1984. While this is a decrease of only two percentage points, it constitutes a 9 percent reduction. For those looking for signs of progress in the battle against drunk driving, it too indicates that in the mid-1980s there was a trend toward fewer dangerous drunk drivers on the road. Unfortunately, it is difficult to accept drawing such an inference from these data. The authors' methodology does not allow them to say whether this decrease is statistically significant or a chance variation. In carrying out longitudinal analysis, it is very important to have trend data for longer than just three years, and the authors are hoping to apply their discriminant analysis to driver deaths before 1982 as well as to data that become available for years after 1984. The more years for which statistics on alcohol-related driver fatalities can be calculated, the more confidence we can have in the conclusions.[1]

The most recent data on alcohol-related fatalities seem to cast more doubt on claims that the incidence of drunk driving is decreasing. The 1986 FARS data in the fifteen "good reporting states" show a 7 percent increase over 1985 in alcohol-related driver fatalities. The increase was even higher among young drivers, whose alcohol-related deaths rose by 17 percent. The vacillations in these national data once again should caution us against reaching premature conclusions about "successes," "failures," and policy impacts. In my view, we are simply not in a position to make a definitive judgment about the impact of the anti–drunk driving countermeasures of the 1980s on the incidence of drunk driving.

Regardless of whether drunk driving is declining, there are a multitude of anti–drunk driving strategies now being deployed or proposed. In Part III we will examine each of the major anti–drunk driving strategies, illuminate the assumptions on which they are based, review the most competent evaluations, and attempt to identify any costs that they may impose.

Chapter 9 examines our primary social control strategy in dealing with drunk driving and other noxious social problems: deterrence through legal threats. We will see that both the probability and the expected cost of apprehension have increased.

Chapter 10 deals with efforts to achieve deterrence through the expansion of civil liability and the use of insurance surcharges for drunk drivers.

Chapter 11 analyzes possible incapacitation strategies against drunk drivers, including jail, house arrest, license suspension and revocation, and automobile impoundment and forfeiture.

Chapter 12 turns to public education strategies, which are closely linked with—but more inclusive than—deterrence. We will examine a variety of efforts to persuade the general public to desist from drinking/driving and to take action to prevent others from drunk driving.

Chapter 13 canvasses a host of opportunity-blocking strategies, which aim to restructure the environment to make drinking/driving less likely to occur. The legal drinking age of twenty-one, earlier closing hours for bars and taverns, and mechanical devices that make a vehicle inoperable by an intoxicated person are examples of opportunity-blocking strategies currently being deployed.

Chapter 14 analyzes treatment strategies, which aim to change the future behavior of those who are arrested for drunk driving. These strategies attempt either to cure the subject's pathological drinking or to persuade the subject to separate his drinking and driving more effectively.

9

Deterrence

Public policy and lawmaking on drunk driving are shaped by background assumptions concerning the nature of the problem and the efficacy of various intervention strategies. The greater the assumed magnitude of the problem and the greater the perceived efficacy of interventions, the greater the willingness to formulate new policies, to intensify old ones, and to reject restraints that might get in the way of progress.

The most popular type of anti–drunk driving policy, the threat and employment of criminal sanctions, is based on assumptions that are difficult to prove empirically. These difficulties do not mean that criminal law strategies do not work. Surely, the criminal law shapes attitudes and, to some extent, conscious decision making. However, it is well to remember that in developing drunk driving policy we are not dealing with a decision whether to criminalize previously legal behavior; rather, the issue is whether enhancing the expected punishments for a behavior that has long been a crime can produce a deterrence gain. It is important not to exaggerate the potential effect that legal threats can have on drunk driving. Incremental enhancements of expected punishment cannot eradicate drunk driving. The realistic goal is marginal decreases, and such decreases, if they can be achieved at all, come only at a price.

Simple Deterrence

Most recent efforts to reduce drunk driving have been based on an explicit or implicit theory of simple deterrence. The theory holds that if the cost of an undesirable behavior can be increased, less of it will be consumed; that is, an increase in the cost of drunk driving will decrease its incidence. Cost is a function of the expected probability of apprehension, conviction, and severity of punishment (Zimring and Hawkins 1973; Blumstein, Cohen, and Nagin 1978; Tittle 1980). If any of these variables is increased, the targeted behavior will diminish. Sometimes a distinction is drawn between legal threats directed at the general public (general deterrence) and threats directed at those who have been arrested for DWI (special deterrence). This distinction will not concern us in this chapter, although it will be relevent to the discussion in Chapters 12 and 13.[1]

For the most part this chapter focuses on simple deterrence, but it is important to point out that escalation and amplification of legal threats may have an indirect and long-term effect on attitudes and values that is independent of the fear of punishment that they produce. As public policy defines drunk driving as a more serious offense and a higher priority, the citizenry may form a more negative view of drunk driving, may become more resistant to temptations to drive drunk, and may become more condemnatory of those who do. In other words, over time new values, norms, and attitudes about drunk driving may evolve. We will return to this theme at the conclusion of the chapter. The first task, however, is to examine the assumptions that seem to lead drunk driving policy toward greater legal threats.

Drunk driving policy is not formulated in a vacuum. Americans often react to undesirable behavior and social problems by passing or amending their criminal laws. When the behavior persists the response is often to make the criminal laws even more severe and to call for tougher enforcement efforts. These dynamics are evident in the way American society deals with problems as diverse as street crime, illicit drugs, and political corruption.

It is not difficult to understand why the idea of escalating both legal threats and enforcement efforts is attractive. First, the notion that people will "consume" less of a behavior if its cost increases is an inherently logical notion that resonates with the economic life of our society. Second, this idea reflects faith in rationality and in the government's capacity to manage the society's social life. Americans seem to have extraordinary faith in the amenability of social problems to rational policy interventions. Without a belief in deterrence, social problems might seem intractible, a conclusion one suspects would be difficult either for American politicians to admit or for American citizens to accept. Third, the effectiveness of simple deterrence cannot easily, if ever, be disproved. A failure to show reductions in the rates of a condemned behavior can be taken as proof merely of the need for further escalations. That a particular crime problem persists year after year or fluctuates without much regard to enforcement levels does not seem to shake the widespread belief that still greater threats will make a difference. Fourth, as Durkheim (1947) pointed out a century ago, the act of denouncing evildoing and evildoers is functional for the condemn-ors; it allows them to draw a line between themselves and "criminals," thus reinforcing community bonds. This observation seems particularly applicable to Americans who define the crime problem, as well as most social problems, in strongly moral terms. The amplification of legal threats against drunk drivers represents a familiar American reaction to social problems.

Deterring Drunk Driving in America

American society has always employed legal threats against drunk driving. The first drunk driving offenses were formulated shortly after the invention of the motorcar. The familiar statutory formula first offense/misdemeanor and second offense/felony was a basic feature of the legal landscape during the 1930s (King and Tipperman 1975). Thus, the deterrence model presently being employed against drunk driving is not new. The current effort is not an attempt to apply legal threats against a previously legal activity but an attempt to achieve significant marginal deterrence by implementing the traditional social control model more vigorously and efficiently.

The major anti–drunk driving thrusts since the early 1970s all have featured deterrence strategies. Deterrence through enhanced legal threats and increased enforcement was the dominant anti–drunk driving strategy of the ASAPs of the early 1970s, of the Presidential Commission on Drunk Driving and citizens anti–drunk driving groups of the early 1980s, and of the state drunk driving task forces and legislative initiatives of the mid-1980s. In recent years most jurisdictions around the country have sought to increase the probability of apprehension by setting up special anti–drunk driving squads, initiating roadblocks, or simply making drunk driving arrests a higher priority. They have acted to increase the certainty of conviction by restricting plea bargaining and opportunities for pretrial diversion. In these efforts they have been aided by the citizens anti–drunk driving groups, which have undertaken "court watch" programs, letter-writing (to judges) campaigns, and the public condemnation of what they regard as unduly lenient sentences.

Possible Barriers to Simple Deterrence

While it seems logical that significantly escalating the costs of a behavior will reduce its frequency, there are some features of drunk driving that might make deterrence though legal threats unusually difficult to achieve. First, if a marginal deterrent effect is to be achieved, the target audience must be aware of increased apprehension probability and sentence severity. Perceptions of risk of apprehension and magnitude of punishment are a complex area for research, one that cannot be surveyed here (see Cook 1980). Dr. Ralph Hingson (1987) of the Boston University School of Public Health surveyed citizen attitudes before passage of tough anti–drunk driving legislation in Maine (in 1981) and Massachusetts (in 1982) and annually thereafter. He found *modest* increases in citizen perceptions that the expected costs of drunk driving had increased. Still, for Massachusetts respondents, "after passage of the law there was some increase in the proportion of respondents who felt the law was adequately enforced, but half of them remained skeptical. Only a fourth of them thought it very likely that a drunk driver would be stopped by the police, and the law had no effect on this perception. If stopped, somewhat more thought they would be charged (59 to 74 percent), taken to court (72 to 80 percent), and convicted (54 to 68 percent)" (P. 595). John Snortum's (1988) comparative research found that Norwegians have far greater knowledge of their drunk driving laws and of the associated punishments than Americans have of their own. My impressions confirm Snortum's observations. For years I have been asking New York University law students whether they know the illegal BAC level in New York State. Consistently, only about 10 percent can give the correct answer. The students also lack knowledge about punishments,[2] although they seem to believe that there is a significant likelihood of being apprehended for drunk driving and although almost all are aware of drunk driving roadblocks.

Another factor standing in the way of further deterring drunk driving is that the non–criminal law costs of drunk driving are already high and might drown out incremental escalations of legal threat. Is it likely that a person undeterred by the possibility of injuring or killing himself, his friends, or his family members would change his behavior on learning that the probability of apprehension had increased and that the expected penalty had risen? Why should a driver discount the probability of an alcohol-related crash but not that of an alcohol-related arrest? One possible, although speculative, answer is that some drivers who are unable or unwilling to admit that drinking impairs driving ability and increases the risk of a crash might change their attitudes and behaviors when they are told that drunk driving creates a risk of governmental condemnation and punishment; in other words, the criminal law might give them a rationalization for behaving as they would wish, in any event, to behave. Another explanation is that people deny or underestimate the risk of a crash even more than they deny or underestimate the risk of an arrest. Still, the fact remains: the criminal law will have to bark very loudly to be heard above the full cacophony of risk.

A third reason why it might be especially difficult to deter drunk driving is that the immediate decision to drive drunk is made when the driver is drunk and not thinking clearly about risks and probabilities. A drunken person may not be able to (1) appreciate the extent of his alcoholic impairment, (2) evaluate his capacity to drive, or (3) reflect on the probability of arrest or expected punishment. However, these impediments to deterrence may not be operative if (1) the decision on whether to drive drunk is made or conditioned when sober and (2) that sober decision affects or conditions the individual's subsequent decision when intoxicated, whether to drive.[3]

The fourth and fifth reasons for skepticism about the marginal deterrent effect of escalating legal threats is that for some offenders drunk driving is infrequent and aberrational while for others it is chronic and habitual; both groups present special deterrence problems. People who fall into the first group may be already deterred or otherwise inhibited from DWI but may on rare occasions, perhaps because of stress or crisis, go on a binge, inadvertently become drunk, or otherwise act out of character. It may be very difficult for shifts in public policy to eradicate an individual's very infrequent and aberrational behavior.

Chronic offenders have already been identified as the hardest to deter. They suffer from a high incidence of alcoholism, alcohol abuse, and psychopathology. Some are also regular drug users and violators of other criminal prohibitions. People for whom alcohol is an addiction, psychological crutch, or way of life are less likely to be either willing or capable of radically changing their drinking habits on being told either that the arrest probability for drunk driving has increased 10, 20, or 50 percent or that the likely punishment has increased from a fine and license suspension to a short jail term, larger fine, and longer period of license suspension.

Strategies for Increasing Deterrence

It is necessary to examine each stage along the path from apprehension to punishment of drunk drivers so that we can determine both what costs are presently being imposed and the likelihood of escalating them.

The Probability of Apprehension

It is frequently said that a significant marginal deterrent effect on drunk driving could be achieved by increasing the probability of arrest.[4] It is no doubt true that in the United States the risk of apprehension for drunk driving is low, probably even lower than that for such other crimes as burglary, car theft, child sexual abuse, tax evasion, and use and dealing of illegal drugs. Still, it is well to keep in mind that the incidences of these crimes are also criticized as intolerably high, despite the arguably higher risks of apprehension (and the threat of much greater punishment).

The probability that a drunk driver will be arrested is determined by the enforcement resources, priorities, and skills of the police. Since drunk drivers are not often reported by victims, notwithstanding recent efforts to enlist citizens' aid in calling in drunk driver sightings to hotlines,[5] they have to be identified by patrol officers either at an accident scene, roadblock, or routine traffic stop or when observed driving recklessly.

A drunk driving arrest necessarily consumes police resources. It may take the arresting officer four hours or even longer, perhaps the better part of an entire shift, to process a drunk driver from initial stop until the completion of the booking procedures.[6] Thus, there are limits to what even a highly motivated police department can accomplish. Nevertheless, the police could increase their productivity by stopping more cars and by identifying more drunk drivers among motorists involved in crashes or traffic stops. Legislation that authorizes police to perform a BAC test on every accident-involved driver would, if followed, obviously improve the apprehension rate. However, the constitutionality of such legislation is dubious.[7]

Local and state police departments could devote more resources (i.e., patrol cars) to traffic patrol. They could establish special anti–drunk driving units. Both regular and special patrols could stop drivers who exceed speed limits by even a few miles per hour, concentrate patrols on roadways with taverns and bars, or surveil the taverns' and bars' parking lots.[8] Los Angeles County, for example, has recently established just such an anti–drunk driving program, involving all twelve of the jurisdiction's police departments. Officers assigned to the units are given special training on identifying drunk drivers and are deployed to designated areas that have had high rates of drunk driving arrests in the past. Program administrators claim a 26 percent increase in arrests during the first month and a 20 percent increase every month thereafter.

Special anti–drunk driving programs such as that of Los Angeles obviously entail costs, in terms of either the diversion of resources from other police priorities or an absolute increase in resources. On busy evening shifts police officers may be called on to respond to suspected burglaries, robberies, and domestic violence. As important as drunk driving enforcement is, these other calls cannot be ignored or slighted. Furthermore, greatly increasing the number of vehicle stops is likely to prove unpopular with the citizenry, who, while favoring tough anti–drunk driving measures, will likely resent being stopped for marginal speeding and minor infractions (see Cressey 1974).

Roadblocks and Other Police Initiatives

We have already spoken of the current popularity of drunk driving roadblocks as a strategy for stopping a greater number of vehicles. Police officers at the checkpoints stop every (or every *n*th) driver on a particular road for brief questioning and inspection. This means that a small number of police officers can stop thousands of vehicles on a single night. Nevertheless, roadblocks have not been very productive in identifying drunk drivers. Because the stops are very brief, only the most obviously intoxicated drivers are apprehended.[9]

In theory, roadblocks' main contribution to deterrence is not their (specific deterrent) affect on those who are arrested but their general deterrent effect on those passing through the roadblock and on the thousands more who see or hear reports of them. Arguably, this policing strategy has the capacity to create a perception that the probability of arrest has dramatically increased. Nevertheless, the marginal deterrent effect has yet to be demonstrated empirically. A 1984 NHTSA evaluation of changes in public opinion due to sobriety checkpoints concluded that "despite the high visibility and awareness of roadblocks, and evidence that they increase estimates of the likelihood that drunk drivers will be picked up, the limited evidence from the self-reported behavioral measures does not indicate that roadblocks have changed the drinking and driving behavior of [survey] respondents."

Some police departments have increased their efficiency in identifying intoxicated drivers by utilizing Alco-sensors, portable breath-testing devices that can be used in lieu of a field sobriety test. These devices give a fairly accurate BAC reading. Some states authorize preliminary breath tests of drivers who have been involved in accidents or who have been stopped for violating a traffic law; the constitutionality of such laws is doubtful, as noted above. Another innovation is the HGN procedure, which involves asking a suspect to stare at an object held directly in front of his face and to follow it out of his field of vision.[10] The HGN test works by measuring the angle at which the subject's eyes begin to exhibit nystagmus—an involuntary jerking motion—when following an object moving from the center of the vision field toward the ear. The closer to the visual midpoint the onset of nystagmus occurs, the higher the BAC. HGN training greatly improves police officers' ability to identify drivers with high BACs. As Alco-sensors and HGN become widely available, more arrests will certainly be achievable.[11]

All of these initiatives have been used in crackdowns against drunk drivers, and the number of drunk driving arrests nationally has increased 50 percent over the past decade.[12] The initiatives demonstrate that the police do respond to pressure; they do shape their priorities according to the wishes of the public; interest groups and public opinion have succeeded in making drunk driving enforcement a higher priority.[13]

Evaluating the Deterrent Impact of "Crackdowns"

More arrests alone do not guarantee a significant marginal deterrent effect. The ASAP experience showed that a large increase in arrests will not necessarily reduce drunk driving, much less the serious and fatal traffic accidents caused by the most dangerous and irresponsible drunk drivers (Zylman 1978).

Deterrence depends on perceptions. It is debatable whether the vast pool of potential drinking drivers could perceive an increase of 10, 20, 50, or even 100 percent in the DWI arrest rate. Indeed, even in Norway, Andenaes estimates that the risk of arrest is only 0.004. Perceptions of arrest probabilities are very likely independent of actual probabilities; in fact, they may be more dependent on publicity and media attention. Therefore, effective publicity for drunk driving crackdowns is vital to a deterrence strategy based on increasing the probability of apprehension.

To a large extent deterrence remains a matter of faith, albeit one supported by a good deal of common sense (see Blumstein, Cohen, and Nagin 1978). Unfortunately, the small number of credible evaluations of anti–drunk driving initiatives (see Cramton 1969; Ennis 1977; National Highway Traffic Safety Administration 1978, 1985; Cameron 1979; Reed 1981) are dwarfed by the number of poorly executed and self-serving "evaluations" by agencies responsible for carrying out anti–drunk driving initiatives.[14] Nevertheless, the small number of carefully executed evaluations is well worth examining.

After the ASAPs were well underway, a sophisticated effort to evaluate them took place. As with many crackdowns before and since, evaluation was difficult since the program consisted of more than thirty local initiatives each of which included a variety of anti–drunk driving strategies. The final evaluation was unable to demonstrate a significant reduction in drunk driving (as measured by single-vehicle nighttime fatalities), despite a huge increase in arrests (Zylman 1976; Insurance Institute for Highway Safety 1981).

Enforcement crackdowns seem to have had greater success in Europe, where they have been studied and analyzed by Professor H. Laurence Ross. Ross's seminal study of the 1967 British Road Safety Act, which made it an offense to operate a vehicle with a BAC in excess of 0.08 and allowed widespread breath-testing (without probable cause), showed that overall fatality rates declined by 25 percent while weekend and nighttime fatalities (those more likely to be alcohol related) declined by two-thirds. However, this apparent deterrent effect dissipated within two years, the number of drunk driving deaths reverting to the preact level. Ross found a similar short-term (several months long) deterrent effect for the French drunk driving roadblock program of 1978 and for initiatives carried out in Canada, The Netherlands, and several ASAP jurisdictions. Wherever Ross has confirmed a deterrent effect, it has slowly evaporated. Thus, as Ross (1982, P. 111) somewhat pessimistically concluded,[15]

deterrence-based policies are questionable in the long run. No such policies have been scientifically demonstrated to work over time under conditions achieved in any jurisdiction. This fact does not mean that such policies are hopeless but rather that success—if achievable—probably will involve something other than what has been done in the past. On the basis of the evidence, it will not suffice to import further elements of the Scandinavian approach into other jurisdictions in the expectation that Norway and Sweden have the answers. Moreover, the option of merely increasing penalties for drinking and driving has been strongly discredited by experience to date. The most hopeful opportunities for further deterrent accomplishments would seem to lie in increasing the actual probabilities of apprehension and conviction of drunk drivers.

Ross's many later evaluations have only strengthened these conclusions. For example, an intense crackdown effort, "the Cheshire Blitz," in a single county in England again showed that short-term reductions in fatal accidents could be produced by changing the perception of the risk of apprehension. Unfortunately, once again fatalities regressed to their normal pattern as the crackdown wound down.[16] The only initiative that has not followed this pattern is the crackdown in New South Wales, Australia. In 1982 the illegal BAC was lowered to 0.05, random breath tests were authorized, and considerable enforcement resources were committed. At the end of thirty-two months fatal accidents had declined 26 percent.

Despite the possible success in New South Wales, I am persuaded by Ross's pessimistic conclusion that deterrence (within the range of enforcement and sanctions so far deployed) is unlikely to provide a successful long-term social control strategy for drunk driving in the United States. I am bolstered in this conclusion by Ralph Hingson's (1987) careful study of major drunk driving crackdowns and punishment enhancements in Maine and Massachusetts in 1981 and 1982, respectively. Hingson concludes that "increased drunk driving penalties, even when coupled with judicial measures to increase conviction, did not initiate sustained drunk driving and fatal crash reductions in Maine or Massachusetts." It is important to be realistic about the capacity of the criminal justice system to sustain a long-term popular perception that the risks of drunk driving have increased. There are many demands on police time and resources. Thus, it is unlikely that drunk driving will be able to maintain perpetually its current high priority with regard to enforcement. Indeed, claims of success themselves will tend to reduce the pressure for activism. Even roadblocks may become less popular as police tire of the effort and other crime problems command attention. Once again, Hingson's (1987) findings are instructive: "Despite increased police arrests for drunk driving, during the post-law period in Massachusetts only one arrest, compared to 2.5 crashes, occurred per 1,000 drunk driving trips reported by survey respondents. Maine's arrest rate was only slightly higher and declined the third post-law year."

These conclusions counsel modest expectations, not pessimism. Ross's evaluations did conclude that a marginal deterrent effect can be produced by crackdowns, at least in the short term. Obviously, short-term victories are preferable to no victories at all. If we could be assured that crackdowns could reduce serious accidents for months or even years, we would probably feel confident in recommending such crackdowns, although we might worry that repeating the same tactics again and again might produce decreasing returns.

Increasing the Process Costs for Drunk Drivers

The cost of drunk driving could also be increased by raising the (perceptions of) postarrest costs. For the most part, we are talking about sentence severity, but *process costs* can also be increased. For example, the National Institute of Justice (1986, P. 20) reports that "many communities hold drunk drivers for four to eight hours following their arrest to ensure that they will be sober when they leave police custody." Such detentions are likely to be perceived as a significant cost of drunk driving by those who have experienced them. The costs are even greater if suspects are routinely arrested and arraigned, rather than released from the police station on desk-appearance tickets or according to a police bail schedule.[17] Police departments may be more inclined to hold drunk-driving suspects in custody since the Massachusetts Supreme Judicial Court upheld a tort judgment against a township whose police officer failed to detain a drunk driver who subsequently injured the plaintiff (*Irwin v. Town of Ware*, 467 N.E.2d 1292 [Mass. 1984]). Process costs can also be increased by a policy of routinely towing drunk drivers' vehicles to impoundment facilities rather than allowing them to be secured alongside the road.[18] While it would obviously be wrong to design pretrial release procedures for punishment purposes, there is no reason either to reject police and processing procedures on the ground that they are inconvenient for arrested drunk drivers or to ignore the incidental deterrent effect of high process costs.

Increasing the Likelihood of Conviction

With the aid of per se and implied-consent laws, drunk driving is not a difficult crime to prove. Moreover, like other criminal offenses, it rarely has to be proved because the overwhelming majority of defendants plead guilty. Despite folk wisdom to the contrary, the conviction rate for drunk drivers is as high as or higher than those for other offenses.[19] In fact, in Goldstein and Susmilch's (1982) Madison, Wisconsin, study, of all DWI defendants in the sample year, 88 percent were convicted of DWI; not a single defendant was acquitted. Professor Joseph Little's (1973) analysis of Vermont DWI defendants found that 58.5 percent of apprehended DWI defendants were convicted as charged and that 89.2 percent were convicted of either the original or a reduced charge. Recent Massachusetts data show that since the laws were toughened in 1982, only 5 percent of DWI defendants have been acquitted.

A 1988 study by New York City's Criminal Justice Agency found that approximately 90 percent of DWI charges resulted in a misdemeanor conviction or transfer to the state court for felony prosecution; less than 10 percent of all DWI defendants had their cases dismissed. According to the UCRs, DWI prosecutions lead to convictions 90 percent of the time, more often than for any other offense. Thus it does not seem possible that deterrence could be bolstered by enhancing the rate of conviction. Furthermore, many administrative costs of drunk driving are imposed regardless of whether the defendant is convicted. For example, a driver's license can be suspended or revoked as a result of an administrative adjudication regardless of whether a DWI conviction is obtained.

The prosecution of drunk driving must be seen in the context of American criminal prosecutions generally. In American jurisdictions the vast majority of defendants plead guilty in exchange for leniency or to avoid greater severity of sentencing. Historically prosecutors have allowed drunk drivers to plead guilty to reckless driving and other traffic offenses. In recent years, however, legislatures and prosecutors have moved to restrict charge bargaining. In many states (e.g., New York) DWI charges are reduced to the lesser-included DWAI offense. Twenty-three states have some type of legislative restriction on plea bargaining, ranging from a flat prohibition to a requirement that the prosecution explain in open court why the DWI charge was reduced (see U.S. Department of Transportation).[20]

Diversion programs have also become less popular, whereas several years ago it was common to offer first offenders the opportunity to complete a treatment program in exchange for dropping the criminal case or reducing the charge to a lesser offense. The clear trend (as recommended by the Presidential Commission on Drunk Driving) is to employ treatment as a probationary condition.

Increasing the Severity and Variety of Sanctions

JAIL

One way to increase the costs of drunk driving is to enhance the punishments that are imposed on convicted drunk drivers. The past decade has seen a major effort to punish drunk drivers more severely. Under the prodding of some citizens' groups, the Presidential Commission on Drunk Driving, and Section 408 of the Highway Safety Act,[21] approximately twenty-five states now prescribe mandatory jail terms for drunk driving: first offenders are typically liable for twenty-four or forty-eight hours of confinement, and repeat offenders face ten days to two weeks. Those who believe in the deterrent efficacy of brief jail terms argue that a credible threat of *any* incarceration will make a difference in peoples' decisions about driving drunk. This argument applies more plausibly to essentially law-abiding people who have never had a jail experience. For the smaller, hard core of high-rate offenders, a substantial percentage of whom have been previously arrested and incarcerated, a threatened twenty-four- to forty-eight-hour jail term is unlikely to be greatly feared.

It is frequently said that mandatory jail sentences will not be carried out and therefore that their threat will not be perceived as credible. This objection is not supported by recent experience. A National Institute of Justice evaluation of mandatory jail sentences for drunk drivers in four jurisdictions found

a dramatic increase in incarceration rates for convicted drunk drivers in each of the four jurisdictions where mandatory confinement has been implemented. This finding is clear and consistent and includes drunk drivers convicted of their first offense. In Seattle, only 9 percent of convicted drunk drivers were sentenced to jail before mandatory confinement was introduced; afterwards, the incarceration rate was 97 percent. In Memphis the incarceration rate was 29 percent before mandatory sanctions and virtually 100 percent afterwards. In Cincinnati and Minneapolis, similar increases occurred. Only California, where judges have discretionary power to impose probation instead of confinement for drunk driving offenses, failed to show a consistent increase in incarceration rates.[22]

While the trend is clearly toward greater use of jail sentences, even mandatory jail sentences are not invariably carried out. Pennsylvania law, for example, imposes a "mandatory" minimum forty-eight-hour jail term on drunk drivers, but it has been interpreted to leave judges with discretion to impose a suspended sentence with or without a diversion program. Thus, almost 60 percent of first offenders are diverted from prosecution altogether. Of 30,198 drunk driving arrestees in 1983, only 2,827 received any jail time.

It would hardly be surprising to find that mandatory DWI penalties are not fully carried out. Prosecutorial discretion and sentencing discounts are basic features of our legal culture. Many studies have shown that mandatory sentences are circumvented; Massachusetts' gun law and New York's "Rockefeller drug law" are two of the best known examples (Feeley 1983). Therefore, one need not seek a special theory of DWI enforcement to account for punishment avoidance and discounts. To the contrary, if some jurisdictions *are consistently carrying out* mandatory DWI sentences, *that would require special explanation,* perhaps based on the mobilization of anti–drunk driving sentiment and strategic exercise of political power by citizens groups.

If all convicted DWI defendants had to serve a jail term, it is likely that more DWI defendants would plead innocent and contest their guilt more vigorously. This would strain prosecutorial and judicial resources. The imposition of more jail sentences also imposes a major burden on jail facilities, which are already experiencing unprecedented crowding (Bulduc 1985). One adaptation has been to permit drivers to serve their sentences on weekends; another has been to avoid the intent of mandatory sentencing laws by checking defendants into the jail at 11:00 P.M. and releasing them at 12:01 A.M. the same night, crediting them with having served two days. Another problem is the concern felt by some jail officials about integrating DWI offenders into the mainline jail population (see U.S. Department of Transportation 1986*a*), for fear that DWI defendants may be vulnerable to the depredations of experienced and violent criminals. Thus, several jurisdictions have chosen to separate DWI offenders in special facilities.[23]

FINES

In spite of the undisputed need for alternatives to incarceration, the American criminal justice system does not take fines seriously. Incarceration is our dominant sanction; all other sanctions, with the exception of probation (if sanction it be), are treated indifferently, if not scornfully. New York State, for example, provides for mandatory minimum fines of $350 for a first offense (maximum $500) and $500–$5,000 for second and subsequent offenses.[24] These statutory fine levels have hardly increased since New York State passed its first DWI statute in 1910! At that time, the maximum punishment for the DWI misdemeanor was also $500 and the fine for a second offense was $200–$2,000 (see King and Tipperman 1975). In other words, DWI fines in constant dollars *have declined significantly* over the course of seventy-five years.

Fines are so low that they are not even the most significant cost of a drunk driving conviction. In most criminal cases, including drunk driving, a nonindigent defendant's greatest costs are his lawyer's fees. A drunk-driving defendant will have to pay his defense lawyer at least $500, more if the case goes to trial. (Perhaps, in some sense, we have delegated to criminal defense lawyers the power to impose financial punishments.) In addition, in recent years a variety of court costs and DWI treatment costs have arisen; these often aggregate to more than the fine. Moreover, defendants may face insurance surcharges.

Unless fines are increased beyond customary levels, there is not much potential for a significant marginal deterrent effect. A person indifferent to injury or death, loss of license, civil suit, insurance surcharges, legal fees, and court costs will hardly be concerned about a $350 or $500 fine. Indeed, fines in this low range trivialize the offense and broadcast the wrong societal message about drunk driving; in effect, they define drunk driving as a traffic offense, not as an offense against the person. To have a realistic chance for a marginal deterrent effect, the typical fine for drunk driving should be drastically increased, say to $2,500–$5,000, perhaps higher. Severe fines of this magnitude would properly mark societal disapprobation and would generate funds to support anti–drunk driving programs.

To impose and collect much more severe fines would require major changes in attitudes and collection mechanisms. Historically our criminal courts have been poor collection agencies. For example, the Government Accounting Office in 1982 reported that the federal courts succeeded in collecting only 34 percent of all fines imposed, and the fine amounts involved were much smaller than the ones I am proposing. It seems that defense lawyers are considerably better at collecting money from defendants than are courts.

The problems of fine collectability should not be minimized. Many people would probably prefer to go to jail for a few days than part with their savings. Many defendants would strive mightily to hide or dissipate their assets. There is no *easy* solution, but I think it is clear that the criminal courts would not be able to carry out this assignment. The most promising approach is either to turn fine collection over to private agencies that have the power of garnishment or to place fine collection in the hands of a special state agency (which is the practice in Sweden).

If fines are to be collected, the job must be done by an agency that has an organizational reason and incentive to succeed. Prosecutorial agencies and courts are likely to see fine collections as a peripheral duty, an annoying distraction from their real business.

Many DWI defendants will be not be able to pay fines of several thousand dollars, at least not if we continue to think in the same way about what it means to be able to pay. This does not mean, however, that they cannot be effectively fined. In England and other European countries, small fines are regularly imposed on and collected from impecunious defendants. The Vera Institute of Justice is currently attempting to implement in Staten Island the European model of day fines. The Europeans (particularly the Germans and Swedes) impose a sanction of so many day-fine units for each offense. The precise value of any individual's day fine depends on his income, in the manner of a graduated income tax. If fines are to become a serious weapon in our deterrent arsenal, a system like this is probably necessary.

LICENSE SUSPENSIONS AND REVOCATIONS

Currently, losing the right to drive is a major cost of a drunk driving conviction. In monetary terms the economic cost of this sanction is probably greater than any of the others. Loss of license could mean loss of job, social life, and dislocation of the defendant's entire way of life. Thus, this sanction might be more dreaded than either jail or a fine.

In recent years a great deal of emphasis has been placed on making license suspension or forfeiture mandatory and automatic on conviction—and even on arrest. While MADD has emphasized jail sentences for drunk drivers, RID has placed top priority on license suspension or forfeiture. Some states have made license suspension mandatory; indeed, some have adopted administrative per se laws, which require the drunk driver to forfeit his license at the police station if he fails the BAC test. The incapacitating effect of these developments is discussed in Chapter 11; at this point, we are concerned with potential deterrence impacts.

Is the threat of license suspension or revocation likely to provide an effective deterrent? One reason to think that license suspensions are not feared much is the vast number of suspensions that are imposed on drivers for failure to pay traffic tickets. Apparently, for large numbers of people, the possibility of loss of license is not enough to motivate prompt and full payment of traffic tickets.[25] Admittedly, however, this type of suspension is merely temporary, while a DWI suspension is likely to remain in effect for some time. Nevertheless, a DWI suspension is considerably mitigated through the issuance of a provisional or occupational license.

As with the other sanctions we have been considering, there are enforcement problems associated with license suspension and revocation. To reflect on the problems of monitoring a license suspension is to be struck by the problematic nature of the driver's-licensing system itself. Why do people voluntarily participate in the driver's-licensing system? Perhaps the most obvious answer is that compliance is relatively cheap. However, if it became difficult to obtain or keep a license, compliance would be more expensive and the incentive to avoid or circumvent the system would increase.

A licensing system, especially one designed to play a significant social control function, has to be backed up by credible threats of sanctions for license violations. It is an offense to drive without a valid license; some jurisdictions specifically make it an aggravated offense to drive while one's license is under suspension because of drunk driving.[26] Nevertheless, the probability of being caught driving without a valid license is small, and the possibility of receiving significant punishment for that traffic offense alone is negligible. Indeed, in New York City tens of thousands of people arrested for driving without a license never appear in court and, in effect, are lost to the criminal justice system. One California study found that only 20 percent of drunk drivers who did not have a valid license because of a previous suspension or revocation were charged with driving without a valid license. Thus, whatever marginal deterrent effect could be achieved by making suspension or revocation of license automatic on conviction of DWI will be tempered by the perception that this sanction cannot be effectively enforced. Therefore, a top priority should be to treat violation of a DWI-related license suspension or revocation as a serious offense.

COMMUNITY SERVICE

Community service is often thought of as an alternative to incarceration, a way of relieving the prison- and jail-crowding crisis (see McDonald 1986). Perhaps its advocates originally viewed it not as a punishment but as a form of symbolic restitution and as a way of integrating the offender back into the community. Nevertheless, in practice its original purpose has been forgotten, and it has come to be seen as a cure for overreliance on jail and prison sentences. Many criminal justice scholars and planners now view community service as a sanction that can be employed as an alternative to incarceration, and they argue that community service should be made strict and onerous. Other people advocate community service as an alternative that can provide some punishment when in the absence of such programs, probation or a suspended sentence would be the likely outcome.

The Presidential Commission on Drunk Driving (1983) and two recent federal laws providing for incentive grants to states that adopt specified anti-DWI measures have stimulated the use of community-service sentencing for drunk drivers. Rhode Island, for example, requires all convicted drunk drivers to serve ten to sixty hours of community service; judges have tended to impose the minimum sentence. To provide placements for four to five thousand offenders per year, the program needs approximately 250 jobs providers, of which half are public agencies. Each offender is required to make his or her own arrangements with one of the participating organizations. Whatever hours the defendant and the organization work out (e.g., service only on weekends) are acceptable to the program administrator. Rhode Island runs its program as a diversion, so that if the defendant fails to complete his service successfully he will be ordered to return to court for sentencing. Program administrators estimate that approximately 15 percent of defedants are returned to courts, although it is revealing that the program administrators do not know what subsequently happens to these defendants.

Community-service sentencing has not yet been proved successful in the United States. Three major hurdles that continue to stymie program developers are (1) liability insurance, (2) locating useful jobs, and (3) management and supervision (see U.S. Department of Transportation 1986). Several studies of community service have shown that the service frequently is not performed. Local communities have not yet developed organizations and administrative systems capable of placing and supervising large numbers of community service–sentenced defendants. Even if they do, it seems highly implausible that the threat of having to carry out a small number of hours of unpaid work would provide much marginal deterrent effect, although it might help to reinforce proper attitudes in the long run.

One might ask whether establishing community service as the basic sanction for drunk driving might undermine deterrence. To say that community service is *by itself* an appropriate response to drunk driving is to define drunk driving as a minor offense. The public would not accept community service as the basic sanction for such crimes against the person as assault and robbery—and probably not for burglary either.

PUBLIC CONDEMNATION

Some advocates of strong anti–drunk driving measures have suggested imaginative sanctions that aim to mobilize community sentiment against drunk drivers. For example, it has often been suggested, sometimes successfully, that newspapers should publish the names of people arrested for drunk driving. Likewise, it has been suggested that drunk drivers be publicly identified (and humiliated?) by a vehicle sticker publicizing their wrongdoing. The theory that impels these proposals seems to be as follows: if potential drunk drivers know that if they are arrested their wrongdoing will be publicized, they will be less likely to drive drunk.

Mobilizing informal public condemnation against drunk drivers assumes the existence of a potential reservoir of condemnation. The creation of such feelings might itself be a job for long-term deterrence and public education. While drunk driving is widely viewed as wrong and irresponsible, it is doubtful that Americans would either shun or express personal outrage, hatred, scorn, or disgust toward friends and acquaintances convicted of drunk driving. Moreover, if public policy explicitly attempted to stimulate and mobilize such citizen sentiment, it might produce an opposite, sympathetic reaction.

Furthermore, it is unclear what actions advocates of public condemnation expect or desire the citizenry to take against convicted drunk drivers. Do they desire friends and acquaintances to denounce and excoriate the drunk driver, cease social relations with him, refrain from employing him (or terminate his employment), or treat him and his family with scorn? Those who advocate this type of sanction desire that community opinion be rallied against drunk drivers. Such an aspiration runs against the public policy of investing the state with a monopoly over sanctioning. In general we do not want the community to take justice into its own hands and to mete out its own informal sanctions. This would be contrary to our aspiration that justice be administered by specialized institutions of government according to formalized and fair procedures.

VEHICLE IMPOUNDMENT, FORFEITURE, HOUSE ARREST, AND ELECTRONIC SURVEILLANCE

There are several new sanctions or controls for drunk drivers which, because they are essentially incapacitating, we will examine in Chapter 11. But they also entail significant costs and therefore should be considered as possible contributors to more effective deterrence. Vehicle forfeiture or impoundment would take away the offender's vehicle, either for a period of time or permanently, thereby imposing a significant financial penalty and some degree of incapacitation. House arrest, especially when backed up with electronic monitoring, would curtail the offender's freedom of movement and therefore his social life.

Long-Term Deterrence

There are many reasons why we should not expect significant marginal deterrence to flow from escalations of legal threats and enforcement efforts. Except when extraordinary publicity efforts are involved, it may take time for people to perceive that the costs of a particular behavior have significantly risen. People may already be habituated to particular forms of behavior and be unwilling and unable to change quickly. Hard-core violators, whose offending has developed over years and even decades, may be particularly inattentive and unresponsive to changing legal threats. The criminal justice system may, in the short run, have great difficulty actually implementing and maintaining higher levels of enforcement and punishment.

For these reasons and others, it is more sensible to think of deterrence as a long-term strategy that operates on the general public and on specific groups of potential offenders. From this perspective, deterrence phases into the expressive and educational functions of punishment. Escalating legal threats may signal to the general population that a particular behavior is worse and more serious than previously thought. In time, general attitudes may come to redefine that behavior as more serious and more culpable. If that occurred, there would be popular support for passing even tougher laws—and for electing police officials, prosecutors, and judges who would enforce them. People will also be more inclined to express themselves as being opposed to drinking/driving, to change their own behavior, and to undertake personal initiatives with children, spouses, friends, and associates. Over time, new norms and patterns of behavior might emerge.[27]

The Scandinavian Experience

Many anti–drunk driving advocates believe that the Scandinavian countries have formulated and implemented a successful deterrence program against drunk driving, and they urge American jurisdictions to follow this example. It is an oversimplification to believe that just by adopting Scandinavian policy, equally low levels of drunk driving could be produced in American jurisdictions. Nevertheless, there is much to be learned from the Scandinavian experience about the interplay of culture, social structure, public attitudes, law, and criminal behavior.

While there are some important differences among the Scandinavian countries, the basic Scandinavian model of deterrence against drunk driving can be characterized by three features: (1) per se legislation making driving with BAC above a certain level an offense in itself, (2) strict enforcement of the legislation, with extensive use of breath and blood tests, including random roadside checks, and (3) stiff sentences, with considerable use of imprisonment and temporary or permanent loss of driver's license (Andenaes 1988).

It has been demonstrated that the Scandinavians, despite significant alcohol consumption, have both strong inhibitions against drinking/driving and lower rates of drinking/driving than do Americans (see Andenaes 1988; Snortum 1988).[28] They express strong support for tough laws against drunk driving, and they demonstrate patterns of personal and group behavior that aim to prevent drunk driving from occurring. For example, it is common for each couple or group of friends, before coming to a party where alcohol is to be served, to designate someone as a nondrinker; similarly, public transportation is often chosen in order to avoid the possibility of subsequent drinking/driving. Thus, Scandinavians presumably have internalized strong anti–drunk driving norms that operate at the following three levels: (1) the formal level of interaction between government and citizenry, (2) the informal level among private individuals in their many social and occupational roles, and (3) the level of individual attitudes, values, and personal controls.

Among social scientists who specialize in deterrence there is a lively debate about whether the Scandinavian laws and enforcement policies have caused the inhibitions against drunk driving or whether inhibitions against drunk driving have caused the strict laws and enforcement policies (see Ross 1975; Votey 1982; Snortum 1988). This debate is unlikely to be resolved. However, whatever accounts for the Scandinavian success, it is hardly likely that there is a particular legal formula that the United States can import with confidence of reaping similar successes. If anything, the research on Scandinavia shows a close link between cultural/social structure, law, public attitudes, and social norms, thus making the prospects for successful transplantation remote.

The crucial question is whether escalation of legal threats beyond current levels can produce significant reductions of crashes caused by drunk drivers and, even if so, whether the benefits of such reductions would outweigh the costs. In reaching a conclusion it is important to remember the many differences between the United States and Scandinavia—and those among the fifty American states (not to mention intrastate differences). American patterns of transportation, recreation, and drinking differ from the Scandinavian, as do the organizational capacities and vulnerabilities of the American criminal justice system.

Moreover, the magnitude of America's many crime problems necessarily places limits on the priority and resources that can and should be devoted to the problem of drunk driving.

It is not surprising to find that the Scandinavian countries have lower rates of drunk driving than the United States. They also have lower rates of all other serious crimes—homicide, rape, armed robbery, and burglary. The generally more responsible behavior of members of those societies cannot be due to tougher criminal laws or stricter criminal law enforcement, since the Scandinavian criminal sanctions with respect to crimes other than drunk driving are quite lenient by American standards. Thus, it seems likely that deep-seated cultural factors explain the different Scandinavian and American rates of drunk driving.

It must be remembered that the current American approach to drunk driving is not all that much different from the Scandinavian approach. We too now universally employ per se laws and widespread breath testing. While the Fourth Amendment prevents random breath testing, we regularly employ roadblocks. We also universally impose license suspensions and revocations on conviction. The greatest difference appears to be in the greater Scandinavian use of jail terms for drunk drivers, although here too some caveats are in order. Except in Norway, drunk drivers with a BAC less than 0.15 are not usually jailed at all.[29] Moreover, during the past ten years there seems to have been a movement in Scandinavia to reduce both the use and severity of incarceration (Andenaes 1988), while the use of jail terms in the United States is on the increase.

Finally, it is important to keep in mind that the Scandinavian countries have neither abolished drunk driving nor solved the drunk driving problem. Andenaes has recently calculated that there may be some four million offenses per year in Norway alone, and he concludes that the Norwegian social control strategies have been more successful (1) in deterring social drinkers than in deterring hard-core alcohol abusers and (2) in preventing drinking/driving than in preventing serious and fatal alcohol-related traffic crashes. The Scandinavians themselves are continuing to cast about for more effective social control strategies.

For these reasons I do not think it advisable to escalate legal threats much beyond current levels, although I do believe that widespread use of vehicle impoundments and home detention (discussed in Chapter 11) would be valuable additions to the deterrence arsenal. It would make sense to distinguish simple drunk driving from aggravated drunk driving, as is done in Scandinavia, and to punish aggravated drunk driving very severely. In addition, serious attention should be paid to enforcing effectively and efficiently those legal threats now on the books. These efforts, combined with more effective administrative processes, would throw a tighter net around the drunk driver—and, one hopes, would lead to a long-term reduction of both drinking/driving and, more importantly, the serious and fatal vehicle crashes that it causes.

Conclusion

Deterrence has an uneasier application to the crime of drunk driving than to rational economic crimes. Drunk drivers are unlikely to calculate closely the costs of offending, and they often offend inadvertently or habitually. Because of the danger to the offender himself, there is always something irrational about drunk driving.

Whatever theoretical doubts can be cast on the capacity of deterrence mechanisms to suppress drunk driving, this remains our most popular anti–drunk driving strategy—and the one that is reflexively embraced by legislators anxious to appear tough on the issue. Citizens' anti–drunk driving groups and their legislative allies have pushed hard and with considerable success to increase the arrest rate and the statutory penalties for drunk driving. A great deal of attention has been given to the imposition of jail terms, and, without doubt, jail has become a possibility, if not a probability, in many jurisdictions. However, because jail space is so expensive and in such great demand, this strategy has limits.

The next most important sanction, license suspension and revocation, is relatively easy to impose but difficult to enforce. The most underemployed deterrent sanction has been fines. Fine levels remain unreasonably low and should be drastically increased. In addition, as we shall see in Chapter 11, greater use of vehicle impoundment and home detention would also increase the financial costs of drunk driving.

In the final analysis, however, while deterrence makes sense, we cannot be confident that any realistic mixture of increased enforcement and tougher penalties will reduce drunk driving, particularly the most dangerous and reckless types of drunk driving, which present the greatest risk of serious and fatal crashes. The most important role of deterrence strategies may be symbolic and long-term, contributing over time to new societal norms about the seriousness and wrongfulness of drunk driving. Such norms would be expressed in support for strong public policy and, more importantly, in internal inhibitions against drunk driving and in the propensity of individuals to stop their friends and acquaintances from driving while drunk.

10

Insurance Surcharges and Tort Liability for Drunk Drivers

This chapter examines recent anti–drunk driving developments in insurance and tort law, including measures to make civil liability easier to prove, permitting punitive damages, imposing insurance surcharges, and expanding liability to third parties responsible for the drunk driver's intoxication.

Drunk Driving and Insurance

Insurance Systems

The dominant purpose of insurance is to spread the risk of fortuitous economic loss among a large number of similarly situated individuals, groups, or enterprises (see, e.g., *Globe Life and Health Insurance Co. v. Royal Drug Co.*, 440 U.S. 205 [1979]; Keeton 1971). Insurance does not require the insured to be free from fault in order to claim coverage, and most insurance covers loss regardless of fault. For example, medical insurance compensates the insured for medical costs despite the insured's unhealthy life-style. By contrast, automobile liability insurance traditionally has protected the insured against the risk of being held liable for injuries caused by negligent driving.

Under the traditional fault system an at-fault driver is liable for property damage and personal injuries he inflicts on pedestrians, passengers, or other drivers; thus, a great deal of effort is expended in determining which driver was at fault (Smith, Lilly, and Dowling 1932; O'Connell and Henderson 1976). While this system has been defended as a deterrent to irresponsible driving, it has often been criticized for its inability to compensate victims of accidents when no driver was at fault or when the at-fault driver was uninsured (Murphy and Netherton 1959). In addition, it sometimes provides incomplete compensation to victims (New York State Insurance Department 1970). During the early 1960s there was tremendous pressure, fueled by an avalanche of academic scholarship, to revamp the entire accident law system according to no-fault liability principles (in general, see Ehrenzweig 1955; Calabresi 1958; Blum and Kalven 1965; Keeton and O'Connell 1965). The reform was only partially successful. Many states did not adopt no-fault systems. Of those that did, many attached significant limitations. For example, most states retained the fault system for losses above a certain threshold.

Although first-party no-fault plans have been criticized for weakening accident law's deterrent effect on irresponsible driving, it seems unlikely that many drivers will feel less inhibited about driving recklessly because the injured party's insurance carrier, rather than their own, will cover losses they cause (see Kornhauser 1985, n. 33). Moreover, in theory no-fault does not eliminate the economic incentive to drive safely. In a pure fault system a driver's insurance rates are a function of the likelihood that other people will present claims based on the insured's driving, or, to get more complicated, on the faulty driving of the insured and of others who use his car.[1] In a pure no-fault first-party system a driver's insurance rates depend on the likelihood that the insured (or a member of his family) will file a claim for injuries to his car and its occupants. In either case, insurance rates are affected by the insured's driving record.

Insurance Initiatives Designed to Reduce Drunk Driving

The current anti-drunk driving campaign includes several proposals to utilize insurance to reduce drunk driving. These proposals include revising the calculation of insurance rates to account for drunk driving behavior, imposing a surcharge on drunk drivers, and denying insurance to drunk drivers.

BASING INSURANCE RATES ON DRIVING PERFORMANCE

The history of automobile insurance evidences a tension between insurance rating systems based on demographic characteristics, such as age, sex, and marital status, and those based on performance characteristics, such as amount and type of driving, number of accidents, and traffic tickets. Performance characteristics have never predominated (in general, see Zoffer 1959), because it is difficult and expensive to monitor insureds' driving habits and records. Furthermore, for marketing reasons the insurance industry has not striven to make automobile insurance "perfectly responsive" to individual risk (see Schwartz 1987).

The recent anti–drunk driving campaign has revived interest in automobile insurance rating based on performance characteristics, but performance-based proposals are inevitably difficult to implement. A major problem is that during a several-year period the majority of drivers are accident and claim free (Zoffer 1959, Pp. 4–5).[2] The rating process is further complicated by the American practice of insuring the vehicle rather than (as in England) the driver. Thus, to predict future accidents and claims, insurance companies would need to consider the joint risks of all the vehicle's drivers.

Given limited resources for data collection, there can be no actuarially accurate formula for factoring prior accident-related claims into present and future insurance rates. Is a claim this year predictive of future claims? Do all this year's claims, regardless of amount, fault, and years of previous claim-free driving, have the same expected impact on future claims? If rates are to be increased, for how long should the increase be effective?

The only practical performance indicators that could play a role in rate setting are imprecise surrogates of dangerousness, such as accidents or traffic tickets. These indicators present substantial problems of under- and overinclusiveness. For example, drivers who have been hit by drunk drivers will legitimately object to being categorized, for rate purposes, with drunk drivers who caused these collisions. Drivers involved in fender bender accidents will object to being grouped with drivers who collided head-on.

Basing insurance rates on traffic convictions is even more controversial. We do not know, for example, how well a speeding ticket predicts future accidents. We surely cannot conclude that a person who receives a single speeding ticket is a certain type of driver. Differences in local traffic enforcement policies have a strong effect on the likelihood of being apprehended for traffic violations. Vast numbers of people who have never been charged with a particular traffic offense have committed the offense on one or more occasions.

Moreover, it should not be assumed that a traffic ticket predicts future driving behavior. An apprehension for a traffic offense might be negatively correlated with future bad driving: the negative experience of apprehension and its aftermath might have a specific deterrent effect on the driver. On the other hand, a traffic ticket might identify the violator as a member of a more dangerous class of drivers. A great deal of empirical research is needed to resolve these competing hypotheses.

Underinclusiveness is also a problem in setting higher insurance rates for drunk drivers and other traffic violators. The chance of a drunk driver being apprehended is extremely small. Many drivers who have never been arrested for or convicted of drunk driving have, nevertheless, on occasion or even regularly, driven while under the influence of alcohol. Some people, classified as "non-drunk drivers," have actually been arrested for the offense but been diverted into a pretrial treatment program or afforded plea bargains to lesser traffic offenses. Thus, categorizing insurance risks according to the vagaries of criminal law enforcement and case processing raises many problems.

INSURANCE SURCHARGES

Surcharging the drivers convicted of certain offenses would be a less drastic solution than setting insurance rates according to performance indicators. Under a surcharge policy an insurance company assesses an additional insurance charge for a drunk driving conviction. Despite its apparent simplicity, there are several reasons why insurance companies do not make a major effort to determine whether their insureds have been convicted of drunk driving. One reason is the high cost of collecting and analyzing criminal justice information.[3] A second reason is the reality of cash-flow underwriting. The insurance industry makes most of its profits from investments, not from the difference between premium dollars paid in and claim dollars paid out. The more cash flow and the longer the float, the more opportunity for investment and profit (Nader 1964). Thus, insurance companies place more emphasis on investment than on rate setting.[4]

Furthermore, it would be very difficult to develop an accurate system to charge a person convicted of drunk driving the actuarially appropriate rate. Representatives of the insurance industry have told me that there are no actuarial data to demonstrate that a person with a drunk driving conviction is a more dangerous future risk than a person without a drunk driving conviction, much less any data to predict the impact, on future traffic claims, of a drunk driving conviction. Granting that drunk driving is dangerous behavior, what indicators would allow us to predict with confidence that a person constitutes a (dangerous) drunk driving risk in the future? that the person is an alcoholic? a binge drinker? a habitué of late night parties?[5] that he has been arrested or convicted of DWI?

Utilizing a DWI conviction as an indicator that someone is a drunk driver produces high rates of false positives and false negatives. False positives are people who have recorded arrests or convictions for drunk driving but who never again drive while drunk. False negatives are people who have never been arrested or convicted for drunk driving but who regularly drive while drunk. Many drunk driving offenses, even if detected, are not recorded as such. Defendants may plea bargain or be diverted to pretrial diversion programs in lieu of prosecution (U.S. Department of Transportation 1986b). Often courts do not forward conviction records to the state department of motor vehicles—or the state department fails to record the information. When convictions are recorded, they do not normally come to the attention of the insurance companies.[6] States do not require motor vehicle departments to notify insurance companies of the insured's convictions. A few states' privacy laws *bar* the release of such information (All-Industry Advisory Research Council 1981). Elsewhere, insurance companies learn of the existence of a DUI conviction only if the insurance broker decides to perform a record check at time of renewal. In the absence of an accident, it is highly unlikely that any investigation will be undertaken.

A record check requires a request to the department of motor vehicles (or to a private data base system such as Equifax)[7] for a copy of the insured's driving record. The information provided will often be incomplete. It is very unlikely, for example, that the record will include traffic convictions in other states. Furthermore, because fairness requires that drivers be given some opportunity to challenge the information's accuracy, surcharging for traffic offenses is complicated and expensive.

Even if the companies did obtain reasonably accurate records of traffic offenses, major questions remain, such as how much the insured should be surcharged, what offenses justify a surcharge, how long the surcharge should last, and whether it is cost effective for the companies to make these calculations. Actuarially sound answers to these questions would require data on the likelihood of future automobile-related claims being filed by people with differing driving records. The industry has not attempted systematically to collect such data, and it would be extremely expensive to do so. Data on traffic violations would have to be regularly collected and correlated against claim records. The effort would be complicated by undetected traffic violations, failure to report accidents, and variations in criminal justice adjudications. To calculate the rate at which drunk drivers have accidents would also require estimating the frequency of drunk driving behavior, a task involving extreme uncertainties.

Practical problems explain only part of the insurance companies' reluctance to impose surcharges on persons convicted of drunk driving. Because profits are regulated, insurance companies may have no economic incentive to surcharge drivers who have traffic convictions.[8] If these drivers are made to pay more for their insurance, and if profits are already at their legal maximum, other drivers must be given a reduction. Yet the companies cannot be sure that other drivers are being properly charged for their riskiness. Furthermore, a system such as this (assuming it were imposed or regulated by a state agency) would be implementing criminal law objectives at the expense of traditional insurance principles. Insurance executives fear that insurance rate setting will increasingly become a battleground for interest groups desirous of implementing their various political and social agendas.

Despite the forces that inhibit surcharging practices, some legislatively mandated automobile insurance rates do take limited account of driver performance under so-called safe driver insurance plans (SDIPs), which increase the rates of drivers who have accident or traffic violations. Under the New York version of SDIP a drunk driving conviction triggers a 75 percent increase in the insurance premium; the surcharge lasts for three years (NY Insurance Law, sec. 2335 [a] [4]). A recent New Jersey law imposes a three-year $1,000-per-year insurance surcharge on convicted drunk drivers (NJCRR, sec. 1:3-1.16 [f] [1] [i] [1985]). The joint underwriters keep 80 percent of this surcharge, and the remaining 20 percent goes to the state agency charged with coordinating and implementing the state's anti–drunk driving campaign. Neither a percentage surcharge nor a flat "insurance fine" is based on the predicted costs of drunk driving; rather, they reflect legislators' feelings about the culpability and dangerousness of drunk driving.

To the extent that an insurance surcharge is meant to punish past behavior or deter future behavior, why not impose the same economic sanction as a criminal fine? One answer is that the criminal courts have not been successful in collecting significant fines (Casale and Hillsman 1985). Thus, it might be thought easier to collect financial penalties indirectly through insurance. However, the marginal deterrent affect of an insurance surcharge might be less than that of a criminal fine, since the former lacks the symbolic content of the latter. A criminal fine is a symbolic statement of societal condemnation, while an insurance surcharge is part of a private contractual relationship involving many factors. Furthermore, insurance surcharges are "voluntary," since a driver can forgo driving or drive a vehicle registered to somebody else (e.g., wife, child, relative, or friend). Unfortunately, he can also drive illegally without any insurance.[9]

DENYING INSURANCE BENEFITS TO DRUNK DRIVERS

Some anti–drunk driving strategists, motivated by the desire to bolster deterrence, advocate denying automobile insurance benefits to drunk drivers. This proposal should not be seriously considered. In jurisdictions with fault systems of automobile insurance, denying drunk drivers the benefits of third-party liability coverage would deny compensation to victims, thereby defeating a primary goal of automobile insurance. To deny liability insurance coverage to drunk drivers would have the perverse effect of punishing some drunk-driving victims as well as some drunk drivers.

Professor Albert Ehrenzweig (1955) proposed a "tort fine" as a way of denying drunk drivers the economic insulation of insurance without imposing hardship on injured parties. Under his scheme states would establish a fund whose managers could seek civil recovery, on behalf of the fund, from a driver engaged in "criminally negligent behavior." The amount of this recovery, as in the case of a criminal fine, would be measured by the defendant's fault and financial resources, rather than by the victim's loss. The plaintiff fund could collect twice, once from the liability insurer and once from the insured. Thus the crash victim would be assured compensation, and the fund could pierce the insurance veil to punish the offender and deter others. Professor Ehrenzweig argued that his proposal would provide better deterrence than traditional tort law because, left to their own devices, some drunk-driving victims either would not sue or would not do so with sufficient vigor.

The efficacy of the Ehrenzweig tort fine proposal is questionable. First, the predicted marginal deterrent effect is dubious, for the reasons discussed above. Second, the administrative costs would likely be quite high. Third, courts might invalidate the plan on the ground that, in effect, it imposes criminal sanctions without the protection of criminal procedures. If it is good policy to impose heavy economic costs on drunk drivers, why not simply increase criminal fines?

Another proposal involves denying first-party insurance benefits to drunk drivers (Fileding 1977), so that, for example, a drunk driver who crashed into a tree, injuring himself and destroying his automobile, would not be compensated by his insurance company. This proposal has been justified on general deterrence grounds: if drivers know that they will not be compensated for injuries sustained while DUI, they will not engage in such behavior. Several states have adopted this policy. New York's no-fault automobile liability scheme prevents a drunk driver from recovering any benefits if it can be proved beyond a reasonable doubt that the driver was intoxicated and that the intoxication caused the injuries (NY Insurance Law, sec. 672 [2]). Whether the law is actually being carried out is another matter.[10]

The deterrence rationale for denying drunk drivers first-party benefits is dubious. If the threat of personal injury itself is insufficient to deter the drunk driver, the threat of being denied insurance benefits in the event of personal injury is hardly likely to be effective. In any event, most drivers are also covered by medical insurance. Logically, deterrence advocates might propose denying drunk drivers this coverage as well. Indeed, taking this strategy to the limits of its logic might suggest denying medical care itself!

Each of these proposed changes aimed at curbing drunk driving suffers from serious problems. Some of the proposals would defeat the purpose of insurance or require a revamping of the insurance industry. Others are objectionable as quasi-criminal sanctions imposed without procedural safeguards. More important, it is very unlikely that any of these proposals could produce a significant marginal deterrent effect.

Enhancing Drunk Drivers' Tort Liability

Tort law generally provides that a person who willfully or negligently injures another person must compensate the victim for both economic losses and pain and suffering. Negligence is the failure to adhere to the standard of care that a reasonable person in the same situation would exercise (Prosser and Keeton 1984, P. 169). Drunk driving almost always involves negligence; the reasonable person does not drive while intoxicated and thereby expose himself and others to risk of injury. Moreover, driving while under the influence of alcohol or drugs is illegal; for this reason, many courts treat this behavior as "negligence per se" (Prosser and Keeton 1984).

The current anti–drunk driving campaign has begun to show interest in tort law. Recent tort law initiatives include (1) defining as negligence all driving with an illegal BAC, (2) awarding punitive or exemplary damages to the victims of drunk drivers, and (3) extending civil liability to those who serve drunk drivers alcoholic beverages.

Defining Drunk Driving for the Purposes of Tort Law

Defining drunk driving has been no easier for civil law than for criminal law. Traditionally, civil law standards basically paralleled criminal law standards. The traditional benchmarks of drunk driving—DUI or DWI—were nebulous standards that did not readily lend themselves to concrete definitions.

The courts have frequently essayed to define the terms "intoxication" and "drunkenness," but, as has been said, the terms are scarcely susceptible of accurate definition for practical purposes, and are so familiar that they define themselves. "Intoxication" is a word synonymous with "inebriety," "inebriation," or "drunkenness," and is expressive of that state or condition which inevitably follows from taking excessive quantities of an intoxicant. To some men, it means being under the influence of an intoxicant to such an extent as to render one helpless, while others speak of a person as intoxicated when he is only slightly under such influence. . . . As far as the infliction of physical injuries upon a third party is concerned, it has been said that a person may be deemed intoxicated within the meaning of a civil damage act when his excessive use of intoxicants has produced such a material change in his normal mental state that his behavior becomes unpredictable and uncontrolled, and when, as a result, slight irritations, real or imaginary, cause outbursts of anger which find expression in acts of physical violence against others. (45 Am. Jur. 2d, sec. 21 [1964])

The criminal law definition of drunk driving was simplified when states adopted per se laws. However, employing a 0.10 percent BAC per se standard in civil law negligence cases raises some problems. The majority of drivers are impaired at a BAC of 0.10 percent; however, some drinkers are not. The presumption that any accident-involved driver with a BAC above 0.10 negligently caused the accident in which he was involved is questionable.[11]

In many jurisdictions driving with a BAC above 0.10 is held to be "negligence per se," a concept whose meaning varies from jurisdiction to jurisdiction. In some jurisdictions it means that negligence is conclusively proved; in others, it means prima facie negligence or only "mere evidence" of a breached duty (Prosser and Keeton 1984, Pp. 200–202). At least one court has held that a 0.10 BAC, although admissible in evidence, does not create a presumption of intoxication (*Burke v. Angies, Inc.,* 143 Mich. App. 683, 373 N.W. 2d 187 [1985]). Intoxication at less than 0.10 BAC is not necessarily nonnegligent; a trial judge might permit a jury to consider evidence of any alcohol consumption as relevant to the ultimate issue of negligent driving.

Punitive Damages

When a tortfeasor's behavior transcends mere carelessness, reaching the level of wanton and malicious conduct, the plaintiff may recover punitive or exemplary damages in addition to compensatory damages (Restatement [Second] of Torts sec. 908).[12] Punitive damages have been criticized by scholars and jurists for providing victims with undeserved windfalls and for imposing freakish punishments on tortfeasors (see *American Surety Co. of New York v. Gold,* 375 F.2d 523 10th Cir. [1966]). In addition, if the risk of punitive damages is insurable, punishment does not fall on the tortfeasor; instead, all automobile insureds pay higher insurance rates.

When juries are asked to consider punitive damages, they have complete discretion to fix the amount. A typical jury instruction on calculating punitive damages is illustrative:

In determining the amount of your award of punitive damages, should you decide in favor of such an award, you should consider any evidence that tends to throw light on defendant's wealth or poverty.

The amount to be awarded as exemplary damages, if you award them, is for your good discretion. The law does not offer any precise formula for determining a ratio between compensatory and exemplary damages. They should not be totally disproportionate to the compensatory damages. You may not base your award upon influences such as passion, prejudice, or undue sympathy for either plaintiff or defendant.

However, in deciding on an appropriate figure, you should give due consideration to the degree of outrageousness of the conduct involved.

The court relies on your good judgment, if exemplary damages are to be awarded, in arriving at a sum which, considering all the circumstances, will serve not only to punish, but also to deter similar wrongdoing in the future. (G. Douthwaite 1981: secs. 2-2, 2-6, at 80, 90n).

The jury is permitted to take into account the defendant's culpability and wealth; awards can vary from one dollar to millions of dollars, depending on a particular jury's assessment or whim. However, the judge has discretion to reduce extravagent awards.

Although states are divided on the issue of availability of punitive damages to victims of drunk drivers, the trend seems to be in favor of allowing them.[13] Proponents of punitive damages believe that these exemplary punishments will deter future drunk drivers. The California Supreme Court explained this rationale in its landmark decision, *Taylor v. Superior Court* (24 Cal. 3d 890, 598 P. 2d 854 [1979]):

The allowance of punitive damages in such cases may well be appropriate because of another reason, namely to deter similar conduct, the incalculable cost of which is well documented. Section 3294 [the California punitive damages provision] expressly provides that punitive damages may be recovered for sake of example, The applicable principle was well expressed in a recent Oregon case upholding an award of punitive damages against a drunk driver. "The fact of common knowledge that the drunk driver is the cause of so many of the more serious automobile accidents is strong evidence in itself to support the need for all possible means of deterring persons from driving automobiles after drinking, including exposure to awards or punitive damages in the event of accidents." (P. 980; (Emphasis in original; footnote omitted)

One can sympathize with the California court's inclination to do something to suppress drunk driving, but, as Justice Clark's stinging dissent points out, permitting drunk-driving victims to collect punitive damages will not affect the incidence of this behavior; deterrence will not be operative, for the reasons previously discussed. Moreover, imposing punitive damages may have some unfair and distorting effects on our tort law system: a jury might label any drunk or drinking driver "willful, wanton, and reckless" and award punitive damages regardless of the defendant's actual driving behavior and the victim's injuries. Punitive damages, in part dependent on the defendant's wealth, amount to a retributive sanction, albeit one meted out by accident law rather than by criminal law. The same result could be better achieved by increasing the fine level in drunk driving cases and by more closely calibrating fines according to defendants' culpability and dangerousness. Criminal fines accrue to the state (and can be earmarked for anti–drunk driving programs), while punitive damages constitute a windfall for the victim. In *Bielski v. Schulze* (16 Wis. 2d 1, 114 N.W. 2d 105 [1962]), the Wisconsin Supreme Court stated: "We recognize that the abolition of gross negligence does away with the basis for punitive damages in negligence cases. But punitive damages are given, not to compensate the plaintiff for his injury but to punish and deter the tortfeasor . . . and were acquired by gross negligence as accoutrements of intentional torts. Willful and intentional torts still exist, but should not be confused with negligence. The protection of the public from such conduct or from reckless, wanton, or willful conduct is best served by the criminal law of the state."

A closely related issue is whether insurance covers—or should cover—punitive damages arising from a drunk driving incident (see Schumaier and McKinsey 1986). Automobile insurance contracts do not exclude coverage for punitive damages (see *Dickinson Law Review* 1980). During the mid-1970s the Insurance Service Office drafted a uniform-exclusion-of-punitive-damages provision, but it did not gain industry acceptance (see Burrell and Young 1978). The majority of courts construe uniform-net-loss clauses of insurance policies to cover awards of punitive damages (Burrell and Young 1978; Schumaier and McKinsey 1986). Some courts, however, refuse, on public policy grounds, to allow insurance coverage because it undercuts the rationale for punitive damages (Prosser and Keeton 1984).

If automobile insurance covers punitive damages, any possible deterrent effect is eviscerated: instead of drunk drivers being sanctioned with exemplary punishment, insurance companies pay the award and pass the cost along via higher rates to all insured motorists. When a drunk driver wantonly injures someone, all automobile insureds are taxed and the victim receives a windfall. Therefore, as the U.S. Fifth Circuit Court of Appeals has explained, there is strong reason to make punitive damages uninsurable: "If that person were permitted to shift the burden to an insurance company, punitive damages would serve no useful purpose. . . . In actual fact, of course, and considering the extent to which the public is insured, the burden would ultimately come to rest not on the insurance companies but on the public, since the added liability to the insurance companies would be passed along to the premium payers. Society would be punishing itself for the wrong committed by the insured" (*Northwestern National Casualty Co. v. McNulty,* 307 F. 2d 432 [5th cir. 1962], Pp. 440–441).

On the other hand, making punitive damages uninsurable also raises serious problems. Insurance provides security against losses, injuries, and catastrophes. If punitive damages arising from drunk driving accidents are uninsurable, people will be uncertain about the consequences of a traffic accident, especially after having consumed alcohol. All drivers would be exposed, without insurance coverage, to the whim and caprice of a jury that might wish to make a statement about the evils of drunk driving. Not only would drunk drivers be vulnerable to devastating financial losses, but so would anyone whom a jury sitting years after the event might brand a "drunk (or otherwise reckless) driver." This could include anyone who had imbibed any alcoholic beverages, or even a person falsely accused of having been intoxicated. Such unpredictable liability would be equivalent to a criminal law that provided that anyone convicted of drunk driving (or of injuring someone as a result of drunk driving) could be fined any amount of money.

Proponents of liberal punitive damage award policies might respond by arguing that persons desiring to avoid *any possibility* of being subject to an uninsured punitive damage award would merely have to decide never to drive while drunk. This argument is unsatisfactory for several reasons. If all of us acted responsibly and competently all the time, we would not need much of the insurance we now have. It is because we sometimes act negligently—or might be found to have so acted—that we purchase insurance. A normally responsible person might, for any number of reasons, operate a vehicle while under the influence of alcohol on a particular occasion. Furthermore, a person who had not been driving under the influence but who had imbibed a few drinks might, because of the vicissitudes of litigation, wrongfully be subjected to punitive damages.

Permitting punitive damages might also be complicated by the refusal of insurers to cover them. If a jury found that the defendant's drunken behavior warranted punitive damages, the insurer might refuse to indemnify either punitive or compensatory damages on the ground that the insured acted wantonly, willfully, and maliciously, thereby disqualifying himself from insurance coverage. If this argument were successful, the defendant might be stripped of all insurance and the likelihood of the victim receiving even compensatory damages might be jeopardized.

Making Alcohol Dispensers Civilly Liable

Because it is so difficult to change the behavior of drunk drivers, perhaps greater success in reducing drunk driving could be achieved by trying to influence the behavior of those who dispense alcoholic beverages to drunk drivers (Mosher 1983). Several anti–drunk driving proposals would impose tort duties on commercial dispensers and social hosts who serve alcohol. Commercial dispensers include liquor stores, roadside bars, and restaurants. Social hosts range from intimate-party givers to fraternities.

CIVIL LIABILITY FOR COMMERCIAL DISPENSERS OF ALCOHOL

At common law, third-party dispensers of alcoholic beverages were not liable for injuries and deaths caused by their drunk customers (Johnson 1962; Keenan 1973). The drinker who caused the subsequent injury constituted an intervening cause superseding the dispenser's causal contribution. Over the years, particularly during Prohibition, many states passed dram shop acts, making liquor dispensers jointly liable for their intoxicated customers' torts.[14] These laws vary in some respects. Some even permit an intoxicated person who injures himself to sue the person who served him (see, e.g., *Christiansen v. Campbell*, 328 S.E. 2d 351 [S.C. 1985]). Some dram shop laws appear to impose strict liability (*North Dakota Law Review* 1983, Pp. 450–451): all the victim needs to show is that a liquor store or tavern sold alcohol to an intoxicated person who subsequently injured him. Some statutes permit punitive damages (see, e.g., *Pfeifer v. Copperstone Restaurant and Lounge*, 693 P. 2d 644 (Or. App. [1985]); Ala. Code, sec. 6-5-71 [1975]; Me. Rev. Stat. Ann. tit. 17, sec. 2002 [1983]).

Unsurprisingly, commercial alcohol dispensers have always opposed dram shop laws, arguing that drinkers (at least adults) should be held responsible for their own actions and that dispensers should not be required to police their customers. After World War II, under pressure from bars and taverns, many dram shop statutes were repealed (*California Western Law Review* 1982). During the past decade, however, the trend has reversed. Several legislatures have enacted new dram shop acts,[15] and several state courts have imposed dram shop liability through common law (see, e.g., *Congini v. Potersville Valve Co.*, 470 A. 2d 575 [Pa. 1983]); *Sorenson v. Jarvis*, 350 N.W. 2d 108 [1984]) by finding that liquor dispensers have a duty of care to the general public or have inferred such a duty from criminal statutes prohibiting liquor sales to intoxicated patrons. The federal government has encouraged states to adopt some form of dram shop liability by, in part, conditioning supplemental highway funding on passage of a dram shop law. Counterpressure by the liquor industry remains very strong, however, and state legislators have reversed several aggressive court decisions establishing dram shop liability (see, e.g., S.D. Comp. Laws Ann., sec. 35-4-78 [1985]).

Courts that have established dram shop liability have been motivated by their perceptions of the magnitude of the drunk driving problem. For example, the Supreme Court of New Mexico, in establishing common law dram shop liability in 1982, stated: "In light of the use of automobiles and the increasing frequency of accidents involving drunk drivers, we hold that the consequences of serving liquor to an intoxicated person whom the server knows or could have known is driving a car, is reasonably foreseeable" (Lopez v. Maez, 98 N.M. 625, 651 P. 2d 1269 [1982], P. 1276). In a similar vein, the South Dakota Supreme Court stated: "We take judicial notice that since Griffin was decided, alcohol has been involved in 50.8% of this state's traffic fatalities from 1976 to 1981; in 1981 alone, 62% of South Dakota's traffic fatalities were alcohol related. This tragic waste of life prompts us to review our conclusion in Griffin. If the legislature does not concur . . . it is the prerogative of the legislature to so assert" (Walz v. City of Hudson, 327 N.W. 2d 120 [1982], P. 122).[16]

The theory underlying dram shop liability is that the threat of civil liability will encourage alcohol dispensers to monitor their customers' drinking behavior. For this to occur, dispensers would have to be able to recognize those customers who pose a significant accident risk to others. How much care can and should we expect from bartenders, waiters, and waitresses, many of whom are young people not long in the liquor business?[17] Can we expect that they be able to determine what it means to be "intoxicated" and to identify customers who have reached this state?[18] The determination is by no means simple, as a recent study by Dr. Peter Nathan, a Rutgers University researcher, concluded:

The study included social drinkers, bartenders, and police officers who were evaluated on their ability to determine whether individuals were drunk. The study indicated that all three of the subject groups studied . . . correctly judged levels of intoxication only twenty-five percent of the time. The accuracy of the ratings by the three groups deteriorated when intoxication increased. . . . The study concludes that the Zane decision [99 N. J. Super 196 (1961)]—that whether a man is sober or intoxicated is a matter of common observation not requiring special knowledge or skill—is clearly in error. . . . Whether a person is sober or intoxicated is not a matter of common observation: rather it requires special skill and special training. (Reported in 2 Dram Shop and Alcohol Reporter 1984 [no. 3], Pp. 1–2)

In a crowded bar a bartender will have little opportunity to keep track of any particular patron's consumption. Indeed, he or she may have no way of knowing whether the patron had done any drinking before entering the bar, how long he intends to stay, or how much he has eaten. Monitoring consumption is further complicated by the common practices of one customer purchasing rounds of drinks for several people and of groups sharing communal pitchers of beer. Servers may have no way of identifying the drivers. Finally, if a customer is not cut off from drinking until he is identified as intoxicated it may be too late to prevent drunk driving.

Taverns, bars, and even many restaurants are in the business of selling alcoholic beverages. Profits depend on creating an attractive atmosphere in which to drink. The goal is not to encourage long evenings of quiet conversation over two alcoholic drinks and several sodas. The best customers are the big drinkers; many run up huge bar tabs. It is highly unrealistic to expect most liquor establishments to police themselves. As Gusfield, Rasmussen, and Kotarba (1984, P. 55) note in their ethnographic study of bar culture: "Asked about the responsibility or obligation of the drinking place toward the patron, the bouncers at That Place and the bartender at the Hermitage absolve themselves of concern by using what one might call the ideology of adulthood, asserting that although most drinkers can manage themselves at drinking with competence, adults also possess the liberty and license to be incompetent. Incompetence is not the responsibility of management because the customers are adults and a person who is old enough to drink is old enough to take care of himself after he stops drinking." Laws regulating size of drinks[19] and prohibiting happy hours and two-for-one nights (e.g., Massachusetts, 204 C.M.R., sec. 4.03 [1984]) may be of marginal help in controlling excessive drinking, but alone they will hardly change bar culture.[20]

While the social and economic forces that sustain our bar and tavern culture are very strong, there is some reason to be optimistic about the potential of expanded dram shop liability to change patterns of alcohol serving and consumption. The establishments with the most to lose from dram shop suits are well-established hotels and restaurants, which have substantial assets and for whom liquor sales constitute only a portion, even a small portion, of overall revenue. They may decide that it makes sense to monitor patrons' drinking more closely.

To protect themselves against potential dram shop liability, many hotels and restaurants—and bars and taverns as well—are signing up to have their bartenders, waiters, and waitresses instructed by one of the rapidly growing number of server intervention programs. These programs, such as TIPS (Training For Intervention Procedures by Servers of Alcohol) provide six to eight hours of videotaped vignettes, leader-facilitated discussions, and server role-play segments: "Servers are first taught the behavioral and psychological cues associated with alcohol's effects on the body, including lowered inhibitions, diminished judgment, slowed reactions, and impaired co-ordination. Next, servers are taught a variety of tactics for controlling the flow of alcohol, even from the first drink. Techniques such as checking IDs to spot underage drinkers, offering food, serving non-alcoholic beverages and stopping service are presented as ways to inhibit overindulgence, impede those approaching their limit, and deal with already intoxicated customers. Finally, servers are given a chance to perfect their skills in role-play situations" (Russ and Geller 1987, P. 952). Many insurance companies, if they provide dram shop liability insurance at all, are requiring their insureds to purchase training packages such as these. As a consequence, TIPS and other server intervention programs are now flourishing.

The reasons why establishments that serve alcohol would wish to purchase server intervention instruction are obvious; there is a desire to obtain liability insurance and to have a "responsible server" defense in the event of a dram shop suit. What is not yet clear is whether these limited educational programs can actually produce positive results. Alcohol abusers are expert at hiding and denying their abuse and at resisting the suggestions and exhortations of others to drink more responsibly. Moreover, without the strong support of restaurant and bar owners and managers, the efforts of bartenders, waiters, and waitresses are unlikely to be successful. Nevertheless, and recognizing the difficulties of changing the way alcohol is marketed and consumed in public, these server intervention programs are among the most positive developments to have emerged from the current anti–drunk driving crusade.[21]

For dram shop liability to produce a significant marginal deterrent effect, there must be a significant probability that lawsuits will be brought. However, drunk-driving victims may not sue alcohol dispensers unless the drunk driver has insufficient insurance to cover the victim's injuries. Moreover, the existence of a secondary pocket will not make any difference unless it is a deep pocket. Normally, there will be no point in suing unless the defendant has liability insurance.

Although few bars presently carry insurance covering dram shop liability, injured victims can be expected, with increasing frequency, to sue bars, taverns, and restaurants as well as injury-causing drunk drivers. Even if the drunk driver's insurance is adequate, the liquor dispenser may be held as a joint tortfeasor. The law does not require exhausting the drunk driver's insurance before dipping into the liquor dispenser's.

Will bars and restaurants be able to purchase dram shop liability insurance, and will they desire to do so? Apparently the market for it has developed slowly, if at all; Minnesota's insurance department has required the insurance industry to offer this type of insurance. Even if such insurance is available, some percentage of liquor dispensers may not be able to afford it—or may choose to do without it, believing that without insurance they are unlikely to be attractive tort targets. Minnesota now requires liability insurance as a prerequisite to being granted a liquor license; other states may follow suit.[22] In that event, however, we return to the dilemma discussed previously; insurance provides compensation for victims, but it undercuts whatever deterrence value the threat of civil liability may have.

Of course, the insurance companies themselves may impose safety standards on the bars, taverns, and restaurants that they insure. Since courts are beginning to look to server training programs to determine whether a bar was negligent in causing a patron's intoxication, insurance companies are increasingly requiring their insured's to put a server training program in place to qualify for liability insurance (*American Bar Association Journal* 1987).

CIVIL LIABILITY FOR SOCIAL HOSTS

As much alcohol is consumed at home as in commercial settings. Here there may be even more cause for optimism about shaping behavior through threat of civil liability and long-term change of attitudes and norms. At small parties, at least, the hosts are in a position to know how much their guests have consumed, their condition at the time of departure, and their means of getting home. They do not have an economic incentive to encourage alcohol consumption. If social hosts could be held civilly liable for the drunk driving accidents of their guests, they might be motivated to arrange and supervise drinking at their parties more responsibly.

While the hosts of small dinner parties may be able to control or monitor their guests' alcohol consumption to some extent, not all parties are of the intimate sort envisioned in the preceding paragraph. Some are fraternity parties, or huge company bashes, or weddings, or wakes, or team celebrations. At these gatherings, an open bar may leave drinkers free to consume as much alcohol as they wish. At such parties it would be difficult to hold any person responsible for a guest's intoxication. If the assigning of blame (beyond the irresponsible drinker's) is appropriate, it is for structuring a situation in which, without supervision, guests can become intoxicated. But we do not yet have a norm in American society that open bars and unmonitored drinking are improper or irresponsible. In the long term, it may be that our prevailing social norms will need to be questioned, but that would be a very major undertaking indeed.

Historically, dram shop liability did not extend to social hosts, perhaps reflecting the view that social hosts cannot be expected to police the behavior of their guests and that to impose such liability would be too disruptive of social relations. Moreover, social host liability might result in the loss of the defendant's personal assets and home (see Graham 1979). Social hosts, unlike commercial dispensers, have no way of passing the costs of tort liability or insurance along to consumers.

Today there is a great deal of interest in extending dram shop–type liability to social hosts, particularly employers and large party givers, and to those who serve liquor to minors. In 1972 both the Minnesota (*Ross v. Ross,* 294 Minn. 115, 200 N.W. 2d 149 [1972]) and the Iowa Supreme Courts (*Williams v. Kleimesrud,* 197 N.W. 2d 614 [1972]) expanded liability to social hosts, but both states' legislatures thereafter amended their laws to exclude social hosts (Minn. Stat. Ann., sec. 340.95 [1980]; Iowa Code Ann. 123.95 [1980]). The Iowa Supreme Court reinstated social host liability under a negligence per se theory, based on the Iowa Alcohol Control Act (*Clark v. Mincks,* 364 N.W. 2d 226 [1985]). New York State imposes criminal liability on commercial and social hosts who sell or serve alcohol to minors (N.Y. Alcoholic Beverage Control Law, sec. 65 [1]).

The most successful nonvendor suits have been brought against employers who have served *already intoxicated* employees at company parties and picnics. Typically, these cases are brought under theories of negligence per se based on violations of the liquor control acts, rather than under common-law or dram shop–act theories. Most of the successful cases have involved employers serving alcohol to minors.[23] However, three recent cases have extended the employer rule to adult employees. *Chastin v. Litton Systems, Inc.* (694 F. 2d 957 4th Cir. [1984]) and *Hallagan v. Pupo* (678 P. 2d 1295 [1982]) extend third-party liability by the usual criminal violation/negligence per se route. However, the Minnesota court in *Meany v. Newell* (352 N.W. 2d 779 [1984]) took a different approach. Citing the special relationship between an employer and employee at common law, it held that the company owed a heightened duty of care to the drunk employee (see Restatement [Second] of Torts 317) and that continuing to serve liquor to an already intoxicated employee constituted a breach of duty, giving rise to a direct-negligence action.

Recently, the New Jersey Supreme Court imposed tort liability on social hosts who knowingly serve intoxicated guests who ultimately cause injury.[24] In *Kelly v. Gwinnell* (96 N.J. 538, 476 A.2d 1219 [1984]) the court said:

> We imposed this duty on the host to the third party because we believe that the policy considerations served by imposition far outweigh those asserted in opposition. While we recognize the concern that our ruling will interfere with accepted standards of social behavior; will intrude on and somewhat diminish the enjoyment, relaxation, and camaraderie that accompanies social gatherings at which alcohol is served; and that such gatherings and social relationships are not simply tangential benefits of a civilized society but are regarded by many as important, we believe that the added assurance of just compensation to the victims of drunk driving as well as the added deterrent effect of the rule on such driving outweigh the importance of those other values. . . Indeed, we believe that given society's extreme concern about drunk driving, any change in social behavior resulting from the rule will be regarded ultimately as neutral at the very least, and not as a change for the very worse; but that in any event if there will be a loss, it is well worth the gain. (96 N.J. 538, 476 A.2d 1219 [1984])

The scope of a New Jersey social host's liability is unclear. The New Jersey Supreme Court noted that the defendant was a social host who knowingly served his guest thirteen drinks in a short period of time. The court also stated that to prevail the plaintiff would have to prove that the host knew that the guest would subsequently be driving. Further, it limited its holding to the situation in which the host directly served the guest. Thus, this decision does not necessarily open the way for suits by victims of drivers who become inebriated at large gatherings where hosts are uninvolved and unaware of each guest's consumption.[25]

Two other courts have adopted social host liability since *Kelly*. In *Clarke v. Mincks* (364 N.W. 2d 226 [1985]) the Iowa Supreme Court held that social hosts may be civilly liable for accidents caused by serving drinks to guests who were already intoxicated. *Clarke* did not add anything to the theory of liability expressed in *Kelly,* but it is a notable decision in at least one respect. The Iowa legislature previously had reversed an Iowa Supreme Court decision (*Williams v. Klemesrud,* 197 N.W. 2d 614 [1972]) that imposed social host liability under the dram shop act. The Iowa Supreme Court's latest decision constitutes a reversal of the legislature's reversal, indicating both the court's intense desire to reduce drunk driving and its belief that it can do so.

In *Ashlock v. Norris* (475 N.E. 2d 1167 [1985]) an Indiana intermediate court of appeals held that a bar patron who procured drinks for another customer who was already intoxicated could be held liable for third-party injuries. *Ashlock* illuminates an often overlooked distinction between vendor and nonvendor liability. The defendant was not a social host but a drinking buddy buying a round for his friends. The plaintiffs sued both the bar as server and the drinking buddy as host. Thus, the court divorced liability from the defendant's status as a server—an identity crucial to liability in *Kelly*. However, since the *Ashlock* court's novel theory has not yet been reviewed by the Indiana Supreme Court, it is too soon to say whether it indicates further extension of civil liability to those involved in drinking episodes.

How likely is it that such a civil liability rule will reduce drunk driving accidents? Admittedly, social hosts at intimate dinner parties are in a better position than commercial dispensers to monitor their guests' drinking, but even so it may be no easy matter to gauge guests' consumption and capacity, nor will all social hosts have the interpersonal skills necessary to stop their friends, clients, bosses, and family members from drinking too much before driving. Some people might, of course, decide to stop serving liquor or to serve less of it. Comprehensive personal injury and homeowner policies cover social host liability, but only to policy limits.[26] Many insureds will no doubt increase these coverages to protect themselves against the risk of catastrophic loss.

Conclusion

The mobilization of tort and insurance law to deter drunk drivers and those contributing to their behavior is an understandable impulse of the current campaign against drunk driving. There is reason to believe, however, that punishment and deterrence through civil law are particularly unsuited to these problems. Although tort law may well have a deterrent role to play in other contexts, it is unlikely to have much effect when the behavior is dangerous to those who engage in it, when the decision processes leading to the behavior tend not to be deliberative, and when damages will be covered by insurance. The tort law is, at best, a very imperfect system of punishment and deterrence because it only applies when damage occurs, and because its effects are significantly blunted by insurance. The use of punitive damages to deter drunk driving seems particularly ill conceived, even more so if the insurer actually pays.

Anti–drunk driving strategists should be cautious about jeopardizing other goals of civil law, most importantly that of providing full assistance to victims of automobile "accidents," but also that of doing justice to defendants in tort suits. The basic constituents of tort and insurance law should not be swept aside without serious consideration of the consequences.

The expansion of dram shop liability seems more likely to yield results. Certain types of well-established restaurants, bars, and taverns will undoubtedly worry about civil liability and higher insurance rates—and will change their serving practices accordingly. The rapid spread of server intervention programs means that a significant percentage of bartenders, waiters, and waitresses will at least have had their consciousnesses raised about liquor servers' responsibility for patrons' irresponsible drinking. At a minimum they will be armed with reasons and justification for trying to prevent abusive drinking. Nevertheless, it would be naive to regard these programs as a panacea. It is one thing to recognize problem drinkers and what is potentially problem drinking; it is another thing to be able to intervene effectively, especially without very strong management support. Many bars will continue to conduct business as usual, pursuing profits from volume sales.

We need to remember that many drunk driving incidents begin at private parties where liquor is plentiful and heavy drinking is encouraged. Large employers have no doubt had their consciousnesses raised by several successful multimillion-dollar lawsuits brought by victims of employees who become drunk at such parties. In the future it is likely that many office parties will be canceled or restructured. Fraternities also will be forced—by university officials, insurance companies, parents of the students, and student activists themselves—to restructure and/or better supervise their social events. Even small-party givers may be encouraged to prevent their guests from overdrinking—or at least from driving away from the party drunk.

Ultimately, the greatest impact of expanded tort liability, as with criminal sanctions, may be the contribution to the long-term reshaping of attitudes and norms. Civil liability educates as well as threatens; it enlists the insurance companies in safety initiatives. Perhaps, even more importantly, it provides people with a justification for acting in ways they know to be responsible.

11

Incapacitation

In other contexts disillusionment with deterrence has led some criminologists to shift their focus to the crime control potential of incapacitation strategies that seek to prevent apprehended offenders from committing further crimes (see Blumstein, Cohen, and Nagin 1978; Greenwood and Abrahamse 1982; Cohen 1983). When offenders are locked up, it is argued, the community is spared the number of crimes they would have committed had they been free. While incapacitation is usually associated with incarceration and, more recently, home detention, drunk drivers could be at least partially incapacitated by separating them from their vehicles either through license suspension or revocation or by vehicle forfeiture or impoundment.

Licensing, License Restrictions, Suspensions, and Revocations

Our traffic law system operates under the assumption that, while driving may not be a right, it is certainly more than a privilege.[1] There is a societal expectation that practically everyone has the capacity to and will operate a motor vehicle. The Supreme Court has recognized that there is a substantial property interest in a driver's license, an interest that cannot be infringed without due process of law (*Dixon v. Love,* 431 U.S. 105 [1977]; *Bell v. Burson,* 402 U.S. 535 [1971]; *Mackey v. Montrym,* 443 U.S. 1 [1979]).

The licensing of drivers did not originate as a strategy for limiting access to a risky or dangerous activity but as a revenue-producing device (Reese 1971). Even our present-day licensing system is not set up to screen out unreliable and unskilled drivers. The test for obtaining an operator's license is very cursory. While an applicant may have to swear that "within the last three years, [he has not] experienced a lapse in consciousness or had any disease, disorder or disability which affects [his] ability to exercise reasonable and ordinary control in operating a vehicle," there is no independent inquiry into the license applicant's character, mental stability, or history of drug use. The applicant need

148

only demonstrate rudimentary knowledge of road signs and rules and minimum driving and parking competence. Almost everything that a person will ever read about traffic safety will be in the driver's manual which is used to prepare for the initial license examination (see Henk, Stahl, and King 1984). The test can be retaken as often as necessary to obtain a passing result. The departments of motor vehicles, which have the responsibility for operating the driver's licensing systems, only weakly monitor a licensee after the initial license has been granted. In most states drivers are not reexamined or investigated, even after serious accidents.[2]

Screening Alcoholics out of the Driving System

In theory drunk drivers could be "incapacitated" by being refused licenses initially. Most states have provisions making "drunkards" or "chronic alcoholics" ineligible for driver's licenses.[3] Yet no effort seems to be made to determine whether a driver falls within these categories. It is unclear how, other than by an applicant's voluntary admission, a motor vehicles department would ordinarily learn that a particular driver is an alcohol abuser. Interestingly enough, the license form does not ask any questions about drinking practices. In any event, efforts to screen alcoholics out of the system at the initial driver's license application stage would probably identify very few alcohol abusers. Most people obtain their first driver's license when they are teenagers or very soon thereafter. Alcohol abuse usually becomes more serious and evident at a later age.

An effort to disqualify "alcoholics," "alcohol abusers," or "problem drinkers" would certainly be futile, for such terms are very plastic and have a great potential to be applied arbitrarily. Those accused of being so afflicted would have to be afforded due process, which would raise many difficulties. It would also discourage problem drinkers from seeking medical assistance. Even if alcohol abusers could be properly identified, denying all of them the opportunity to operate a motor vehicle until they were "cured" (a determination requiring additional hearings) would be seriously overinclusive. Richard Zylman (1976), among others, has argued that not all alcoholics have bad driving records and that not all of them drive while drunk. Analysis of the accident records of hospitalized alcoholics shows that the majority were crash free during the year prior to hospitalization (Zylman 1976). In the final analysis, it is inconceivable that America's estimated ten million alcoholics and alcohol abusers could be screened out of the licensing system and, even if they were, that such disqualifications could be enforced. A more modest proposal is to make restricted licenses a much greater part of any traffic regulatory system. Drivers with alcohol or drug problems might be issued restricted licenses that would permit driving only during certain times of the day or just along certain routes (e.g., from home to work). The terms of the restriction could be reviewed periodically in light of the individual's driving experience, work record, and progress in treatment.

Once a driver has been arrested for DWI and an investigation has revealed a history of alcohol abuse, the state's interest in removing the defendant from the road is greater and the defendant's interest in avoiding the risk of being a false positive is weaker. The defendant has demonstrated his unwillingness or inability to separate his drinking from his driving and has revealed himself as a threat to the community. At that point I believe that it would be entirely appropriate to revoke his license, as long as the offender subsequently could obtain a hearing to determine whether his abusive drinking had been cured.

License Suspensions and Revocations

There are more than 150 million persons licensed to drive in the United States. People cooperate with the licensing system because licenses are awarded liberally and for only small cost. Moreover, up-to-date licenses are useful for identification purposes. Conformity with the licensing system requires little effort. Any proposals to make licensing requirements more stringent or to lower the threshold for suspension or revocation should consider the possibility that more people would drive without valid licenses, perhaps threatening the viability of the entire licensing system. Thus, while license restrictions, suspensions, and revocations have an important role to play in tracking, controlling, and incapacitating drunk drivers, it is important to recognize both the limits of social control via licensing and the need to provide credible legal threats for violations of licensing restrictions.

License suspension is a common punishment for drunk drivers. In New York State in 1984, for example, there were 81,566 suspensions or revocations for drunk driving and refusal to take the Breathalyzer test—and an even greater number for driving without insurance (25,362) and for failing to pay traffic tickets (346,336). These statistics suggest that there is a sizable subgroup of the population that does not regard license restriction as a serious sanction.

License suspension is often meant to be only partially incapacitating. First offenders are usually eligible for provisional or conditional licenses which permit driving for essential purposes, such as commuting to and from work. To abolish conditional licenses would create vast enforcement problems. There is no point in imposing draconian suspensions or revocations to which most offenders cannot be expected to conform. For all but the most incorrigible offenders, some sort of provisional license during the suspension period makes sense.

Inevitably, some drivers whose licenses have been revoked and suspended will fail to abide by the terms of their driving restrictions. In addition to taking a chance on driving with an invalid license, there are many schemes for fraudulently obtaining valid licenses. The driver's licensing system is enormously porous; there are many ways to obtain licenses fraudulently (see U.S. Department of Transportation 1979). One common scheme is to obtain multiple licenses from different states. In the event that one license is suspended, the other(s) can be used.[4] Until recently driver's licenses did not require photos, so it was difficult to prevent use of fraudulently procured licenses. Drivers whose licenses have been revoked or suspended may, through fraud, be able to obtain another license under the same or a different name. Furthermore, the integrity of the licensing system is only as good as the integrity of the documents (usually birth certificates) that are used to get licenses. Most licenses are readily obtainable with a birth certificate. Since forged and purloined birth certificates are readily available, false driver's licenses can be easily obtained.

People can drive without a license. I suspect that hundreds of thousands—perhaps millions—of illiterates, illegal aliens, and others have never obtained licenses but drive regularly. Our licenses do not have to be displayed on the car and in some states do not even have to be carried on the person.[5] Driving without a valid license is not typically treated as a very serious offense.[6]

Ultimately, the law must keep its promises, and license suspensions, forfeitures, and restrictions must be backed up with credible punishments if they are to deliver their deterrent and incapacitating effects successfully. Most jurisdictions prescribe a jail sentence for driving without a valid license, but jail is rarely imposed. In reality, there is not sufficient jail space to enforce two million license revocations and suspensions a year with a significant jail sentence. Necessarily, home detention, large fines, and vehicle forfeiture or impoundment have to play a major role as sanctions for violating license restrictions.

A recent California study revealed that two-thirds of drivers whose licenses had been suspended and revoked operated their vehicles in violation of license restriction (National Transportation Safety Board 1984; also see Willet 1973). This finding is not surprising given the importance of driving for participation in economic and social life; nor is it inconsistent with an incapacitation effect. The sizable minority of restricted drivers who do not drive at all are fully incapacitated. Those who drive anyway almost certainly drive less often, less far, less dangerously, and less drunk. A 1986 California study found that persons whose licenses had been suspended for test refusal had 72.2 percent fewer crashes during the six-month suspension period than during the six preceding months, a significant incapacitating effect (Traffic Tech, NHTSA Technology Transfer Series 1986). Thus, licensing restrictions, suspensions, and revocations should continue to be considered one of the core sanctions for drunk driving, but the temptation to make these restrictions more draconian should be resisted with healthy realism about the social control limitations of license sanctions. Moreover, it is vital that in implementing licensing sanctions there be a will and capacity to enforce those sanctions with credible backup punishments.

Vehicle Forfeiture and Impoundment

Forfeiture laws empower the government to seize contraband, instruments or fruits of crime. Traditionally, forfeiture proceedings were civil rather than criminal proceedings, a situation predicated on the legal fiction that the government's action was directed against the asset rather than against the asset's owner. The 1968 Racketeer Influenced and Corrupt Organizations (RICO) Act, revived the idea of criminal forfeiture. It provides for forfeiture of the proceeds of racketeering activity as part of the criminal proceedings. With civil and criminal forfeitures becoming increasingly important sanctions, especially in drug and organized-crime cases, the government has been able to seize cars, boats, planes, real property, and businesses. If drug smugglers' vehicles can be forfeited as instrumentalities of crime, why not drunk drivers' vehicles? While vehicles simply facilitate drug transactions, they are essential to drunk driving.

Alaska, North Carolina, and Texas currently have statutory provisions for forfeiting drunk drivers' vehicles. The Alaskan statute (Alaska Stat., sec. 28.35.037) authorizes forfeiture on either a second conviction for DWI or refusal to take the chemical test. The state must demonstrate (by a preponderance of evidence) that the forfeiture of the motor vehicle will deter the convicted person from future drunk driving, deter other potential violators, protect the safety and welfare of the public, or serve as an expression of public condemnation of the serious or aggravated nature of the convicted person's conduct. The Alaskan law also provides a forfeiture remission to protect secured parties and nonoffending vehicle owners. Apparently, the law has not been used. The attorney general's office stresses both the importance of cars to social and economic life in Alaska and the time-consuming, complex procedures involved in effecting a forfeiture.

North Carolina (N.C. Gen. Stat., sec. 20-179 [c]) authorizes vehicle forfeiture on (1) a second DWI offense (within seven years), (2) driving with an operator's license previously revoked for DWI, or (3) causing serious injury as a result of operating a vehicle while impaired. However, like the Alaskan statute, this North Carolina law indicates reluctance to deprive a drunk driver of his automobile. Forfeiture is not allowed if the vehicle is primarily used by a member of the defendant's family or household for a business purpose or for driving to or from work or school; moreover, the interests of a secured party or innocent owner must be protected. These provisos more or less swallow up the rule, at least when the defendant has a family. Inquiries to the attorney general's office have revealed that only one DWI forfeiture has actually been carried out under the statute.

The Texas statute (Texas Code Annot., sec. 6701L-1) permits vehicle forfeiture as a sanction for DWI or involuntary manslaughter if the defendant (1) committed the offense while on probation for involuntary manslaughter or (2) has three or more previous convictions for DWI or involuntary manslaughter. This statute is also likely to have little practical effect, since very few offenders have been convicted of DWI either while on probation for involuntary manslaughter or after having accumulated *three previous* DWI convictions.

To carry out a vehicle seizure in a drunk driving case, it is not necessary for a state to have an explicit forfeiture provision covering drunk driving offenses. General forfeiture provisions (e.g., New Jersey Stat. Annot. 2C:64-1) could be used to seize a DWI offender's vehicle. Recently, for example, the Brooklyn district attorney was able to forfeit the vehicle of a crash-involved repeat drunk driver under the general civil forfeiture statute (*Holtzman v. Bailey,* 503 N.Y.S. 473 [1986]).[7]

In addition to serving retributive and deterrent functions, forfeiture might provide something of an incapacitating effect if it keeps a defendant from driving. Admittedly the offender is free to replace the forfeited vehicle, but this is time consuming and expensive. Vehicle forfeiture (like license revocation and brief jail terms) should be seen as one strand in a web of sanctions that must be spun around the drunk driver. Vehicle forfeiture need not be imposed as an alternative sanction; rather, it should supplement license revocation, fine, and jail. It could even be made a condition of the defendant's probation that he not purchase, lease, or borrow any motor vehicle for a period of time.

Since forfeiture has become such a popular sanction in drug cases, why has it not caught on as an anti–drunk driving remedy? My hunch is that there is an unarticulated but deep-seated feeling that forfeiture is too harsh a sanction for drunk driving. It cannot be happenstance that drug offenders' vehicles regularly are forfeited and that only a handful of drunk drivers' vehicles have ever been forfeited. Prosecutors—and perhaps the larger society—must assume or believe that drunk drivers are less culpable and/or less dangerous than drug sellers. This assumption or belief might be difficult to justify, since drunk drivers more directly put life at risk than do drug sellers.

The Alaska, North Carolina, and Texas statutes evidence great concern for the consequences of vehicle forfeiture on the offender's family. This is surprising, because our jurisprudence of sanctions usually does not take into account impacts on family members and other third parties. Sentencing laws do not admonish judges to refrain from imposing a jail or prison sentence if the defendant's family would be inconvenienced or harmed. All criminal sanctions have negative implications for an offender's family. If the offender is fined, his family loses income that could have purchased food, clothing, and vacations. If the offender is jailed, the family has to forgo the offender's company, affection, and paycheck. The offender's conviction may disgrace his or her family and diminish its social and economic standing.

The burden of a vehicle forfeiture should obviously not fall on creditors and innocent third parties. The victim of a car theft should not have his vehicle forfeited because the thief was a drunk driver; nor should a finance company have its security interest forfeited (thereby drying up car loans or increasing everyone's interest rate).

What if the vehicle the drunk driver was operating belonged to his parent, spouse, or friend?[8] If the state could show that the owner was negligent in lending the vehicle to someone whom he should have known either had been or would be drinking, forfeiture would not seem unfair. Lenders should be required to assume the risk that their vehicle might be forfeited in a drunk driving proceeding just as they assume the risk that it might be destroyed in a crash. If this rule made vehicle owners less prone to lend their cars to persons whom they believe might drive drunk, so much the better. The liability of parents might well be even stricter. There should be a presumption in favor of forfeiture when minor children drive drunk, because parents might be said to have an affirmative obligation to prevent this from occurring.

Impoundment

Impoundment is a well-known feature of traffic enforcement. Police departments have substantial experience impounding vehicles that have been abandoned, used in crimes, overparked, and so forth.[9] Indeed, a person arrested for drunk driving will often have his vehicle towed away and impounded. To reclaim it he will have to pay the towing and storage fees and show proof of ownership, registration, and insurance. Impoundment can also be accomplished by fitting the vehicle with tire clamps ("shoes") or by seizing its license plates.

Impoundment, like forfeiture, is a symbolically appropriate sanction for drunk driving, a vehicle-related punishment for a vehicle-related offense. However, it is a less severe sanction than forfeiture, since, after the impoundment period expires, the vehicle is returned. Impoundment incapacitates to the extent that it prevents or reduces the defendant's driving. Some defendents would be fully incapacitated, while others, because they have free access to another vehicle, would hardly be incapacitated at all. Thus, impoundment should be supplemented by license suspension or revocation.[10]

For first and second DWI offenses, California provides for impoundment for not less than one or more than thirty days (at the owner's expense); a third conviction allows up to a ninety-day impoundment (West's Annotated California Vehicle Code, sec. 23195). However, a 1984 amendment requires that, before imposing an impoundment, the court *consider* whether it will result in the offender's or a family member's loss of employment, in diminished ability to attend school or obtain medical care, in loss of the vehicle because of inability to pay impoundment fees, or in unfair infringement on community property rights. This is another example of ambivalence about punishing drunk drivers. The statute seems to say that if employment of vehicle impoundment as a sanction would have punitive or incapacitative consequences it should not be imposed!

The pertinent Delaware statute permits vehicle impoundment following conviction for operating a motor vehicle while the operator's license is suspended or revoked for a DWI offense or for refusal to take a BAC test (Dela. Code Ann. 21, sec. 2756). For a first violation the minimum duration is ninety days; a subsequent impoundment carries a year minimum. The statute allows for surrender of the vehicle plates in lieu of impoundment.

Oregon provides for up to 120 days impoundment (1) on a second DWI conviction or (2) for driving with a license suspended or revoked because of a DWI offense (Ore. Rev. Stat., sec. 484.222). The statute further provides for *mandatory* 120-day registration suspension and return of license plates of *all vehicles owned by the defendant*. If the owner is someone other than the offender and can prove by clear and convincing evidence that he or she lacked knowledge that the defendant was operating the vehicle while under the influence, his or her vehicle will not be impounded. This means that parents will be able to avoid impoundment of their vehicles if their children are apprehended for DWI.

Impoundment is a potentially useful drunk driving sanction. It properly calls attention to the irresponsibility of operating a vehicle while under the influence of alcohol and inconveniences the defendant's driving activities. Thus, it seems strange that, despite the encouragement of the federal law and the authorization of many states' laws, impoundment is almost never used. It is my impression, based on interviews with motor vehicle personnel, that there is a widespread feeling that impoundment is too harsh a penalty. However, police and transportation personnel also point to practical problems: police liability for damage done to impounded vehicles, registration to an owner other than the driver, and extensive paperwork.

Home Detention and Electronic Monitoring

In Chapter 9 we noted the drive to impose short jail terms on drunk drivers in the context of its potential deterrent effect. Although incarceration is also the basic incapacitating strategy, twenty-four- to forty-eight-hour jail terms obviously do not incapacitate drivers very long. Much more might be achieved through the use of home detention, especially if enforced by electronic monitoring systems (see Ball and Lilly 1986).

The idea of home detention (or, in the pretrial context, "house arrest") is not entirely novel. On occasion, judges have imposed home detention as a condition of bail or probation. During recent years the jail crowding crisis around the country has stimulated a great deal of interest in home detention and electronic monitoring. Today several thousand people are subject to this sanction, many of them because they were convicted of drunk driving (Petersilia 1987).

Home detention has much to commend it as a sanction. It is easily adaptable to the requirements of particular offenders. Thus, it can be imposed around the clock or just during evening hours. For most drunk drivers it would make sense to impose home detention during the hours when the majority of drunk driving occurs: after nightfall on Fridays, Saturdays, and Sundays. The drunk driver could be subjected to this sanction for a substantial time period, say six months or longer.

The incapacitating payoff could be significant. If the offender is at home, he is not on the road driving while drunk. Suppose the basic sanction for drunk driving was that the convicted offender remain at home after 7:00 P.M. either every night of the week or just on weekends. If such a sentence could be enforced, the possibility of his being a recidivist during this period would be eliminated. In fact, the Linn County, Oregon, home detention program found that none of the sixty drunk drivers were rearrested for drunk driving, as compared with 15 percent rearrests for those on regular probation (Petersilia 1987).

Admittedly, enforcing home detention presents difficulties. Vastly overburdened probation departments hardly have the resources to make evening visits to the offender's home—or even to make regular phone calls. In fact, probation has traditionally been a 9:00 A.M.–5:00 P.M. program. For home detention to emerge as a major sanction in our social control armamentarium, probation departments or some new agencies would have to develop effective round-the-clock monitoring.

The recent development of electronic monitoring equipment makes supervision of home detention more feasible (see Lilly, Ball, and Wright 1986).[11] There are several versions of this equipment on the market. The basic technology works by attaching a signal-emitting bracelet to the offender's ankle or wrist. The signal is relayed via the offender's home telephone to the monitoring agency's computer. If the offender removes the bracelet or leaves his house, the signals cease and the computer indicates a probation violation. The violation can be confirmed by a phone call and/or a home visit.

Florida has been the pioneer state in developing home detention/electronic monitoring programs. Joan Petersilia (1987) describes the Palm Beach, Florida, program. "House" arrest sentences are calculated on the basis of three or four days home confinement for each day the convicted driver would have spent in jail. Most participants are drunk-driving offenders, who are given a choice of thirty days on monitored home confinement or ten days in jail, the latter being the mandatory minimum sentence under the Florida law for a second drunk driving conviction. While on home confinement the offender is required to (1) pay $5 a day for the monitoring equipment, in addition to the standard probation fee, (2) maintain a working telephone, (3) remain at home during the established curfew hours, and (4) report weekly to the monitoring office to have the transmitter inspected, pay probation and monitoring fees, and discuss any problems with respect to probation or home confinement.

The three arguments that I anticipate being made against this sanction are that it is (1) too harsh, (2) unenforcible, and (3) too intrusive. In my view none of these objections is convincing. Six months of weekend nighttime home detention seems well within the range of punishments traditionally thought appropriate for drunk driving. Drunk driving involves the risk of serious personal injury. Therefore, in judging whether a particular punishment is disproportionate, we should look to the punishments prescribed for crimes such as assault and robbery. These offenses invariably carry the possibility of maximum prison terms of more than a year. By comparison, being restricted to one's home at night, while inconvenient and disruptive of social life, is not as painful and onerous as a felony prison term.

The enforcement of home detention is made much easier by the electronic monitoring technology. It is now technologically possible to verify the offender's compliance with the home detention sentence. The tougher enforcement problem comes after a violation is uncovered. Will the probation department be able to maintain a credible threat against violating the terms of the home detention sentence? This may be a difficult challenge. Probation departments are extremely overburdened; nationally, over the past decade their caseloads have grown even more than the jail population. Harried prosecutors resist the idea of prosecuting as a probation violation a home detention violation that does not result in either an arrest or traffic accident. Furthermore, judges with an eye on jail crowding resist pressures to impose jail terms on home detention violators. If home detention is to emerge as a significant sanction, these prosecutorial and judicial attitudes have to be overcome. Criminal justice personnel will have to be convinced that unless such alternative sanctions as home detention are backed up by credible jail threats, they will not be effective. In other words, these personnel must come to understand their roles in systemic terms. However, changing attitudes alone will not be sufficient; greater resources are also necessary.

The privacy and civil-liberties objections to home detention are not convincing. The monitoring equipment does nothing more than indicate the offender's presence in his home. This provides no more information than could be learned by personal surveillance. Indeed, it provides less information. Personal surveillance would reveal who enters and exits the offender's home, what rooms he uses, when he goes to bed, and when he awakens. Perhaps some critics would argue that requiring an offender to attach a bracelet to his body is the most offensive part of home detention. Nevertheless, it seems to me that an offender who could be made to wear a jail or prison uniform is not worse off for being made to wear a bracelet. Such bracelets are thin and relatively unobtrusive. They do not cause pain, and they do not restrict any activities.

Incarceration

Short twenty-four- to forty-eight-hour "shock" jail terms obviously have only the most limited incapacitating effect. However, as we saw earlier, the criminal law has already defined both recidivist DWI and

DWI resulting in injury or death as felonies deserving at least modest incarceration. Thus, if attention to DWI remains high, there will be increasing numbers of DWI offenders incapacitated in jail or prison. Beyond that, to follow our earlier discussion, it would be appropriate to specify significant jail terms for certain aggravated-DWI offenders as well.

It might also be reasonable to use modest terms of incarceration for drivers who build up long records of serious offenses and crashes; these are high-risk drivers for whom severe retributive and incapacitating sanctions would be appropriate.[12] Goldstein and Susmilch (1982) point out that a small number of irresponsible, incorrigible, and dangerous drivers are known to the police in every jurisdiction; approximately one-third of impaired drivers judged responsible for their serious-injury accidents had extensive prior records of both traffic violations and accidents leading to license restrictions. They are like serious accidents waiting to happen. If this is so, would it not be appropriate for the state to take some sort of preemptive action against them? This could be done via the criminal justice system by imposing the maximum felony sentences prescribed for repeat drunk driving, or it could be done administratively by license revocations.

Conclusion

Incapacitation can play an important role in the total effort to control drunk driving. The key to incapacitation is separating the defendant from his vehicle. This can be accomplished through judicious use of license restrictions, suspensions, and revocations. While license restrictions, suspensions, and revocations must serve as a standard DWI sanction, it is important not to overload the licensing system with demands that it cannot meet. Increasing suspensions and revocations must be matched by increased resources for enforcement and by credible sanctions for those who violate license restrictions. Short-term vehicle impoundment would be a very useful supplement to license suspension, adding to the costs of drunk driving and inconveniencing the offender in a way that might reduce his driving and focus his attention on the nature of his offense. Forfeiture, a more extreme penalty, might be a potent sanction, but it should be reserved for the most serious cases of aggravated drunk driving and injury-causing offenses. Home detention, backed up by electronic surveillance, has potential to provide a workable midrange incapacitating strategy. It should become a standard sanction for drunk drivers, but effective monitoring and enforcement will also need to be developed. Prolonged incarceration is an appropriate response to aggravated- and recidivist-DWI offenders.

12

Public Education and Drinking/Driving

The changing of attitudes and norms is the best hope for reducing drunk driving over the long run.[1] If more people regarded drunk driving as irresponsible and dangerous, there would be less drunk driving, more informal control mechanisms, and more support for formal counter-measures. We have already noted that deterrent strategies may have a long-term effect on attitudes and norms. In this chapter we turn to nonpunitive educational efforts aimed at the same goal. Public education encompasses systematic mass media efforts and community information campaigns by citizens action groups such as RID, MADD, and SADD.

Information Campaigns

Public education stresses the positive side of social control. It urges conformity to legitimate rules and norms because conformity is responsible citizenship as well as a contribution to one's own life and health. Public education is similar to some forms of rehabilitation in its emphasis on rational persuasion, but it differs from DWI treatment programs in being directed at the general public rather than at apprehended drunk drivers.

We tend to associate public education campaigns with public health efforts. The public health services have used the mass media to inform the public about the risks of heart disease, smoking, failure to wear seat belts, and promiscuous sexual behavior. The assumption behind such efforts is that if people know the facts about health and safety, they will understand that self-interest requires them to conform to legitimate norms (Wallach 1984).

Although tracing the effects of public education campaigns is no easy matter, at least some of the health campaigns of the past twenty years seem to have produced positive results. The percentage of Americans who smoke has declined (Warner 1977; Federal Trade Commission 1979), and concern over heart disease and cholesterol seems to have

160

affected eating habits. On the other hand, seat belt campaigns have not had any discernible effect in increasing usage (Insurance Institute for Highway Safety 1981).[2] Some scholars have emphasized that efforts to influence behavior by mass persuasion tend to be ineffective because people process information selectively, tuning out or rejecting messages they do not want to hear. Thus, even if an information campaign is successful in providing an individual with "the facts," there is no guarantee that his behavior will change (Lazarsfeld, Berelson, and Gaudet 1948). People must have knowledge on which to base a change of behavior. They must be persuaded to want to change their behavior, and they must be shown how to change (Hochheimer 1981).

Public education is carried out through print and electronic media and by face-to-face encounters. Not surprisingly, the biggest campaigns have taken place on television, the medium with the largest audiences and greatest capacity for vivid communication. American television stations must provide some free time for communications in the "public interest, necessity, and convenience" (see Barrow 1975). Some television and radio stations have donated free time for PSAs to agencies such as the NIAAA or NHTSA for messages on alcohol abuse and drunk driving. Sponsors of PSAs can also purchase television, radio, magazine, and newspaper time for their messages. The liquor industry has not objected to stations with which it does business also donating or selling time to anti–drunk driving campaigns, as long as those campaigns (and their sponsors) do not support the drive to ban alcohol advertising from the air.

Some corporations apparently consider public interest advertising to be good public relations. Ads by large corporations, especially the insurance companies and some beverage alcohol producers, denouncing drunk driving and urging greater responsibility project a corporate image of public spiritedness.[3] MADD and other anti–drunk driving groups have been reasonably successful in attracting corporate support.[4]

Public Education versus Drunk Driving

At first blush, drunk driving, a behavior dangerous on its face, would seem ideally suited to a public education campaign. Unlike drug use, it is not the centerpiece of any subculture.[5] It has not been romanticized in song and film, and it has not attracted a constituency that favors legalization or glorifies it as "authentic" or legitimate behavior. There is a solid national consensus against drunk driving; no one speaks in its favor. Moreover, anti–drunk driving campaigns appeal to self-interest;

if you drive while drunk, you greatly increase the chance of injuring yourself, a family member, or friend.

There have been periodic public education campaigns against drunk driving for many decades. Since shortly after World War II, the NSC has sponsored anti–drunk driving commercials and advertisements; the most famous exhorts "If you drink, don't drive. If you drive, don't drink." NHTSA has sponsored various anti– drunk driving campaigns since the early 1970s. One of its major campaigns has been aimed at mobilizing the efforts of people —parents, other family members, friends, peers, and bartenders—who are in a position to stop someone from drunk driving. This campaign's slogan, "Friends don't let friends drive drunk," is by now very well known (see Grey Advertising 1975*a*, 1975*b*). The Distilled Spirits Council of the United States (1975) has sponsored anti–drunk driving messages ("If you drink, drink responsibly"), as have insurance companies and other organizations and businesses.

Has public education had a significant effect? Most students of the subject agree that it has not: educational campaigns may increase information and knowledge, but they have little effect on changing behavior (Haskins 1969; Blane and Hewitt 1977). In fact, the U.S. Department of Transportation has decided to phase out all advertising money for PSAs "because of a report that concluded that there is no proven link between advertising blitzes and saving lives (Evans 1987). This pessimistic conclusion can be tempered with the observation that the most important effects of media campaigns may well be indirect and long-term. Rather than producing startling behavior changes in a week, month, or year, such messages may work over much longer time frames, perhaps in conjunction with other social trends (e.g., the health movement). There are, however, several reasons to doubt the capacity of public education to reduce drunk driving.

Information about the Dangers of Drunk Driving Is Already Well Known

People have long been told that drunk driving is dangerous. This is not obscure, arcane, or technical information. We are dealing with behavior that is dangerous on its face and about which people are warned by parents, teachers, media announcements, friends, and lovers. Many people who occasionally drive while under the influence may readily admit that drunk driving is dangerous. Indeed, they almost always drive sober. Their problem is not lack of information about the hazards of drunk driving but occasional failures in coping with peer pressure, stress, or reverie.

Frequent drunk drivers, who are almost certainly alcohol abusers, also do not need to be informed that drunk driving is dangerous. It is likely that they have been told innumerable times that they drink too much and are jeopardizing their own and others' health and welfare. If they regularly drive while drunk, they have probably learned to rationalize their behavior, perhaps having convinced themselves that they can hold more liquor than the average fellow, or that they are not really drunk, or that they can effectively compensate for their intoxication, or that they cannot control their behavior. Every time they complete a drunk driving trip successfully, their confidence in their drinking/driving capability is reinforced. Perhaps they rationalize that "while the dangers of drunk driving are real, they don't apply to me."

Attitudes toward Drunk Driving Are Already Quite Negative

Public opinion polls generally show that Americans favor tough sentences for all criminal offenders, including drunk drivers. One interesting 1967 poll reported that 44 percent of the respondents answered affirmatively the following question: "In three or four European countries, a person who drives a car after having more than one drink of alcoholic beverages is sent to jail. Would you like to see such a law in this country or not?" In actuality, no European country criminalizes, much less incarcerates, a driver for having imbibed more than one alcoholic drink. That 44 percent of American respondents would agree to such an extreme proposal suggests either a deep wellspring of antipathy toward alcohol and/or drunk driving or the extraordinary powers of suggestion that are embedded in survey questions.

The U.S. Department of Transportation's 1968 *Report on Alcohol and Highway Safety* found that "a majority of those interviewed were of the opinion that laws for the control of drunken driving should be stricter and more actively enforced." Moreover, "two thirds of surveyed drivers were of the opinion that present penalties are too lenient and almost half were in favor of legislation to jail individuals who drive after more than one drink." Almost two decades later the same preferences continue to be expressed. A 1981 survey found that 82 percent of respondents favored "tougher sentences for drinking and driving," and in 1985 65 percent of respondents favored sentencing drinking drivers to jail "even if they have not caused an accident" (Survey Research, Consultants International 1986).

The Anti–Drunk Driving Message Is Ambiguous

Smokers are told that smoking causes emphysema and lung cancer and are exhorted not to smoke. Drivers are told that seat belts are an important safety device and are urged to wear them. People who drink and drive are told that drinking and driving are both alright and that even drinking/driving is alright if it is not excessive. People are not really meant to follow the injunction "If you drink, don't drive." What is meant is, "If you drink excessively, don't drive." This is a vague exhortation that starkly contrasts with such simple messages as "Don't smoke" and "Wear seat belts."

What constitutes responsible drinking/driving? There are a minority of heavy and deviant drinkers whose interpretation of this standard, even if they tried to follow it, would differ markedly from the majority's interpretation. Quite clearly, more specific information is necessary if even the first stage of the behavioral change process is to be reached. Why not have PSAs tell people exactly how many drinks it is safe to consume before driving? One can understand the hesitancy of experts to be pinned down to a specific number that can be safely consumed during a specified time period. Indeed, given widespread *underestimation* of the amount that can be lawfully consumed, announcing a fixed, "safe" number of drinks might encourage light drinkers to increase their consumption. A norm that permits people to drink and drive— "but not too much,"—is bound to be frequently exceeded by inadvertence, bad judgment, and rationalization. But a norm that tells people not to drink and drive at all is unrealistic and smacks of discredited prohibitionism.

Inability to Act on One's Knowledge

Even if a person knows that excessive drinking/driving is dangerous and irresponsible, he may be unable or unwilling to monitor his drinking and driving properly because his thought processes are clouded by alcohol or because he may fear losing face before his peers (or in his own eyes) by admitting that he is too intoxicated to drive. After a certain amount of alcohol consumption, he may no longer be able to appreciate the extent of his impairment. Having many times driven after considerable drinking, he may believe that he is capable of driving competently. Hard-core alcoholics and alcohol abusers may be unable (or may believe themselves to be unable) to conform their behavior to a moderate drinking/driving standard, even if they "want" to conform.

The PSAs will most likely be most compelling for those people who do not drink and drive—and for social drinkers who previously lacked accurate information either about the alcoholic content of beer or about the ineffectiveness of coffee and showers to counteract intoxication. With education, as with deterrence, the most irresponsible and dangerous drunk drivers are most difficult to influence.

Proalcohol Advertising

The anti–drunk driving and anti–alcohol abuse messages delivered through public education campaigns may be diluted, counteracted, or even overwhelmed by "proalcohol" advertising. The alcoholic beverage industry spends more than $1 billion per year advertising its wares. Although by voluntary agreement most distilled spirits are not advertised on television,[6] there is extensive television advertising of beers and wines. Between 1970 and 1982 the alcoholic beverage industry increased its expenditures on advertising by 231 percent.

Mobilizing Restrainers and Controllers

One promising public education strategy involves efforts to convince the citizenry to stop their friends and acquaintances from drunk driving. To be successful this strategy does not require that people change their own personalities, habits, or occasional lapses from responsibility. Instead, it requires that they take responsibility for preventing a friend's or acquaintance's drunk driving. Since the mid-1970s, NHTSA has aimed PSAs at people who are in a position to prevent or restrain people from drinking/driving—thus the slogan "Friends don't let friends drive drunk." One television commercial shows a man sprawled out, apparently dead. The picture pans to another young man who explains: "Cinderella here had nine drinks this evening. He wanted to drive home, but I made him sleep here. He'll have quite a head tomorrow, but at least he will be alive." The caption, "Friends don't let friends drive drunk," is printed over the screen. The goal is to establish norms that make it socially acceptable, even socially required, to tell friends and family members not to drive because they have drunk too much, to find them alternative means of transportation, to invite them to sleep over, or to otherwise prevent their drunk driving.

A similar educational strategy, albeit one bolstered by threats of civil liability, is being directed at restaurant and bar owners, managers, and employees and at large corporations that traditionally sponsor holiday parties. These institutions are urged not to serve inebriated patrons and guests and to call cabs for those too intoxicated to drive safely. Whether such exhortations will be effective remains to be seen. It should certainly be easier to convince the corporations to structure and supervise their parties differently, since they have every incentive to minimize civil liability and insurance costs and to appear responsible. As noted in Chapter 10, bars face a dilemma, since profits depend on alcoholic beverage sales and since heavy drinkers are the best customers.

Beyond Information

By themselves, sporadic PSAs alerting the public to such public health risks as drunk driving are probably not enough to create substantial behavioral change. Communications experts stress the importance of providing the target audience with practical information and strategies for changing behavior. As Hochheimer (1981) points out, it is not enough to tell people not to let their friends drive while drunk; the audience must be instructed on practical strategies to accomplish this objective. What should a concerned friend say and do? What happens if the would-be drunk driver protests, becomes angry, resists, tries to leave? The media campaign can supply ideas: call a cab, drive the drunk friend home, take his keys away, order him a full meal. Such suggestions are commonsensical, but the campaigns can encourage the belief that such actions are legitimate and even morally compelled.

Likewise, drinkers need to be instructed on how to prevent themselves from driving while under the influence. Naturally, one way is always to drink moderately. But *how* does one drink moderately? by bringing only a certain amount of money to a bar? by making a pledge not to drink more than a certain number of drinks? by seeking counseling? Different strategies are probably necessary for different age groups and types of drinkers. No strategy seems promising for abusive drinkers whose consumption is regularly or periodically out of control.

It would be a mature step forward to recognize that there will always be a good deal of drunk driving, owing to both the normal life pattern of alcohol abusers and alcoholics and to the occasional lapses of light and moderate drinkers. The alcohol abusers must be introduced to strategies they are capable of implementing. It should not be assumed that they are hopelessly irresponsible, lacking all capacity to act in their own self-interest and in the interests of the larger community.[7] While such individuals may lack substantial control over alcohol and be either unwilling or unable to change their drinking practices, they may be able to change their driving practices.

In addition to urging heavy drinkers to choose alternative means of transportation, perhaps they could be instructed on how to drive more safely when intoxicated—for example, reduce speed, stay in the inside lane, and so forth. I offer this as a serious suggestion, in the same vein as efforts to provide information on birth control and safe sex. If possibly injurious behavior is going to occur, we ought to do what we can to ameliorate the costs as much as possible. Teenagers can be instructed on how to engage in sex more responsibly and safely. Alcohol abusers could be instructed on how to drive more safely. Both proposals are vulnerable to the criticism that they encourage the very behavior we wish to prevent. Indeed, it may be true to speak of responsible teenage sexual activity and safe drunk driving is to legitimate and perhaps encourage those activities. Nevertheless, such initiatives may well contribute overall to reducing the total costs associated with these activities. We can only speculate about whether they would do so. Safer drunk driving would not negate criminal liability. Safety would be its own reward, so DWI would not be "encouraged." In any event, experiments with such initiatives should be encouraged. The only way to determine whether such innovations could have a positive impact is by mounting and evaluating demonstration projects.

The Role of Community Groups

The grass roots, anti–drunk driving movement can play a critical role in making public education campaigns more effective. There is research to demonstrate that behavior change is much more likely when there is personal contact in addition to media exposure. The success of groups such as Alcoholics Anonymous and Weight Watchers suggests that behavior change frequently is more successful in a group setting. Thus, the Stanford Heart Disease Project demonstrated that people who were exposed in groups to discussions and demonstrations on measures for preventing heart disease were much more likely to change their behavior than were persons exposed solely to media messages (Maccoby et. al. 1977). However, researchers also found that the group exposed solely to public health messages improved its attitudes and behavior more than did the control group that was not exposed to any special health campaign.

Groups such as MADD, RID, and SADD have been very imaginative in bringing programs to schools and other community organizations. At the local level they have increasingly defined their role in terms of public education (Weed 1987). Often in coordination with state-sponsored anti–drunk driving task forces and projects they have developed and disseminated educational packets for children as young as elementary school students. They have worked with both junior high school and senior high school students to develop practical strategies to help the latter groups both in resisting peer pressures to drink and in restraining friends from drinking/driving. They have passed out all kinds of promotional literature and devices—bumper stickers, pens, and shopping and litter bags—containing information and exhortations about drinking/driving. One of SADD's primary activities is to have high school students and their families sign "Contract for Life: A Contract for Life between Parent and Teenager."

TEENAGER: I agree to call you for advice and/or transportation at any hour, from any place, if I am ever in a situation where I have been drinking or a friend or a date who is driving me has been drinking.

PARENT: I agree to come and get you at any hour, any place, no questions asked and no argument at that time, or I will pay for a taxi to bring you home safely. I expect we would discuss this issue at a later time.

I agree to seek safe, sober transportation home if I am ever in a situation where I have had too much to drink or a friend who is driving me has had too much to drink.

Conclusion

The NSC has sponsored media campaigns against drunk driving for many decades. Public education was a key feature of NHTSA's ASAP initiative during the early 1970s, and it continues to be a priority. State anti–drunk driving programs are increasingly utilizing the media, and private corporations, especially insurance companies, are regularly placing anti–drunk driving advertisements.

The capacity of mass media campaigns to change behavior, at least in the short run, is probably quite limited. The assumption that when provided with accurate information about health and safety people will cease acting recklessly and irresponsibly is dubious; one need only reflect on our apparent inability to reduce illicit drug use through educational campaigns. This is especially true when societal opinion about the behavior under attack is already fixed.

Public education efforts should look to the long term. Perhaps it is too late to change the behavior of people already committed to deviant life-styles or activities; still, public education can shape the perceptions and values of the next generation. For this reason, it especially makes sense to aim anti–drunk driving messages (and anti–alcohol abuse messages) at young people, beginning at very early ages. Efforts by the citizens anti–drunk driving groups to design curricula and programs for the early school years are an important step.

In all education campaigns, it is important to recognize that behavior change requires more than information and exhortation. Strategies must be communicated. People must be shown how to avoid those situations in which ultimately they will either drive while drunk or drive with someone who is drunk. Communicating and demonstrating strategies is also crucial for convincing third parties to take action to prevent their family members, friends, associates, and customers from driving while drunk.

13
Opportunity Blocking

This chapter examines a diverse array of strategies that aim to restructure the environment so that drunk driving will be more difficult to commit. We first examine a technological solution to drunk driving: preventing a vehicle from being operated by someone who is intoxicated. Next we turn to a series of strategies that aim to shape drinking practices: regulating drinking promotions at taverns and bars, making twenty-one the national minimum purchase age for alcohol, and increasing the taxes on alcoholic beverages.

A Technological Solution to Prevent the Drinker from Driving

In theory, the best anti–drunk driving counter measure would be a device that makes it impossible—or at least very difficult—for someone who has been drinking to drive a vehicle. If such a device could be developed, nobody's attitudes, values, or drinking habits would have to be altered. The drunk driving problem would be substantially eliminated simply by a technological fix that reconfigured the environment. In fact, for more than twenty years students of drunk driving have speculated about the feasability of just such a device, and NHTSA has invested in certain experimental designs.

Today we appear to stand at the threshold of this dream becoming a reality. Guardian Interlock Systems of Denver, Colorado, claims to have developed an alcohol-sensitive automobile ignition system that would lock the starter system of a car if the driver's alcohol level rendered him unsafe to drive.

The device consists of a tube into which the driver must breathe, and an alcohol sensor that allegedly determines the alcohol level of the driver. Each time the car is started the driver exhales into the tube continuously for four seconds to stimulate the alcohol sensor. If the driver's alcohol level is in an acceptable range to drive, Guardian claims that a green light will appear on the device and the car will start. A yellow light is an indication to the driver that his alcohol level is nearing the legal limit and he should use caution in driving, but the car will continue to start. If the driver's alcohol level is above the legal limit, a red light is supposed to appear, the car's ignition system will lock, and the car will not start.[1]

The Interlock System is currently being tested in Cincinnati, Ohio, where it has been installed in two hundred probationers' vehicles,[2] and in several California communities. California, Oregon, Washington, Texas, and Michigan have each passed a package of legislation authorizing sentencing judges to order the Interlock System installed in certain DWI cases. The Interlock System costs $468 to rent. It must be installed by the manufacturer. The latest version even claims to be able to code the probationer's breath so that he cannot enlist a friend's help to fool the device. The probationer is required to bring his car in for servicing every thirty days so that the system can be checked. If there is evidence of tampering the probation department is notified.

It may take several years before the Interlock System's effectiveness can be adequately assessed. Meanwhile, it is likely that more jurisdictions will make the Interlock System a sentencing option. It might even be cost effective to pay the costs for indigent defendants because any comparable sanction would probably cost the state more money.

If the Interlock System is effective in preventing drunk driving, should it, like seat belts, be required for all vehicles? Those opposing such a requirement will no doubt argue that this would impose an unnecessary expense on the majority of drivers who never drive while drunk. On the other hand, we already impose various automobile safety devices that would not be necessary if drivers always drove safely and lawfully. Moreover, making the Interlock System mandatory would reduce the number of drunk-driving victims. Unfortunately, the history of auto manufacturers' opposition to seat belts and air bags makes it unlikely that the Interlock System, even if proved effective, would ever be required as a mandatory feature on all vehicles. Thus, its role in the foreseeable future will be as a sentencing option for convicted drunk drivers.

Regulating Access to Alcohol: Time, Manner, and Place

The best strategy for blocking the opportunity to drive while drunk would be a device, like the one described above, that makes it impossible for someone with a BAC above a preset level to operate a vehicle. A second-best solution would be to reconfigure the environment to make it more difficult for people to get drunk. Some analysts (Aaron and

Musto 1981) believe this could be done by regulating liquor stores, bars, and taverns.

Alone among Western societies, the United States tried to prohibit beverage alcohol manufacturer sales entirely. (Gusfield 1963; Kobler 1973; Clark 1976). The Eighteenth Amendment and the Volstead Act outlawed the manufacture and sale—but not possession, consumption, or home production—of most types of alcoholic beverages. The massive societal evasion that occurred under Prohibition has become part of American folklore—speakeasies, bootlegged alcohol, corruption, mob dominance, and business as usual. Today, it is widely believed that Prohibition was a failure and that people continued their drinking habits despite the law. Thus, the legacy of the "the noble experiment" is a deep-seated pessimism about possibilities of regulating alcohol (Room and Mosher 1979–80; Moore and Gerstein 1981).[3]

Revisionists have demonstrated that popular belief in Prohibition's failure is exaggerated (Aaron and Musto 1981). Beverage alcohol consumption decreased significantly during Prohibition, probably 30–40 percent. Perhaps more important, alcohol-related problems, such as cirrhosis and "alcoholic psychosis," declined.[4] This means that an overall decrease in beverage alcohol consumption was reflected in reduced consumption by heavy drinkers as well as social drinkers.[5]

Given that prohibition is not a political possibility, the options available for possibly reducing consumption are raising taxes, limiting the number of people who are eligible to purchase alcohol, limiting the number of liquor stores, and regulating bars' and taverns' promotional tactics, hours of operation, and serving practices.

Regulation under Alcoholic Beverage Control (ABC) Laws

After the repeal of Prohibition, the Twenty-first Amendment left regulation of alcohol to the states, which in some cases delegated responsibility to county governments. In most states regulation was put in the hands of ABC agencies. While the original theoreticians of this system of control apparently envisioned ABC agencies exerting influence to limit alcohol problems (Aaron and Musto 1981), for the most part the agencies have not functioned this way. The ABC agencies primarily define their function as raising tax revenue and promoting an orderly market in the sale and distribution of alcoholic beverages.

One could ask more of the ABC agencies (see National Institute of Alcohol Abuse and Alcoholism 1978; Bonnie 1985). They could, for example, be asked to license fewer liquor stores and bars, perhaps taking accessibility via public transportation into account. Several researchers have found a relationship between the per-capita number of on-premises liquor outlets and various alcohol-related problems, including cirrhosis (Harford et al. 1979; McGuiness 1979; Colon 1981). It is conceivable that reducing the number of taverns would decrease drunk driving, although an opposite effect is also possible; drivers might seek out taverns at ever farther distances, thereby increasing the number of miles they drive while drunk (Waller 1976). In any event, the political impediments to reducing the number of taverns seem substantial, probably insurmountable.[6]

The ABC agencies could try to impose practices consistent with responsible and moderate drinking. For example, they could require bars to do one or more of the following: purchase Breathalyzer machines;[7] pass out cocktail napkins with warnings about drunk driving;[8] provide employees with training in identifying and controlling abusive drinking; close at earlier hours; cease offering "two-for-one" nights, happy hours, and similar promotional schemes;[9] and serve food as well as alcohol. In addition, they could more strictly monitor conformity to the minimum age laws.

Promotions such as happy hours and two-for-one nights are the functional opposite of a tax on alcoholic beverages; they constitute a large discount which encourages customers to drink a lot and quickly. Even worse is the custom of serving doubles just before closing time. It might make sense to ban alcohol sales entirely an hour before closing.

Realism about the success of such proposals requires a few caveats. First, most alcohol that is sold in the United States is not sold in restaurants, bars, and taverns; it is sold in package stores to persons who will do their consuming at home. The ABC laws have very little effect on this type of drinking. Furthermore, while bars and taverns typically pay lip service to responsible drinking, they often act otherwise. They have a strong economic incentive to sell as much alcohol as possible. It is naive to believe that they can make up for decreases in alcohol consumption by selling more food and soft drinks. The culture and economics of bars and taverns make significant change in serving and drinking patterns unlikely (see Gusfield, Rasmussen, and Kotarba 1984). Moreover, in many states the ABC agencies are captives to the industry they are mandated to regulate.

Minimum Drinking Age

Another strategy to prevent intoxication—and therefore intoxicated driving—is to prohibit (1) young people from purchasing alcoholic beverages and (2) commercial venders and social hosts from serving alcoholic beverages to young people. The temperance movement focused on older drinkers, not on youth (Mosher 1980; Wagenaar 1983). Minimum-drinking-age laws did not appear until after repeal of Prohibition. Subsequently, a crazy quilt of laws appeared. Some states set eighteen as the minimum drinking age, while others chose nineteen or twenty-one. Many states have different minimum purchase ages for different types of alcoholic beverages. Some states criminalize only the sale or service of alcoholic beverages to minors, while other states criminalize the act of purchasing.

Between 1970 and 1976 (probably in response to passage of the Twenty-sixth Amendment, extending the right to vote in federal elections to persons eighteen years old and older), twenty-nine states reduced the minimum drinking age. Studies showed an increase in alcohol-related fatalities for the eighteen-to-twenty-year-old group (Wagenaar 1983). Some states, prodded by the citizens anti–drunk driving groups, reversed direction and moved their minimum drinking age upward to nineteen, twenty, or twenty-one.

The move to prohibit anyone under age twenty-one from purchasing alcoholic beverages for either on- and off-premises consumption is a Prohibition-type anti–drunk driving strategy. In theory, prohibiting a particular age group from purchasing alcohol will result in that age group's reduced consumption and incidence of intoxication. Advocates also predict a spillover effect, so that teenagers one and two years below the minimum age also will drink less (Smith et al. 1984).

As the states began elevating the minimum legal purchase age to twenty-one, the number of fatalities involving younger-aged drivers decreased. The anti–drunk driving establishment was quick to claim success. Nevertheless, research evaluations were confounded by a general decline in fatality rates for all drivers.[10]

The citizens' groups argued that differing minimum-age laws led to a great deal of drunk driving along state borders as young drivers sought out bars in the lower-minimum-age jurisdictions. Thus, they urged Congress to pass a national uniform minimum drinking age of twenty-one. Ultimately, in 1984, Congress, under the aegis of its spending power, chose to attempt to increase the minimum purchase age by providing that any state that by September 1986 did not have a minimum drinking age at least as high as twenty-one would lose 5 percent of its highway safety funds.[11] By the end of 1986 all but eight states had responded to this financial incentive.

This is yet another example of the federalization of the drunk driving problem—and one that provoked a sharp negative reaction from many states and from the National Conference of State Legislatures. In a suit challenging the constitutionality of the law, South Dakota argued that the minimum-drinking-age law violated both constitutional limitations on Congress's spending power and the Twenty-first Amendment. The district court rejected these arguments, and the Court of Appeals affirmed the decision. The case ultimately was resolved in the U.S. Supreme Court.

In *South Dakota v. Dole*, 107 S.Ct. 2793 (1987) the Court, in an opinion by Chief Justice William Rehnquist, held that Congress's action was lawful unless prohibited by the Twenty-first Amendment. He then found that the Twenty-first Amendment only prevents Congress from *directly regulating* beverage alcohol. According to the Chief Justice, financial inducements to further the federal interest in traffic safety do not constitute regulation, unless they are far more coercive than the minimum-drinking-age condition for receipt of federal highway safety funds:[12] "When we consider, for a moment, that all South Dakota would lose if she adheres to her chosen course as to a suitable minimum drinking age is 5% of the funds otherwise obtainable under specified highway safety grant programs, the argument as to coercion is shown to be more rhetoric than fact. . . . Here Congress has offered a relatively mild encouragement to the States to enact higher minimum drinking ages than they would otherwise choose. But the enactment of such laws remains the prerogative of the State not merely in theory but in fact."

Meanwhile, the debate among researchers continues. The majority of studies have found that raising the drinking age has resulted in a 4–8 percent reduction in fatalities (Cook and Tauchen 1984; Saffer and Grossman 1987). However, Mike Males (1986) has demonstrated that the most influential empirical study of the issue (Williams et al. 1983) is not replicable when data from a slightly longer time frame are utilized. Because Males's study is so important, it is worth reviewing his findings in some detail.

Males points out that during the past decade large decreases in under-twenty-one-year-old-driver fatal accidents occurred in nearly all states, regardless of whether the states had raised their minimum legal drinking age.

Single state studies have claimed that raised drinking ages have produced young-driver fatal crash reductions of 31 percent in Michigan, 11 percent in Maine, 47 percent in New Jersey, 12 percent in Florida, and 27 percent in Illinois. But studies done under identical circumstances could claim with equal justification that *not* raising the drinking age reduced young-driver fatal crashes by 30 percent in Louisiana, 31 percent in Vermont, 28 percent in Pennsylvania, 54 percent in Oregon, and 18 percent in Indiana. Studies that do not examine MLPA [minimum legal purchase age] change effects on a multi state basis over time should be viewed as having extremely limited value. (Males 1986, Pp. 187–188)

The Williams et al. study examined the change in age-specific fatality rates in (a) nine states that raised their MLPAs during the 1976–80 period against (b) comparison states that did not do so. Males adopted the same strategy but extended the time series to 1983. If the MLPA had a positive effect on teenage drunk driving, then, when compared with the non-MLPA states, the MLPA states should show a greater percentage reduction in nighttime vehicle fatalities vis-à-vis daytime fatalities. These results did not materialize.

Five of the nine MLPA-increase states show the larger decline using data through 1980; five of the nine comparison state show the larger decrease through 1983. The average decrease in the two categories of states is virtually identical. For every one of the matched pairs of states the net decrease in nighttime fatal crashes among drivers of the affected age group reported in 1980 for MLPA-increase states is less—and usually much less—than the net decrease shown in the HS study. The discrepancy excedes 25 percent in the Massachusetts-Connecticut, Minnesota-Wisconsin, and Tennessee-Kentucky matches. (Males 1986, P. 191)

The conclusion of this study is that the MLPA increases have no effect on young drivers and that any decrease in nighttime fatal crashes in the MLPA-increase states was due to a general trend that affected drivers in the just-older control groups as well as those in the affected age group.

Males's study is also supported by a variety of other data and by common sense. For example, despite the fact that youth under eighteen are prohibited from drinking in all states, surveys show that a substantial majority of high school students drink; indeed, almost 10 percent might be termed alcohol abusers. Apparently prohibition does not interfere with a massive amount of drinking among members of this age group. There is every reason to believe that the lack of adherence to prohibition is much greater among those eighteen to twenty-one years old. Moreover, a great many stories in the popular press report that college students are adapting their drinking practices rather easily to the new MLPAs. Furthermore, the absolute prohibition of illicit drugs has hardly prevented their widespread use among young people.

Even if a national minimum purchase age of twenty-one may work, I have serious doubts about the desirability of this policy. Only a small portion of young people in the eighteen-to-twenty-one-year-old age group are alcohol abusers; females in this age group are not nearly as significant drunk driving risks as are males older than twenty-one. Why should those young people—and especially young women—who drink responsibly be penalized because of the minority of irresponsible young people?

The individuals affected by the increased minimum purchase age are generally adult in their life-styles, if not always in their social habits. The majority live on their own. Some are college and university students, others are well established in the work force or the armed forces. A significant number are married and/or parents. These young adults are likely to think of themselves as grown-up and entitled to the rights and privileges of full citizenship, including the right to purchase and consume alcoholic beverages. In no other Western society are citizens as old as twenty-one denied equal access to alcoholic beverages.

Those who advocate a minimum drinking age of twenty-one argue that it is appropriate to deny eighteen-to-twenty year olds the right to purchase and possess beverage alcohol in public because this age group presents an elevated risk of alcohol-related traffic accidents. However, this is not true (Wagenaar 1983). The higher accident rate of young drivers appears to be a function of their lack of driving skill rather than of their propensity to drive while drunk (Zylman 1973). We noted in Chapter 5 that roadside surveys have shown that young drivers have low rates of drunk driving, much lower, for example, than those of the next older age group, those aged twenty-one to twenty-four. Beginning drivers are by definition inexperienced. Logically it might make more sense to raise the *driving* age to twenty-one.

Drinking and driving are two activities that must start sometime; it seems unwise to start both activities at the same time (see Zimring 1982). It is probably harder to delay drinking than to delay driving. Long before the age of majority, drinking can begin surreptitiously at home and with friends. Indeed, some families may wish their children to become accustomed to drinking alcohol at home in modest amounts. By contrast, driving is not an activity likely to begin surreptitiously.

A further criticism of making the drinking age twenty-one is one that could be directed at all prohibitionist strategies: they discourage habits of moderation essential to responsible use. There is evidence to show that ethnic and cultural groups that expose their young people to alcohol earlier—for example, in rituals or in settings with food and celebration—have fewer alcohol problems than those groups that prohibit consumption until a mature age. The explanation seems commonsensical. Societies that place stringent prohibitions on alcohol send out the message that alcohol is a dangerous drug, typically leading to intoxication and abuse. Such a message may well result in a self-fulfilling prophesy; that is, young people who repeatedly hear and internalize such messages and expectations will act out the expected behavior.

There is also the additional and significant problem of enforceability. Just as under both Prohibition and the current prohibitions on heroin, cocaine, marijuana, and other drugs, there will be much evasion of the minimum-drinking-age law. It will certainly not be difficult for young people aged eighteen to twenty-one to obtain alcoholic beverages; they can rely on older friends, on false identification, and on careless, indifferent, or complicitous sales personnel and bartenders. Those most highly motivated to drink will be least deterred by the law. To the extent that those aged eighteen to twenty find it more difficult (time consuming) to obtain alcohol, they may substitute other drugs, such as marijuana and cocaine. Furthermore, there is something disquieting about starting so many young people off as criminals. We may be constructing a circle of prohibitions around young people that makes law violation practically inevitable.

Increasing the Price of Alcohol through Taxation

Yet another strategy for preventing intoxication—and therefore intoxicated driving—is to make this condition more expensive to achieve. If alcohol problems, including drunk driving, are positively correlated with total alcohol consumption, then one strategy for reducing drunk driving would be to increase the cost of alcohol so that less of it will be purchased and consumed. Ironically, over the past twenty years, the United States has followed the opposite policy. Between 1960 and 1980 the real cost to the consumer of a bottle of liquor declined by 48 percent; of beer, by 27 percent; and of wine, by 19 percent (Cook 1981; Cook and Tauchen 1982). Until 1985, federal tax rates on alcoholic beverages were last changed in 1951, when they were set at $.29 per gallon of beer, between $.17 and $3.40 per gallon of wine (depending on alcoholic content and type), and at $10.50 per proof gallon of distilled liquor. In 1985 the federal excise tax on distilled spirits was increased by 19 percent, but the overall tax on alcoholic beverages is now (in real terms) at its lowest level since the repeal of Prohibition (Hacker and Jacobson 1986).

There is an impressive corpus of research to suggest that the demand for alcohol is relatively elastic at all levels of consumption (Ornstein 1980; Cook and Tauchen 1982).[13] Cook and Tauchen (1982) have shown that there is a negative correlation between the rate of state taxation of alcohol and cirrhosis mortality, the latter of which is an excellent surrogate variable for alcohol consumption by heavy drinkers. More precisely, Cook and Tauchen found (vis-à-vis states that did *not* raise their liquor taxes) that increases in state liquor taxes were consistently associated with reductions in the cirrhosis mortality rate—and in per-capita alcohol consumption. In addition, Cook (1981) found a negative correlation between the rate of alcohol taxation and fatal vehicle accidents. More recently, Saffer and Grossman (1987) have used econometric techniques to show that if beer taxes had been maintained at the 1951 level, 15 percent fewer lives would have been lost in fatal crashes.

What are the policy implications of these research findings? Would it be good policy to fight drunk driving by increasing taxes on alcoholic beverages? The United States has a long history of taxing beverage alcohol, a history that dates to the beginning of the republic. Indeed, up till the passage of Prohibition, liquor taxes were a major revenue source for the federal government. The states also have a long history of alcohol taxation. According to Hyman et al. (1980), of all consumer expenditures for alcoholic beverages, just over one-third go to government as tax receipts. Distilled spirits are taxed much more heavily than beer or wine, although spirits are no more likely to produce alcohol problems than are wine and beer (Moore and Gerstein 1981). Increasing alcohol taxes so that they are equivalent in real dollars to what they were thirty years ago would be a reasonable policy choice, as would increasing beer and wine taxes to the same rate as that for distilled spirits.

Nevertheless, significant tax increases on beverage alcohol would raise difficult questions (O'Hagan 1983). Most people who would be penalized by higher alcoholic beverage prices would be non–alcohol abusers. Light and moderate drinkers who never drive while drunk would pay more for their innocent enjoyment of alcoholic beverages—or have to consume less—in order to bring about a reduction in the consumption of heavy drinkers. Moreover, this type of tax would disproportionately burden low-income drinkers who would be forced to consume less, to switch to cheaper brands, or to give up other goods and services.

Furthermore, if beverage alcohol taxes were increased, the incentives for home brew and bootlegged alcohol would increase. Even in today's market, a certain percentage of beverage alcohol is bootlegged—that is, diverted from the regulated market and sold without payment of taxes. If taxes significantly increased, the bootlegged portion of the market would also increase, and some number of consumers would begin (or increase) their own production. This might foster organized crime and threaten public health. While such objections are not trivial, given our long history of excise taxes on alcohol, striving to at least maintain the level of such taxes in real dollars seems sensible and justifiable.

Conclusion

The ideal solution for reducing drunk driving is an Interlock System which makes vehicles inoperable by drunk drivers. While the development of such a system may be at hand, caution is advised. Technological "fixes" directed at crime have appeared throughout the twentieth century, and none have proved effective. Moreover, even if the Interlock System is effective and tamper proof, will it be politically possible to implement it universally?

If we cannot stop people who are drunk from operating their cars, then we need to prevent people from getting drunk. Using taxation to make intoxication more costly appears to be a sensible approach to this end. It is difficult to see any strong arguments against raising liquor taxes (at least up to their mid-1950s level) and to bringing the taxes on beer and wine up to the level of taxes on distilled spirits. This method of discouraging alcohol consumption would be essentially the same as government policy on cigarettes and perhaps might have similarly salutary results. Prohibiting irresponsible tavern practices and promotions should also be an uncontroversial and sensible policy initiative.

The one opportunity-blocking strategy that the United States has willingly embraced is the minimum purchase age of twenty-one. In effect, this strategy reenacts Prohibition for a single age cohort that will, after all, someday become eligible to purchase and drink alcoholic beverages. The willingness to treat young adults as children when it comes to adult vices reflects a schizophrenia in American society. On the one hand forbidden fruits are treated with more and more glamour, while on the other hand there is a rigid public morality that exhorts young citizens to practice abstinence of all sorts. This latter approach is completely oblivious to the changing nature of young adulthood in American society.

14

Rehabilitating the Offender

Rehabilitation, the effort by a change agent to change a target's attitudes and behavior, is a major theme in the sociology of social control and in the social control of drunk drivers.[1] Strategies to rehabilitate drunk drivers can be divided conceptually into those that stress underlying problems of personality and emotion (therapy) and those that stress "the facts" (education). The first approach is associated with treatment programs to cure pathological drinking, while the second is associated with educational programs to cure poor judgment. Many anti–drunk driving programs have elements of both approaches.

It should not come as a surprise to learn that a majority of people arrested for drunk driving can plausibly be labeled alcoholics, alcohol abusers, or problem drinkers. Light drinkers are not likely to exceed prohibited BAC levels, at least not very often. Unfortunately, this is not good news for strategists and policy makers. Alcoholics and problem drinkers are a notoriously intractible treatment group, frequently denying their alcohol problems despite overwhelming contrary objective evidence and the exhortations of family, friends, and treatment personnel.

·This is not the place for a lengthy review of the state of alcohol treatment programs. While research and treatment experimentation continue, there have been no breakthroughs in the search for a cure for alcoholism (Saxe et al. 1983). As a 1976 editorial in the *Annals of Internal Medicine* stated, "the treatment of alcoholism has not improved in any important way in 25 years . . . only a minority of patients who enter treatment are helped to long-term recovery" (see Polich, Armor, and Braiker 1980; Saxe et al. 1983; Vaillant 1983).

If the rehabilitation of drunk drivers is dependent on cures for pathological drinking, prospects for progress in the social control of drunk driving seem dim. Because treatments for alcohol abuse have proved only marginally effective at best, it is not surprising that both anti–drunk driving advocates and policymakers wishing to do something immediate about drunk driving have focused on the offender's drinking and driving rather than on his drinking alone. This chapter focuses on the efforts to "treat" drunk driving in "drinking/driver schools," which aim to convince the offender to be a safer driver by separating his drinking from his driving. However, before turning to an examination of the schools, it is worth focusing on one type of alcohol-abuse treatment because it demonstrates how DWI enforcement can be used as a lever to coerce offenders into treatment programs.

Antabuse

The most controversial form of alcohol treatment is antabuse (disulfiram), a form of drug therapy. Antabuse does not cure alcohol craving or dependence but causes unpleasant physiological effects, such as respiratory difficulty, nausea, vomiting, and sweating, when alcohol is ingested while the drug is active. After taking antabuse the patient's desire to drink is dulled by the thought of getting sick. Unfortunately, many patients are not able to succeed in this therapy. It requires a commitment not to drink any alcohol, which is beyond the capacity of many alcohol abusers. As Dr. George Vaillant (1983) points out, unlike Alcoholics Anonymous, antabuse takes alcohol away from the patient and offers nothing in return. Because this leaves an enormous void in the alcoholic's life, the temptation to quit therapy is very great.

There is some suggestion in the ASAP evaluations that antabuse treatment produces slightly lower recidivism rates than do other therapies; even if this is true, this treatment is hardly a panacea. Antabuse can properly only be prescribed for severe alcoholism. It is not generally applicable to DWI offenders.

Some anti–drunk driving programs (see Marco and Marco 1980) have offered certain DWI defendants the choice of going to jail or submitting to a year of antabuse treatment. The defendant has been required to obtain an antabuse prescription from a doctor and to bring it to a monitoring location where, under the monitor's observation, he takes a daily dose for one year.

Using a drunk driving arrest to coerce alcoholics into an antabuse program raises moral and legal problems (Marco and Marco 1980). The idea of coerced medical and psychiatric treatment has been sharply and effectively criticized as inconsistent with due regard for an individual's autonomy and personhood (Von Hirsch 1976). The advocates of such treatment—especially in the case of those treatments, such as antabuse, that entail medical risks—must shoulder a heavy burden of proof. The fact that antabuse treatment does not produce results significantly better than those of other therapies suggests that offenders should not be coerced into this treatment.

This does not mean that antabuse should not have a place in the constellation of drunk driver rehabilitation strategies. It would be entirely appropriate for a judge to (*a*) require as a condition of probation that a DWI defendant enroll in a recognized alcoholism treatment program and (*b*) tell the defendant that antabuse is an option for some alcoholics. However, the defendant should not be forced, by threat of incarceration, to undergo this drug therapy.

Using an antabuse program as an option for diversion from the criminal justice system illustrates a major theme in DWI enforcement. There is constant pressure from the treatment community to divert drunk drivers from the criminal courts into treatment programs. The alcohol treatment community views drunk driving as a manifestation of an alcohol problem and a drunk driving arrest as an opportunity to pull alcohol abusers into treatment. In 1980, 29 percent of all admissions to NIAAA-funded treatment programs were DWI related (Saxe et al. 1983). As Weisner and Room (1984) note, "perhaps no other agency is as well situated to provide a steady flow of clients as the criminal courts. The coercion of the court assures that the referred case arrives and can often be used to induce the client to pay for treatment . . . by mid-1982 drunk drivers began to be one of the dominant treatment groups throughout California." Many jurisdictions require an alcoholism assessment for every drunk-driving defendant. These routine assessments usually seek to label drunk drivers as either social or problem drinkers,[2] although this dichotomy, like any such labeling, does not exactly capture reality.[3]

In any event, the medicalization of the drunk driving problem is unlikely to provide effective social control. Indeed, if it means diverting drunk drivers completely from the criminal justice system, it is likely to undermine social control efforts. In addition, in certain cases it has the potential to coerce into intrusive therapies individuals who would not freely choose to submit to them.

The Drinking/Driver Schools

For reasons of expense, administration, and perceived urgency, the majority of DWI defendants in treatment have been channeled through drinking/driver schools, most of which are based on the Phoenix prototype, established in Phoenix, Arizona, in 1964 (Steward and Malfetti 1970) in response to several tragic alcohol-related crashes (another reminder that the anti–drunk driving movement did not emerge full grown during the 1980s). Originally, of an offender pool of about 250 defendants, between 30 and 100 people were sent to the Phoenix course each month. Failure to comply was punishable by a ninety-day license suspension.

The Phoenix schools are an ingenious effort to provide mass drunk driver rehabilitation in a short time frame. A 1983 survey by the National Association of State Alcoholism and Drug Abuse Directors identified 1,514 programs in forty-five reporting jurisdictions; thirty-nine of these jurisdictions "guestimated" that they served 532,000 persons annually. Several million Americans have probably passed through the drinking/driver schools since their emergence during the 1970s. If this is so, they should be regarded as a major institution of social control, analogous to the county jail or state mental hospital.

New York State's Drinking/Driver Program

To understand what the drinking/driver schools entail, it is useful to describe one such program, New York State's drinking/driver program. From 1975 to 1983 the program processed more than 185,000 people; it currently handles about thirty thousand people per year. All DWI offenders, whether problem drinkers or social drinkers, are eligible, except for about 10 percent who are ineligible because of (1) court order, (2) two or more previous DWI or DWAI offenses accompanied by personal injury, or (3) participation in the program during the past five years. Participants are eligible for a conditional license, refund of one-half the fine, and early restoration of the regular driver's license. The program charges $75 or $85, depending on the county.

New York's drinking/driver program comprises five two-hour sessions and two three-hour sessions. There are two instructors, an alcoholism counselor and a highway safety specialist. The program's goal statement claims that its intention is not rehabilitative but educative and diagnostic. This modesty probably reflects a shrewd political judgment that it is unwise to make a claim that, if unconfirmed, might provide an argument for terminating the program. Other Phoenix-type programs, with essentially the same curriculum, claim to be in the business of producing graduates who do not drive while under the influence.

The classes provide a good deal of factual information about such matters as the deterioration of driving skills at different BAC levels, the inability to counteract the effects of alcohol with coffee or cold showers, and the penalties for repeat drunk driving in New York State.

Students are required to fill out (1) twelve-hour diaries covering the period before their DWI arrest, (2) weekly drinking chronicles, and (3) Life Activities Inventories dealing with various issues of personal and social adjustment. They must also fill out the MAST, which is used, in conjunction with the other information and personal interviews, to screen out problem drinkers.

Session 1 is an introduction to the program. The MAST test is administered. The instructor urges the students to discuss the circumstances of their DWI arrests. Typically, the students express both a great deal of hostility toward the police and resentment at being treated like common criminals. Session 2 deals with traffic safety. A film, *The Final Factor,* points out that many factors contribute to traffic crashes and that the best way to avoid an accident is to take control over those factors that are controllable. Alcohol as a traffic problem is not discussed until the end of the session.

The third session addresses alcohol as a traffic safety problem. The film *Drink Drive Rationalize* deals with the dangers of drinking/driving and with such wrongheaded myths as that one is able to drive better while intoxicated or is able to counteract the effects of intoxication by chugging coffee. The fourth session deals with the physiology of alcohol and with alcohol as a drug. The film *Chalk Talk* deals with the physiology of alcohol. The instructors administer the Alcohol Opinion Survey, which contains a list of true/false statements about the properties and effects of alcohol, and engage the students in a spirited discussion of the survey questions.

The final segment of *Chalk Talk,* shown in session five, deals with alcoholism as a disease and with the difference between social drinkers, problem drinkers, and alcoholics. The instructors identify drinking patterns symptomatic of alcoholism and ask the class to discuss people they know who have drinking problems.

The sixth session stresses that alcoholism is a *disease,* not a moral failing. The aim is to make it easier for problem drinkers to admit the existence of a problem. The message is that alcoholism is nothing to feel guilty about and that it can be treated. Alcoholics Anonymous is described and strongly recommended. At the end of the session the film *Driving under the Influence* is shown in order to remind the class that they are not participating in the drinking/driver program because they consumed alcohol but because they mixed drinking and driving. The last class provides a summary of the course. The students are left to ponder the messages presented in the film *The Decision Is Yours.*

Sixty-eight percent of offenders enrolled in it complete the seven-week New York drinking/driver program. The remaining 32 percent are referred for clinical observation; of these, approximately three-quarters are retained for treatment. Offenders involved in this subsequent treatment phase are graduated from the program on recommendation of treatment personnel. But the program's leverage on the students really lasts only until the expiration of the six-month license suspension period. Once the license is returned, the original motivation for participating in the program disappears.

Evaluation of Treatment Programs

Perhaps the main contribution of the 1970s federal ASAP was the implementation of a major drunk driver rehabilitation effort (Ellingstad 1976). Local programs were permitted to develop autonomously, without NHTSA's central direction. Many local ASAPs utilized a drunk driving arrest to divert drunk drivers into treatment. Defendants were screened by treatment personnel and, depending on diagnosis and eligibility, assigned to a DWI school, an outpatient alcohol-abuse program, or an inpatient facility. Successful completion of the diversion program sometimes meant eligibility for charge reduction, full or partial remittance of the fine, or a conditional license.

If they were assigned to treatment, most (62 percent) drunk drivers, whether problem drinkers or social drinkers, were channeled into drinking/driver schools. Group therapy and Alcoholics Anonymous were the next most frequent treatment placements, receiving 7 and 6 percent of referrals, respectively. Other treatments accounted for 15 percent of referrals.

The ASAPs produced an impressive corpus of evaluation research on the effectiveness of both drinking/driver schools and other treatment programs (Ellingstad and Springer 1976). The leading evaluators, James Nichols, Elaine Weinstein, Vernon Ellingstad, and David L. Struckman-Johnson (1978), reviewed all of the state-level ASAP rehabilitation program evaluations. They also analyzed aggregate combined data from the local ASAPs and launched their own experimental study of eleven ASAPs. Despite many claims of success by local ASAP projects, the researchers' conclusions were quite discouraging:

1. Over the years from 1971 to 1976 more than 200,000 arrested drinking drivers were referred to ASAP education rehabilitation programs in 35 localities. Approximately one-third were diagnosed as social drinkers and one half as problem drinkers (the rest could not be classified).

2. Over a period of three years, a review of 35 project-level studies of overall rehabilitation efforts (without careful controls) showed 51% reporting

positive results (Ellingstad and Springer 1976). When these studies were categorized relative to the quality of the study, however, it was found that the majority of studies (25) fell into the "inadequately controlled" category. The proportion of inadequate studies that reported positive results was greater than the proportion of adequate studies.

3. Almost 90% of the social drinkers in ASAP referral programs were assigned to educational programs. Type of school made little difference for social drinkers.

4. Inter-project analyses of aggregate rearrest data suggest that problem drinkers exposed to rehabilitation programs have the same rearrest rates as problem drinkers not exposed to rehabilitation.

The short-term rehabilitation experiment involving eleven ASAP sites also produced discouraging conclusions. DWI offenders classified as moderate drinkers were randomly assigned to treatment and control groups. A number of serious traffic arrest categories were combined to measure recidivism. The results of survival analysis (percent of each group remaining arrest free at each point in time after treatment) showed no difference in the rearrest rates of the two groups.

Almost all of the carefully executed evaluation studies of DWI treatment programs have reached the same conclusion as the ASAP evaluators (see, e.g., Ross and Blumenthal 1974; Michelson 1979). The NHTSA-sponsored Comprehensive Driving under the Influence Project in Sacramento, California, was the best-planned, -executed, and -evaluated of the treatment experiments. More than three thousand DUI offenders were randomly assigned to (1) a four-session education program, (2) a take-home study course, or (3) a no-treatment control group. When rearrest for DWI or reckless driving was used as the dependant variable, there were no significant differences between any of the groups.

A more recent evaluation study by Robert Holden (1983) reached the same conclusion. He evaluated NHTSA-sponsored educational and therapy programs in Memphis, Tennessee, from September 1976 to the end of 1980. DWI offenders with no previous record of alcohol-related driving were eligible for the program. About 85 percent of the participants were referred via diversion and the rest via probation. Clients were randomly assigned to one of the following four conditions: (1) control, (2) drinking/driver schools, (3) drinking/driver school and one and one-half hours of group therapy (for problem drinkers), or (4) probation supervision, drinking/driver school, and (for problem drinkers) group therapy. Each subject was followed for a minimum of two years after court referral.

Holden found that for social drinkers the control group had the lowest rearrest rate! Among problem drinkers, offenders assigned to probationary supervision plus education/therapy had the lowest (17.6 percent) rearrest rate, but the controls were second lowest. For social drinkers the effects of each factor on DWI were nonsignificant, as were the interactive effects of the two factors. In other words, the rearrest rates of all four social drinker treatment groups can be considered equal. Thus, neither probation nor education had a demonstrable rehabilitative effect.

Why the Drinking/Driver Schools Fail to Reduce Recidivism

The drinking/driver schools provide a great deal of knowledge about drunk driving, in a format that is well designed and, at points, very dramatic. It seems hard to believe that a person, other than a chronic alcohol abuser, could be exposed to such materials without being impressed with the dangers and irresponsibility of drunk driving. Therefore, it seems incredible—indeed, almost perverse—that the drinking/driver schools do not have a positive effect on future recidivism and alcohol-related crashes. What explains the lack of demonstrable success?

It is important to emphasize that for all DWI offenders the rate of rearrest is small, approximately 6–8 percent within one year. Perhaps this small recidivist minority represents an intractible alcohol-abusing, antisocial group for whom the drinking/driver schools' treatment is too weak. For the rest of offenders the experience of arrest, jail pending release, lawyers' fees, higher insurance rates, and social stigma may produce a strong short-term suppressant to drunk driving, one that cannot be enhanced by a treatment program.

Perhaps the essentially educational Phoenix-type curriculum is incapable of producing attitudinal and behavioral change. The theory behind such treatment must be that if offenders are informed of the dangerousness of their behavior, they can be persuaded to separate the components of—or at least moderate—their drinking/driving. This type of strategy makes sense for social drinkers but not for problem drinkers, whose abuse of alcohol is complex. Social drinkers, however, have undoubtedly been told (and probably would readily agree) that drunk driving is dangerous and irresponsible. Since they do not regularly drive while drunk, the experience of being arrested by itself might be significant enough to bolster their resolve not to repeat their crime. This does not mean, of course, that they will never violate the law again. Resolve might not be enough. At some future point they might find themselves in the throes of depression, reverie, or peer group pressure and thus might drive while drunk.

The Future of Rehabilitation

As in many other areas of crime and justice (see Sechrest, White, and Brown 1979), rehabilitation of drunk drivers is now on the defensive.[4] The 1983 Presidential Commission on Drunk Driving objected to diversion programs on the ground that they delay both the disposition of the criminal case and imposition of license restrictions and that their effectiveness cannot be demonstrated. This is fair criticism.

Nevertheless, the DWI treatment programs have not gone out of business. Instead of being utilized as diversion programs, they are being deployed as a condition of probation or as a condition for obtaining an occupational license. They have also achieved a good measure of fiscal independence by charging defendants a fee. They may have reached a point of institutional development such that, like public schools, prisons, and jails, their survival is assured regardless of evaluation researchers' negative findings. Brown, Zelhart, and Schurr (1975) astutely note that

there appears to be an impaired driver reeducation movement underway and we doubt that it will be halted by negative findings which employ the PROVE IT MODEL [of evaluation research]. Moreover, the evaluator employing such a strategy finds himself in an uncomfortable position. If the program is an established and continuing one and has the commitment of the treatment staff, the goverment and the public, the question is not one of "go versus terminate" as the persons involved in the program base their commitment upon their experiences. . . . Under these conditions a more appropriate question for the evaluation to focus upon is: how can we improve the program so that its major objectives and subobjectives are more effectively realized?

The use of drinking/driver schools and other treatment programs as conditions of probation creates serious pressures for probation departments and courts. Nationally, probation caseloads are already at an all-time high. As the backlog of drunk drivers on probation increases, it will become harder for already hard-pressed probation departments to provide effective supervision—or, perhaps, *any* supervision. In many jurisdictions they may be unable effectively to supervise the offender's participation in rehabilitation programs, especially in the case of those programs that extend over many months. Furthermore, while unsatisfactory program participation theoretically should lead to termination of probation and imposition of a nonprobationary criminal sanction, the reality (at least in major metropolitan areas) is that neither busy prosecutors nor courts will be much interested in prosecuting offenders who have violated probation by failing to participate satisfactorily in a treatment program.

Conclusion

Rehabilitation programs have long figured prominently in the effort to reduce and control drunk driving. This is a natural consequence of the medicalization of alcoholism and alcohol abuse. The United States has a huge alcohol treatment establishment; there is no likelihood that it will be dismantled or discarded in favor of some other approach to alcohol problems. Thus, it is inevitable that drunk driving will relate, in one way or another, to the treatment networks dealing with alcohol abuse. The major strategies for dealing with alcohol abuse—individual and group psychotherapy, counseling, disulfiram—are also being used for individuals who have been referred after a DWI arrest. One may hope that over the long term these alcohol-abuse treatment programs can assist more and more patients in overcoming their alcohol-related problems. But we should not be deluded about the possibility of a quick fix.

It is not surprising that the drinking/driver schools have emerged as the most common treatment response to DWI. These well-defined programs can be delivered at modest cost over a relatively short time period. Unfortunately, evaluation researchers have consistently shown that the schools do not reduce recidivism. The schools should therefore be terminated, or major experiments should be undertaken with new designs and curriculum. Only through an array of demonstration projects will it be possible to find a format that might work, at least with regard to certain subgroups of DWI offenders.

15

Conclusion

Several major themes reverberate throughout this review of the criminology, criminal jurisprudence, and social control of drunk driving in the United States. The first is the curious paradox of doing more and knowing less. The second is the ambivalent attitude of law and public opinion toward drunk driving. The third is the willingness to mount a multifaceted social control agenda that goes far beyond simple deterrence strategies. The fourth is the institutionalization of a self-sustaining anti–drunk driving movement. The fifth is the recognition that there are limits to what can be accomplished through directed social change.

Doing More and Knowing Less

Social scientists and those who engage in public policy analysis, including myself, have an unquenchable thirst for information and studies. American pragmatism embodies the belief that if only a social problem can be properly understood it can be eradicated. We seem to believe that at some future point enough studies will reveal the mosaic, so that all the disparate bits and pieces of information will coalesce into a single picture. But experience tells us that reality is not like that. Research and information on drunk driving is generated by diverse individuals, centers, organizations, and government agencies. Their work is not of a whole cloth. They make different assumptions and have different biases, vested interests, and competencies. Over time enough studies accumulate to substantiate all hypotheses. Good work is drowned out by the mediocre, and objective analyses by advocacy research. The way research studies are funded, executed, consumed, and publicized reflects the politics of social problems. As research accumulates, the facts seem more rather than less elusive.

Most of the major empirical issues involving drunk driving remain unresolved. I believe that the research fairly well shows—and it is certainly consistent with common sense—that alcohol abusers are the most frequent and, more important, the most serious offenders. But the

191

term alcohol abuse includes many different types of abusive and irresponsible drinking, some of it by people who ordinarily are social drinkers. The more one examines the problem, the more one sees the complexities: there is no single type of drunk driver and no single type of drunk driving problem. It is difficult to formulate coherent and efficient legal and social policy without a clearer vision of the typology of drunk drivers—who they are, their drinking patterns, their driving patterns, their rates of offending, their dangerousness.

The extent of drunk driving is muddled by the tendency to equate drinking/driving with drunk driving and by the difficulty of adequately sampling a representative group of drivers on representative roads at representative times of the day and night. Moreover, a single statistic conceals a great deal of variation among places, subgroups, sexes, and age cohorts. Consequently it is difficult even to say whether drunk driving is decreasing in the United States. There are certainly hopeful signs of modest decline, but a tough-minded analyst probably would not be willing to say more than that drunk driving does not seem to be increasing.

The problems of measuring the effects of drunk driving control initiatives are also substantial. Traffic fatalities have declined since the early 1970s, but we do not understand why. The fifty-five-mile-per-hour speed limit, safer vehicles, greater seat belt usage, and blunderbuss anti–drunk driving initiatives are all possible contributors, but the specific contribution of each is not known. Since hardly any traffic safety initiative is carried out by itself, it is almost impossible to attribute beneficial impacts to one countermeasure rather than to another. Moreover, the absence of data on nonfatal accidents makes it difficult to say whether traffic safety is improving across the board or whether there are only fewer fatal accidents.

A further problem in assessing the affects of DWI initiatives concerns the independent variables—the measures themselves. Frequently, the anti–drunk driving initiatives that purportedly are being evaluated were never really carried out—or were not carried out as intended. Often, it is difficult to say what, if anything, is actually being subjected to evaluation. Even when initiatives are implemented, they usually are not carried out in a way that maximizes the potential for evaluation. Most regrettably, there are hardly any experimental studies with random assignments and well-defined control groups. Thus, evaluators are forced to do the best they can by attempting to control for possible variables that might have contaminated the results. Good evaluations are difficult to carry out; basic errors in research design are common. Moreover, evaluation research is part art and part science; there is always more than one way to carry out an evaluation, and different techniques may yield different results.

What all this means is that public policy does not proceed according to systematic experimentation and accumulated experience. In the real world, very few intervention strategies are ever eliminated; they are often likely to attract an entrenched interest group or constituency. New initiatives are added to the list of old ones. The same strategies that were judged ineffective in the 1970s ASAP experiment have been enthusiastically employed in the 1980s anti–drunk driving campaigns. In particular, there is an unshakable belief that enhancing legal threats, enforcement, and sanctions will substantially reduce the problem. Likewise, there remains a general reluctance to conceptualize drunk driving as part of the overall highway safety problem that can be best addressed by making safer cars and better roads.

Ambivalence toward Drunk Driving

Throughout our analysis of drunk driving we have encountered ambivalence in assessing both the culpability and dangerousness of drunk driving. It is a myth that until recently Americans did not regard drunk driving seriously and that they now do. Attitudes have always been ambivalent. This follows from ambivalent attitudes about alcohol itself. America is an alcohol-rich society, and yet it carries the legacy of Puritanism and of an almost one-hundred-year-long temperance movement. We tend to believe that alcoholic beverages are a positive feature of our culture, social system, and personal lives; this is especially clear when we compare the social approval of alcohol with the social condemnation of practically all other drugs. Yet we recognize and regret extensive alcohol problems. In recent decades we have become less judgmental about alcohol problems and more inclined to see them as beyond personal control. Even our attitudes toward drunkenness are ambivalent. As a society we seem by no means prepared to denounce drunkenness as an unmitigated evil. Apparently there is a place for drunkenness in our culture, as long as it does no harm.

Given our attitudes toward alcohol, it is hardly surprising to find ambivalent attitudes toward drunk driving. Americans continue to treat drunk driving as, in effect, a serious traffic offense. The basic legal response to drunk driving was set early in the century and has changed very little over time. Statutory penalties are no more severe today than they were decades ago. The main punishment has traditionally been loss of license, although this sanction has been tempered through plea bargaining and the availability of limited-use and occupational licenses.

Fines are no greater today than they were decades ago. While the popularity in some jurisdictions of shock jail terms is new and represents a symbolic denunciation of drunk driving, the debate about the proper punishment of drunk driving really encompasses a quite limited range of penalties. For example, practically nobody advocates making first-offense DWI a felony or even a serious misdemeanor—that is, punishable by up to one year in jail.

Part of the reason that drunk driving is not treated more seriously is that in the standard case no harm occurs. Our criminal jurisprudence is just beginning to focus in a sophisticated way on the criminality of reckless risk creation. Nevertheless, one can understand the resistance, months after a harmless drunk driving incident, to label the (now contrite and sober) offender a dangerous criminal. Such a hard-nosed response would require a policy perspective that does not fit easily with the decentralized and personalized administration of criminal justice.

Another obstacle to redefining drunk driving as a more serious offense, perhaps as a low-to-mid-level felony, is that the line separating noncriminality from criminality is blurry in the minds of most Americans. If most Americans believe that they could be convicted of drunk driving after one, two, or three drinks, they obviously will not favor defining the offense as a felony or serious misdemeanor. Such behavior is simply too prevalent, and in common experience it does not seem dangerous. Perhaps if it became clear that drunk driving usually requires four, five, six, or more drinks, it would be easier to mobilize sentiments against offenders. The more egregious the behavior, the more deviant it is and the less it resembles ordinary behavior. Furthermore, it would make sense to give greater emphasis to the reckless-driving component of drunk driving. People may be more ambivalent about the culpability of irresponsible drinking than about the culpability of wanton driving.

Unfortunately, emphasizing the distinction between drinking/driving and drunk driving does not sit well with anti–drunk driving advocates. They fear that such a message will lull people into the belief that a few drinks before driving is safe, and they also fear (1) that even a few drinks are not safe or (2) that a few drinks will "spill over" into many drinks. Thus, Americans are admonished "Don't drink and drive." This position may be entirely sensible and, ultimately, more protective of life and property than a "Don't drive drunk" policy. However, it ensures that drunk driving will continue to be perceived as common behavior not suitable for severe punishment.

Public opinion toward dangerous drunk driving that results in death or serious injury is not restrained. Such cases evoke the most angry and condemnatory reactions. Almost inevitably the defendants are alcohol abusers and sociopathic personalities whose behavior was flagrantly reckless and outrageous. Citizens, prosecutors, and judges do not empathize or sympathize with such defendants. For these reasons it would make sense to formulate an aggravated-drunk-driving offense to cover the most egregious forms of drunk driving,—regardless of whether injury occurs—and to define harmless episodes unaccompanied by dangerous driving as low-level misdemeanors or traffic offenses.

Multifacetedness of Anti–Drunk Driving Control Strategies

Drunk driving has stimulated an extraordinarily multifaceted array of social control initiatives. Even the simple deterrence initiatives—roadblocks, special police drunk driving units, mandatory jail terms and license revocations, restrictions on plea bargaining, punitive tort damages, and insurance surcharges—are quite diverse. In addition to punitive threats, there is a wide range of anti–drunk driving programs based on public education and treatment. In fact, to a substantial extent the treatment of drunk drivers has been aggressively pursued by the vast alcohol treatment community, which has striven to make drunk drivers part of its domain.

In Part III I have recommended a few sanctions and strategies that are not currently being used widely, if at all. Much higher fines and vehicle impoundments would make it more costly to be apprehended and convicted of drunk driving. To further guarantee that the convicted drunk driver will be incapacitated with regard to future drunk driving, he should lose both vehicle and license. Home detention is also extremely well suited to be employed as a drunk driving sanction.

While simple deterrence and incapacitating strategies are likely to be the core of any comprehensive anti–drunk driving program, the long-term goal is to reach a point when anti–drunk driving norms are widely internalized throughout the population. Then social control would not be so dependant on governmental initiatives and could rely on less intrusive, informal interpersonal controls and on personal choices and inhibitions. All of the efforts against drunk driving taking place today can contribute to changes in norms, attitudes, and behavior over the long term.

One positive step in the effort to shape norms can be seen in governmental initiatives to encourage responsible drinking practices. Prohibitions on happy hours, two-for-one promotions, and chugalug contests are good ideas. Earlier bar and tavern closing hours should also be considered. Police resources should focus more on bar and tavern parking lots during late-night/early-morning hours. We are dealing with a strong and easily abusable drug, and efforts to promote its mature and responsible use are appropriate and sensible and do not infringe in any serious way on people's freedoms. Server intervention courses, stimulated by developments in dram shop liability, also provide a very useful starting point for changing restaurant and bar norms—and therefore societal norms—regarding alcoholic beverage consumption.

I have more doubts about making twenty-one the minimum purchase age. Our experience with Prohibition and with the prohibiting of marijuana, cocaine, heroin, and an array of other narcotics and dangerous drugs does not make me sanguine about the probabilities of a successful prohibition on beverage alcohol consumption by those less than twenty-one years old. Furthermore, this kind of prohibition may convey the wrong message about alcohol consumption—by linking drinking with intoxication and out-of-control behavior. I prefer policies that emphasize responsible drinking contexts and practices.

Finally, and most important, continuous attention must be paid to making cars safer to drive and more protective when crashes occur. The reason that we are anxious to prevent drunk driving is to protect drivers, passengers, pedestrians, and other road users from being injured or killed. A direct route to this goal is to place drivers and passengers in vehicles that can survive serious crashes, including head-on collisions. Air bags are the most promising technology for meeting this goal, and they should become a standard feature of all automobiles sold and driven in the United States. We would do well to remind ourselves continuously that *drunk driving is first and foremost a transportation problem.*

If the Interlock System proves effective, it could be the single most important anti–drunk driving weapon in our arsenal. It should become a standard response to drunk driving. Beyond that, depending on cost, consideration should be given to making it a mandatory safety feature on all vehicles.

The Institutionalization of a Self-sustaining Anti–Drunk Driving Movement

The future for more effective social control of drunk driving is bright because of the citizens' anti–drunk driving movement, the institutionalization of state anti–drunk driving programs, federal recognition of drunk driving as a national problem, and the continuing role of NHTSA.

The importance of the citizens' anti–drunk driving movement cannot be exaggerated. While drunk driving was recognized as a social problem before the emergence of this movement, the modern-day movement has greatly increased the visibility of the drunk driving problem and given expression to a reservoir of anti–drunk driving sentiments. By putting a human face on the victims of drunk driving, the citizen activists have mobilized the public's attention and sentiment. Relentless lobbying has led to passage of hundreds of state laws and several major federal laws. In effect, the citizens' movement has made drunk driving a politial issue that many legislators, prosecutors, and even judges cannot afford to ignore. The citizens' groups continuously pressure political leaders at all levels of government to pass legislation, to provide funding, and to vigorously enforce the laws. MADD, RID, and SADD are very well established. Their existence assures that pressure to maintain and increase anti–drunk driving efforts will not diminish in the short term.

The war against drunk driving has been further institutionalized by the creation of new governmental units to wage it. Many states have appointed anti–drunk driving task forces and established anti–drunk driving agencies or programs. These specialized agencies provide an institutional base for a sustained campaign against drunk driving. They do not depend on periodic mobilization of public sentiments and voluntary efforts, and they will not lose interest in drunk driving when other issues come to the fore of the public problems agenda. Their raison d'être is to launch programs to reduce drunk driving. Moreover, in many cases their long-term survival is guaranteed by funding formulas that allocate to their operations a portion of the fines paid by drunk drivers.

New York State, for example, established the Stop-DWI Program within its department of transportation in 1982. A specialized Office of Alcohol Countermeasures with a staff of twenty provides coordination and technical back-up services to local Stop-DWI programs in every county. Each county must have such a program and appoint a DWI coordinator who is required to submit an annual plan for combating drunk driving. Following the plan's approval the county receives a 50 percent rebate on all fines it collects from drunk drivers. The coordinator can allocate (via his or her approved plan) these funds to law enforcement, treatment, courts, public education, and so forth. Thus, the agencies responsible for drunk driving control have been given economic incentives to keep the issue a top priority.

Recognition of drunk driving as a national problem and priority also augurs well for the future of social control initiatives. Achieving federal recognition marks the coming of age of a social problem. The 1968 U.S.

Department of Transportation report on drunk driving was a vital step in forcing the nation to come to terms with drunk driving. Responsibility for developing an anti–drunk driving agenda was delegated to NHTSA, a unit within the department. NHTSA instituted the ASAP programs, which provided both a great deal of important information and research and models for many of the anti–drunk driving programs that are flourishing today. NHTSA also provided grants to MADD and other citizens' groups. It continues to sponsor research on all facets of drunk driving.

While NHTSA is the federal agency most heavily involved in dealing with drunk driving, other institutions and agencies also have a role. The president and Congress have established a week in December as an annual anti–drunk driving week, thus contributing to the symbolic attack on drunk driving. Congress has, in effect, been prodded to legislate a rather elaborate program of anti–drunk driving policies by offering highway safety grants to states that comply. The National Institutes of Health, the National Institute of Justice, and NIAAA are also involved in supporting anti–drunk driving programs and research.

The Costs of Social Control

The social control of drunk driving is not costless. The most important costs are infringements on liberties of nondrunk drivers. Drunk driving roadblocks are a particularly troubling social control strategy. They ignore a core value of American freedom and a key restraint on American police—that is, that there must be probable cause for the police to stop, investigate, and search. The roadblocks adopt a new standard—that is, that it is proper for police to carry out dragnet searches and investigations of the general public as long as everyone is treated the same way and notice is provided. The same rationale might permit the police to decide that, because guns and knives are a serious problem, they will henceforth stop all citizens and force them to walk through metal detectors, arresting those found with weapons in their possession. While such a practice, like drunk driving roadblocks, might contribute to societal safety, it would exact a heavy price in reduced liberty.

Establishing a minimum drinking age is an anti–drunk driving strategy similar to but less drastic than roadblocks. Admittedly the states have the right and obligation to regulate the sale of alcoholic beverages to children, but the attempt to raise the minimum age to include young adults up to age twenty-one is troubling. It limits the rights, opportunities, and social life of millions of responsible citizens in order to prevent drunk driving by a small percentage of irresponsible persons. Sacrificing the freedom of the many to prevent the criminal irresponsibility of the few is a large cost to pay to possibly reduce the drunk driving of the few. If taken to its logical extreme, this strategy would lead us back to a program of prohibition, which, given the failure of our current drug prohibitions, is not a happy prospect.

I also find troubling the increasingly mechanical character of the criminal justice system's processing of drunk drivers. It is true, of course, that the entire American criminal justice process, at least from the point of arrest, is more or less a guilt-stamping machine, but that characterization is nowhere more blatant than in the defining and processing of drunk driving cases. Drunk driving is now defined in a way that makes guilt on arrest practically automatic, especially if the arrestee's BAC is above 0.10. Acquittals or charge reductions are treated as mechanical failures, to be fixed and overcome. Administrative and even criminal penalties are deployed to coerce arrestees to provide incriminating BAC evidence. Arrestees are given the dilemma of either providing the state with evidence necessary to convict them or being punished administratively (or criminally), perhaps more severely. Legal counsel is considered an impediment to—not a constitutional protection in—the making of this decision.

There is little comfort and much inconsistency in the argument that, because drunk driving is only a traffic offense, we need not worry about extraordinary police practices and assembly line justice. It is precisely because drunk driving is not and should not be regarded as only a traffic offense that the willingness to disregard important liberties is so disturbing. If a first drunk driving offense (not resulting in injury) were defined as an administrative violation, some concerns about the undermining of important values of criminal jurisprudence and constitutional law would be alleviated. It would still be possible to revoke the offender's license and, possibly, impound his car. In addition, of course, he could be criminally prosecuted for reckless driving or for any specific traffic violations.

There are also economic costs to the campaign against drunk driving. Jailing vast numbers of drunk drivers is extremely expensive. Each jail bed costs approximately $80,000 to construct and perhaps $10,000–$20,000 per year to maintain. Prisons are already becoming the largest item (after education) in state budgets, and jails may soon occupy a similar place in county budgets. While jailing is no doubt meant to symbolize societal concern with drunk driving, one- or two-day sentences may actually signal that drunk driving is a trivial offense, especially when one considers the lengthy sentences doled out for offenses regarded as serious. The same signal is given when jail officials provide drunk drivers with the opportunity to serve their sentences in surroundings more comfortable than those of "real" criminals or give them the opportunity to reduce the actual amount of time they spend in jail.

The Limits of Social Control

In dealing with drunk driving and other social problems, it is well to remember that total victory is not achievable. The coexistence of widespread alcohol availability and near universal reliance on vehicular transportation ensures that drunk driving will always be a significant threat to highway safety. As long as our society has a lot of alcohol and driving, we will have drunk driving. A certain amount of hand wringing and anger is probably healthy; as Emile Durkheim long ago pointed out, it contributes to the solidarity of the majority of people. In the final analysis, however, positive results require persistence, resources, and imagination. Success will not come in grand victories but in small achievements.

It is a healthy sign that the anti–drunk driving movement has sought social control strategies from outside the criminal justice system—in the treatment world, public education, and civil law. This diversification is much more promising than the usual impulse merely to throw more police and incarceration at a problem. Nevertheless, government can only achieve so much. In the final analysis, like other irresponsible, antisocial behaviors, excessive drinking and driving is shaped by cultural and social attitudes and values and, short of a technological breakthrough such as the Interlock System, will only be significantly reduced by profound changes in norms, attitudes, and values.

Governmental interventions can make a difference—but only marginally. Policymakers and analysts would do well to be modest in their expectations and claims. At a minimum, it is important for government to be sure that it is not contributing to the social problems it is trying to cure—and that it at least is setting the right examples (e.g., with its own holiday parties and personnel policies regarding alcohol, drunk driving, or air bags). Government can and should set a tone, promulgate messages, and define as wrong and deviant such behaviors as drunk driving, but it is a mistake to promise a governmental cure or solution. The inevitable failure to fulfill extravagant promises leads to cynicism about government's capacity to achieve anything. Politicians and their constituents must accept the inevitability of long-term struggle to achieve more effective social control.

Notes

Introduction

1. An early-1980s survey by the U.S. Department of Health and Human Services found that "one in three Americans surveyed last year felt that alcohol caused problems in his or her family." See *Fifth Special Report to the U.S. Congress on Alcohol and Health from the Secretary of Health and Human Services* (December 1983), P. v.

2. SADD essentially has no national organization. Its chapters often are started by students in response to a lecture or a drunk driving tragedy. Such groups are often short-lived unless they become a special interest of a particular school administrator. Interview with Professor John D. McCarthy, Center For Study of Youth Development, Catholic University, Washington, D.C.

3. Presidential Commission on Drunk Driving (1983, P. 12):

Citizen Support: Grass roots citizen advocacy groups should be encouraged to continue fostering awareness of the DUI problem, to co-operate with government officials, prosecutors and judges to deal more effectively with the alcohol-related crash problem, and to encourage the development of personally responsible drinking/driving behavior.

Task Forces: State and local governments should create task forces of governmental and non-governmental leaders to increase public awareness of the problem, to apply more effectively DUI laws, and to involve governmental and non-governmental leaders in action programs.

National Body: A non-governmental body of public and private leaders should be established at the national level to ensure a continuing focus on efforts to combat driving under the influence.

4. Borkenstein (1985, P. 8) notes that "nearly all persons or organizations involved in the early North American research and activities were physicians, chemists, lawyers, police, traffic engineers, insurance interests and traffic educators. The social and behavioral sciences were completely ignored, or at least neglected."

5. For the most part I have not included foreign research but have approached drunk driving as an American social problem. *Social Control of the Drinking Driver* (1988), edited by Michael Laurence, John Snortum, and Franklin Zimring, presents several important essays on deterrence research in Europe that readers with a specialized interest in deterrence will find valuable.

Chapter One

1. "Alcohol acts on virtually every cell of the body, but the central nervous system is the target most affected. Alcohol's influence is profound—from personality disorder created by chronic drinking to the distorted judgment of the drunken driver. Current research is converging on explanations for some of these effects and their underlying biological mechanisms, but a comprehensive understanding of an individual's response to alcohol is still elusive" (U.S. Department of Health and Human Services 1983, P. 25).

2. "The traditional unitary disease concept of alcoholism has been challenged by the observation that there may be multiple patterns of dysfunctional alcohol use, which result in multiple kinds of disability. . . . An alternative approach characterizes alcohol dependence along a continuum of severity, with no clear demarcation between the beginning of alcoholism and the end of social drinking" (*Fifth Special Report to the U.S. Congress on Alcohol and Health from the Secretary of Health and Human Services* [December 1983], P. 100).

3. There exists an extensive network of programs and treatment professionals (U.S. Department of Health and Human Services 1983) to deal with alcoholism and alcohol abuse. "In 1977, although approximately 1.6 million alcoholics and problem drinkers received treatment from private and public sources and over 600,000 alcoholics participated in meetings of Alcoholics Anonymous, at least 8 to 10 million other alcoholics and problem drinkers did not receive any treatment" (Saxe et al. 1983).

4. The enormously influential 1967 President's Commission on Law Enforcement and Administration of Justice recommended that drunkenness in itself should not be a crime, that civil detoxification programs should be developed, and that comprehensive treatment programs should be established. In 1968 the U.S. Department of Transportation's historic *Alcohol and Highway Safety Report* noted that the commission's recommendation on the decriminalization of public drunkenness "point[s] to a far more sophisticated legal approach to the problem of alcohol abuse in general, and may have particular applicability to pedestrians and drivers who drink so heavily that they pose actual or potential threats to the public safety" (P. 100).

5. A major victory for the proponents of decriminalization was approval of the Uniform Alcoholism and Intoxication Treatment Act by the National Conference of Commissioners on State Laws in 1971 and by the American Bar Association in 1972. Under the act, the alcoholic was not to be criminally prosecuted; all laws that included drinking or drunkenness as an element of the offense were prohibited, except those banning drunk driving or controlling the purchase or sale of alcoholic beverages.

6. This is primarily attributable to the influence of the American Law Institue's Model Penal Code, sec. 2.08, which provides that intoxication is a defense to the extent that it negatives the mental element required to establish the offense, except that intoxication is not a defense to a crime defined in terms of reckless conduct. When this provision was issued it was considerably more

liberal than the prevailing law in many states, which did not permit voluntary intoxication to be raised as a criminal defense.

7. A 1982 government survey found that fifty-seven million Americans had used marijuana and that twenty-two million had tried cocaine, including 28% of young adults. In 1984 over 60% of high school seniors reported use of an illicit substance (Peele 1987).

Chapter Two

1. Perhaps our historical perspective is too short. The Enno Foundation For Highway Traffic Control introduced its 1949 study of "The Motor Vehicle Driver: His Nature and Improvement" by stating: "Mobility is the essense of American living—and the motor vehicle is the nation's prime source of mobility. Our economic, social, cultural, and recreational activities are dependent to a great extent on gasoline. At the wheel, many an American tends to transform himself into a god. After all, can't he make the power of a hundred horses pull himself and his passengers speedily forward?"

2. For some interesting writing on the automobile's role in American society, see Jerome (1972), Flink (1975), Lewis and Goldstein (1983), Eastman (1984), and Halberstam (1986).

3. One study sponsored by the Insurance Institute for Highway Safety (1982) examined all emergency room–treated facial injuries in a midwestern county for one year. Almost half of the severe facial fractures and lacerations were associated with vehicle crashes. The study estimated that nationally each year there are 625,000 hospital-treated facial injuries resulting from highway crashes. An earlier study (Smart and Sanders 1976) found that half of all acute spinal cord injuries (5,000 annually) result from motor vehicle crashes.

4. In 1986 the highway death toll was 48,560.

5. Congress established a temporary maximum national speed limit of fifty-five miles per hour in 1974 and made it permanent in 1975. See National Maximum Speed Limit, 23 U.S.C., sec. 154(a)(1). The Surface Transportation and Uniform Relocation Assistance Act of 1987 (P.L. 100-17) changed the maximum speed limit to sixty-five miles per hour. The Transportation Research Board (1984) estimates that two hundred to four thousand lives are saved every year because of the fifty-five-mile-per-hour speed limit. The reduction may be produced by a combination of the following effects: (1) motorists have better control; (2) there is less variability in speed and thus a more uniform, orderly, and predictable traffic flow; and (3) the energy released in lower-speed crashes is less, so injuries are less serious. See also U.S. Department of Transportation, NHTSA, "The Life-Savings benefits of the 55 mph National Speed Limit," report of the NHTSA/FHWA Task Force (October 1980).

6. Federal motor vehicle safety standards are promulgated by NHTSA pursuant to the 1966 Motor Vehicle Safety Act. See 49 Code of Federal Regulations, pt. 571. According to Leon Robertson (1983), between 1975 and 1978 more than nine thousand people per year avoided death as a result of these standards.

7. In 1979 NHTSA began its National Accident Sampling System (NASS). NASS investigates a probability sample of *all police-reported accidents* in the United States. See the U.S. Department of Transportation's *Report on Traffic Accidents and Injuries for 1979–1980* (1982).

8. Perhaps things are changing. A Purdue University study of new car buyers' attitudes has found that safety considerations "play more of a role in purchasing decisions than previously thought" (AAA Foundation for Traffic Safety, Falls Creek, Va., "The Effect of Automobile Safety on Vehicle Type Choice: An Empirical Study," unpublished). Each of the "Big Three" American automobile manufacturers has promised to equip up to one million 1990 cars with air bags.

9. These were not the first federal expressions of interest in highway safety. In 1924 Secretary of Commerce Herbert Hoover convened a national conference on street and highway safety. In 1936 President Franklin Roosevelt convened an Accident Prevention Conference whose report, *Guides to Highway Safety,* recommended that automakers should improve interiors. Ten years later President Harry Truman called a highway safety conference and urged industry action to encourage state and local safety efforts. President Dwight Eisenhower, in whose administration the massive interstate highway system was built, spoke out on highway safety on several occasions. Congressional interest in highway and traffic safety was formally initiated in 1956 by the Subcommittee on Health and Safety of the House Committee on Interstate and Foreign Commerce. In the following decade there were more than a dozen hearings before various House and Senate committees. For a chronicle of the federal role in highway safety, see U.S. Senate, 90th Congress, 2d sess., Committee on Government Operations, *Federal Role in Traffic Safety,* report of the Subcommittee on Executive Reorganization, Senate Rep. 951 (January 24, 1968).

10. National Traffic and Motor Vehicle Safety Act of 1966, P.L. 89-563 (September 1966); Highway Safety Act of 1966, P.L. 89-564 (September 1966).

11. Consider the Ford Pinto case; the design of its gas tank created a substantial risk of explosion in the event of rear-end collision. Ford concluded that it would be cheaper to settle wrongful death claims and other injury cases than to redesign the car (Epstein 1980; Dowie 1985). Vehicle failures, recalls, and charges of safety violations remain major issues to the present day. Safety-related defects or failure to comply with federal motor vehicle safety standards resulted in more than 5.6 million vehicles being recalled in 1985; this was down from 7.2 million recalls the year before. See Highway and Vehicle Safety Report, vol. 12, no. 13 (March 17, 1986), P. 5.

12. Some studies estimate that air bags could save as many as ten thousand lives per year. The Insurance Institute for Highway Safety recently estimated that "there would be an estimated 7,750 fewer fatalities by 1990 if all cars are equipped with driver side airbags, assuming a 30 percent use of manual belts by front seat occupants" (Insurance Institute for Highway Safety, "The Public Prefers Airbags," status report, vol. 22, no. 1, [January 24, 1987], Pp. 1–6).

13. For a critical account of developments at NHTSA under the Reagan Administration, see *Public Citizen* (1982).

14. *Motor Vehicles Mfrs. Assoc'n v. State Farm Mut. Auto. Ins. Co.*, 463 U.S. 29 (1983).

15. *State Farm Mut. Auto. Ins. Co. et al. v. Dole*, 802 F.2d 474 (D.C. Cir 1986).

16. As of July 1987 twenty-nine states had passed mandatory seat belt use laws.

17. For an early, systematic, and thoughtful analysis of driver behavior and misbehavior, see ENNO Foundation For Highway Traffic Control report *The Motor-Vehicle Driver: His Nature and Improvement* (1949).

18. The Figgie Report, *On Fear of Crime* (A.T.O., Inc. 1980, P. 18) found that "crime is on the increase in the U.S.—but as distressing as the rapid rise is, . . . the incidence of crime is far outstripped by the fear of crime. This study reveals that four out of ten Americans are fearful they will become victims of violent crimes, such as murder, rape, robbery or assault. It also reveals that four out of ten Americans feel unsafe in their everyday environments—their homes, their neighborhoods, their business districts and shopping centers—due to the fear of crime."

Chapter Three

1. The citations provided in the report indicate that the California study is nine pages plus tables and that the New Jersey study is twenty-three pages. In his exhaustive attempt to reexamine the research underlying the 1968 report, Richard Zylman (1974) learned that the New Jersey department actually presented data *on all drivers tested and found to have been drinking*—not on all single-vehicle fatalities, as the 1968 report suggested.

2. Elsewhere, the report stated that "during the last thirty-five years, in every area of the nation in which the presence and concentrations of alcohol among individuals responsible for initiating crashes has been investigated systematically, alcohol has been found to be the largest single factor leading to fatal crashes." No citations are offered. The impression that a systematic corpus of studies exists is inaccurate.

3. As for pedestrians, the report located only Haddon et al.'s (1961) study, which found that 40 percent of New York City adult pedestrian fatalities had BAC levels at or above 0.10.

4. "Reckless driving shall mean driving or using any motor vehicle, motor-cycle or any other vehicle propelled by power other than muscular power or any appliance or accessory thereof in a manner which unreasonably interferes with the free and proper use of the public highway, or unreasonably endangers users of the public highway. Reckless driving is prohibited. Every person violating this provision shall be guilty of a misdemeanor" (New York Vehicle and Traffic Law, sec. 1190).

5. A real opportunity for research is available in the diaries that "students" in drinking/driver schools are often required to prepare. The student must

recount what he did in the twenty-four hours leading up to the DWI arrest.

6. The problem of extrapolating results from the fifteen "good reporting states" to the rest of the United States should not be minimized. Is there reason to believe that, with respect to alcohol involvement, fatal crashes in Mississippi differ from crashes in California or Massachusetts? Since these states differ in per-capita alcohol consumption, in percentages of abstainers, and in cultural values concerning drunkenness and reverie, there is good reason to reject the hypothesis that the percentage of accidents that involve alcohol in these states is the same.

7. For an explanation of comparative negligence, see Keeton et al. (1984), sec. 67: "Under pure comparative negligence, a plaintiff's contributory negligence does not operate to bar his recovery altogether, but does serve to reduce his damages in proportion to his fault."

8. From time to time large police departments have attempted to develop training programs on recognizing the presence of alcohol and/or illicit drugs in traffic accidents. According to the August 3, 1987, *Highway and Vehicle Safety Report* (vol. 13[23], Pp. 6–7), Los Angeles has developed a program to train select officers as drug recognition experts. The officers are trained to look for a pattern of symptoms that can identify a specific drug, drug category, or combination of drugs.

9. In England the police have authority to test every crash-involved driver for BAC. Some American states are moving in the same direction. New York Vehicle and Traffic law, sec. 1193-a, provides that any person involved in a traffic accident must submit to a preliminary breath test. If that test produces probable cause to suspect drunk driving, the driver must submit to a full-scale BAC test. The constitutionality of administering such a preliminary breath test without probable cause is dubious (see Chapter 8).

10. There is an interesting counterpressure. To demonstrate that their countermeasures are working, anti–drunk driving advocates and programs feel a need to show a declining number of alcohol-related fatalities. Thus, they must simultaneously show their success and the continued magnitude of the problem.

Chapter Four

1. Moderate drinking is defined as "drinks at least once a month, typically several times, but usually with no more than three or four drinks per occasion." Heavy drinking is defined as "drinks nearly every day with five or more per occasion, or about once weekly with usually five or more per occasion." Because people are likely to understate the amount they drink, the percentage of heavily drinking males may be as high as 21 percent.

2. Many studies have found the opposite—that is, that drunk drivers tend to be disproportionately less educated and to be drawn from lower socioeconomic groups (see, e.g., Wolfe 1975).

3. Goldstein and Susmilch (1982) found that over a six-year period in Madison, Wisconsin, drunk driving fatalities occurred almost exclusively from

late Thursday night to late Sunday night. Strangely enough, for this sample there were fewer drunk driving fatalities on Saturday than on Thursday, Friday, and Sunday.

4. Unfortunately this important study unaccountably remains unpublished. The manuscript version I was able to obtain is entitled "Summary of Findings, 1986 United States Roadside Breathtesting Survey," by Arthur C. Wolfe, Ph.D.

5. The FBI collects, compiles, and publishes arrest data on drunk driving. In 1984, according to its Uniform Crime Reports (1985), there were 1.8 million drunk driving arrests. While these arrests provide important data on the characteristics of drunk drivers, they cannot be taken as representative of all DWI offenders. As a group, arrested drunk drivers must be worse drivers, more dangerous, and more drunk than nonarrested drunk drivers. Whether a driver is stopped and, if stopped, investigated for alcohol is at the police officer's discretion. Thus, who is arrested depends on the enforcement priorities and biases of thousands of state and local police departments around the country. Furthermore, certain subgroups are disproportionately vulnerable to arrest. For example, the police are much more alert to the offending of young men than to that of women or older men. Young men are not only the main grist for the criminal justice system; they are the most likely to hassle police officers, and they are the worst drivers. Nevertheless, sixteen-to-twenty year olds are less frequently arrested for DWI than for any other UCR offense.

6. Harrington's (1972) longitudinal study of young drivers in California showed that 85 percent of the men and 56 percent of the women had either an accident or a conviction during the first four years of driving. Of the 2,229 fatal and personal injury accidents, drinking was reported for 6 percent of the men and 2 percent of the women.

7. Office of the Commissioner of Probation and The Division of Alcoholism, Department of Public Health, "An Evaluation Of Drunk Driving In Massachusetts Under Chapter 373, Acts of 1982" (unpublished mimeo, August 1, 1984). Of previous non–drunk driving criminal charges, 16.8 percent were for offenses against the person, 26.8 percent were for property offenses, 9.8 percent were for drugs usage, 28.5 percent were for public order offenses (including family abuse), and 20.8 percent were for criminal traffic offenses excluding drunk driving.

Chapter Five

1. Even before there were motorcars, Americans punished drunken operation of trains, as well as drunken comportment on the public streets.

2. Note, however, that the Maine Supreme Court struck down a statutory reformulation of first-offense DWI as a noncriminal traffic infraction of "operating under the influence" (OUI), on the ground that the "civil" OUI proceeding retained sufficient criminal characteristics to require its treatment as a criminal proceeding, thereby necessitating appropriate constitutional safeguards. See *State v. Freeman,* 487 A.2d 1175 (Me. Sup. Jud. Ct. [1985]).

3. The Supreme Court's seminal decision in *Powell v. Texas* (392 U.S. 514

[1968]) rejected the defendant's claim that it was unconstitutional to punish a chronic alcoholic for being drunk in public. The Court indicated great concern that a decision in Powell's favor would undercut the assumption of individual responsibility that is essential for criminal law. Justice White's concurring opinion argued that even if chronic alcoholics could not help appearing in public once they began drinking, they could still be held morally blameworthy for failing to take, before they started drinking, precautions that would assure their nonappearance in public after they became intoxicated.

4. Model Penal Code, sec. 2.08: "(2) When recklessness establishes an element of the offense, if the actor, due to self-induced intoxication, is unaware of a risk of which he would have been aware had he been sober, such unawareness is immaterial."

5. The code's approach has been vigorously criticized by Professor Paul Robinson (1985). He would permit voluntary intoxication to negate reckless risk creation but would establish a new offense, "dangerous intoxication": "(1) Definition of Offense. An actor who would have been guilty of the offense charged or any lesser included offense but for the defense of intoxication negating an element, is guilty of the offense of Dangerous Intoxication. (2) Affirmative Defense. It shall be an affirmative defense to the offense of Dangerous Intoxication that the actor proves that at the time he was intoxicating himself he did not have the culpability required by an offense or lesser included offense for which he gained a defense."

6. The gravamen of the DWI offense is the *potential* for dangerous driving, a point nicely illustrated by a recent Michigan case (*P. v. Walters*, 160 Mich. App. 396, 407 N.W. 2d 662; Mich. Ct. of App. [1987]) which held that the defendant's normal driving was relevant only to show that he was not impaired and that it would not preclude a conviction for DWI. The court stated that "normal driving is not necessarily inconsistent with the factual conclusion that a driver's ability was impaired."

Chapter Six

1. See *Papachristou v. City of Jacksonville* (405 U.S. 156 [1972]): "Where, as here, there are no standards governing the exercise of the discretion granted by the ordinance, the scheme permits and encourages an arbitrary and discriminatory enforcement of the law."

2. Some statutes, for example, Wisconsin's, use the word "operating" rather than "driving"—thus the offense of "operating under the influence."

3. Interesting laboratory research shows that those who mistakenly think they have consumed alcohol display many signs of intoxicated behavior.

4. *Commonwealth v. Connolly* (474 N.E. 2d 1106 [1985]) reversed a conviction based on a faulty DWI jury instruction:

However, the judge went too far when, following Model Instruction 5.10, he charged the jury that "being under the influence . . . means that a person . . . was influenced in some perceptible degree by the intake of alcoholic beverages, and he exacerbated that error when he explained his statement by hypothesizing a case in which a person drinks liquor, drives, and as a result of liquor suddenly feels 'slightly light headed,' 'slightly depressed,' or 'slightly happier' than that person would feel in the absence of liquor . . . ."

The Commonwealth must prove beyond a reasonable doubt that the defendant's consumption of alcohol diminished the defendant's ability to operate a motor vehicle safely. The Commonwealth need not prove that the defendant actually drove in an unsafe or erratic manner, but it must prove a diminished capacity to operate safely.

5. Due process requires that criminal statutes be reasonably definite as to the persons and conduct within their scope. In determining whether a criminal law is void for vagueness, a court must determine (1) whether the law gives fair notice to those persons subject to it and (2) whether the law adequately guards against arbitrary and discriminatory enforcement (LaFave and Scott 1985; see also *University of Pennsylvania Law Review* 1960).

6. The passage actually speaks of "greater impairment than is required by the lesser offense of driving while ability impaired." New York's greater and lesser included driving offenses, DWI and DWAI, are hopelessly confused. DWAI is driving while one's ability is impaired. In *People v. Cruz*, (399 N.E. 2d 513 [1979]), the New York Court of Appeals defined driving while intoxicated to mean driving while one's ability to drive is impaired. Subsequently, a few New York courts have struggled to define DWI as very impaired and to define DWAI as merely impaired. In applying the laws, police officers and the prosecutors obviously have enormous discretion.

7. In *State v. Edmundson* (379 N.W. 2d 835 [1985]), the South Dakota court upheld a conviction for DWI that was based on the police officer's "expert opinion" that the defendant was intoxicated at the time of arrest: "the officer's knowledge, skill, training, education and experience with past DWI arrests was sufficient to qualify his opinion that . . . [defendant] was intoxicated" (379 N.W. 2d, P. 840).

8. 23 U.S.C., sec. 408(e)(1), states: "For purposes of this section, a state is eligible for a basic grant if such state provides—(C) that any person with a blood alcohol concentration of 0.10 percent or greater when driving a motor vehicle shall be deemed to be driving while intoxicated."

9. In England it is illegal to drive with a BAC in excess of 0.08, and in some jurisdictions, such as New York State, a BAC greater than 0.05 operates as a rebuttable presumption of driving while one's ability is impaired, the lesser included drunk driving offense. If the New York defendant is under twenty-one, a 0.05 BAC is prima facie evidence of DWI.

10. Nevertheless, data might show that for certain categories of drivers, especially young inexperienced drivers, even lower levels of intoxication are dangerous. Thus, Maine makes it an offense for a driver under twenty-one to operate a vehicle with a BAC greater than 0.02. In my view, such a strategy is preferable to raising the minimum drinking age to twenty-one, a strategy that attempts to interdict drunk driving in an even more attenuated way than do the per se laws.

11. A study based on driving performance on a test course showed that "many drivers are significantly impaired at blood alcohol levels well below the

80mgms/100 ml limit [0.08]." In particular, "the willingness to take risks . . . was . . . demonstrated by our drivers by their attempts to negotiate hazards when their angle of approach was clearly unsuitable" (Driver performance began to deteriorate at a 0.025 BAC. (Flanagan et al. 1983, P. 206). Studies also have shown reaction-time increase that is due to drinking; one study revealed a 6 percent increase in reaction time at BAC 0.07–0.08 (Carpenter 1962). "Vision per se is not greatly affected by alcohol at BACs of less than .10%, but above that, it becomes impaired in most persons" (U.S. Department of Transportation, *Alcohol and Highway Safety: A Review of the State of Knowledge, 1984,* 1985). However, "[T]he major conclusion that can be drawn from existing research on the fundamental nature of alcohol's effects on the nervous system is that there is insufficient knowledge to develop any practicable model for predicting a specific effect on behavior."

12. For example, defendants frequently challenge a breath testing result on the ground that the machinery was not properly approved and certified by the designated state agency as required by state law. In *State v. Anderson* (M447325, Ore. Dist. Ct., Multnomah Cty. [1987]), the district court ordered a number of breath test results to be suppressed because the Intoxilyzer model used to obtain the tests had not been properly certified. The model differed from earlier, approved Intoxilyzer models with respect to the wavelength used by the radiation beam.

13. The breath test provides an estimate of the BAC at the time the test is given. The effect of alcohol dissipates over time, so that if a significant amount of time transpires between the arrest and the test, it is possible that the test would underestimate the BAC present at the time the defendant was driving the vehicle. In England the courts have recently accepted a mathematical formula for estimating backward from the test result to the BAC present at the time of the arrest. It is also possible that a defendant's breath test might *overestimate* his intoxication at the time he was arrested. Imagine the following: a defendant rapidly downs four or five drinks and starts to drive home. He is immediately stopped by the police who, smelling alcohol on his breath, take him to the station for testing. By the time the defendant is tested, more than one hour has passed. Since it takes a certain amount of time for alcohol to move from the stomach into the bloodstream, the defendant may have a higher BAC at the time he is tested than he would have had at the time he was stopped.

14. I suspect that there is a strong possibility that the widespread dissemination of BAC tables might lead to *more drinking/driving* because many people underestimate the number of alcoholic drinks necessary to bring them over the prohibited BAC level. For the past several years I have been asking students, friends, colleagues, and associates how many drinks they think are necessary to bring the drinker over the illegal BAC level. The response is invariably two or three, clearly an underestimate. Perhaps if people knew the truth they would be encouraged to drink up to the legal limit.

15. See also *Clayton v. State,* 652 S.W.2d 810 (Texas, 1983) (DWI is an offense that dispenses with the requirement of a culpable mental state); Ex Parte Ross, 522 S.W.2d 214 (1975) (a culpable mental state is not required either for

DWI or involuntary manslaughter); *State v. Grimsley,* 444 N.E.2d 1071 (Ohio, 1982) (DWI is a strict liability offense); *People v. Teschner,* 394 N.E.2d 893 (Illinois, 1979) (DWI is a strict liability offense); *State v. Duenke,* 352 N.W.2d 427 (Minn., 1984) (an unlawful intention or state of mind is not an element of a DWI charge). But see *Morgan v. Municipality of Anchorage,* 643 P.2d 691 (1982) ("there must be joint operation of conduct and intent; to convict, the state must prove that the defendant both intentionally consumed alcohol and intentionally drove his car; but we do not believe that a person who both intentionally drinks and intentionally drives must be aware that he is under the influence of alcohol").

16. See, for example, New York Vehicle and Traffic Law, sec. 1224: "The drinking of alcoholic beverages, in a motor vehicle being driven upon the public highways is prohibited. Any operator or passenger violating this section shall be guilty of a traffic violation." Hawaii Revised Statute, sec. 291-3.1, states: "(a) No person shall consume any intoxicating liquor while operating a motor vehicle upon any public street, road, or highway. (b) No person shall posess, while operating a motor vehicle on any public street, road, or highway, any bottle, can, or other receptacle containing any intoxicating liquor which has been opened, or a seal broken, or the contents of which have been partially removed. (e) Any person violating this section shall be guilty of a misdemeanor."

17. See New York Vehicle and Traffic Law, sec. 1195(b) and (c); and Conn. Gen. Statutes Ann., sec. 14-227(a)(d)(3). Under Connecticut law a BAC greater than 0.07 but less than 0.10 constitutes an infraction.

18. New York State's Pattern Jury Instructions state: "I charge you that a person's ability to operate a motor vehicle is impaired when he has voluntarily consumed alcohol to such an extent as to diminish or reduce his ability to operate the motor vehicle, even in the slightest degree. If the consumption of alcohol has any effect at all, even the slightest, upon the physical or mental ability of the defendant to operate the motor vehicle, this is sufficient to constitute driving while impaired" (Vehicle and Traffic Law, sec. 192[1]).

Chapter Seven

1. While there are those commentators who fail to find a persuasive philosophical justification for punishing a person more severely because he has previously been convicted of a crime (see, e.g., Fletcher 1978), others argue that treating recidivists more severely is merely a decision to withhold leniency (Morris 1974) mercifully extended to defendants who do not have a significant prior record. Still others argue that, by recidivating, the offender fortifies our confidence in a predictive judgment that he is dangerous. In my view, these justifications for sentence enhancement are persuasive. Moreover, whatever the rationale, current American sentencing practice permits previous criminal record to serve as an aggravating sentencing factor. As long as this is generally acceptable, there seems no reason not to make recidivist drunk driving a more serious *substantive offense* than a first offense.

2. In *Rummell v. Estelle* (445 U.S. 263 [1980]), the Supreme Court upheld a

mandatory life sentence for three crimes of fraud that netted the defendant $230. However, in *Solem v. Helm* (463 U.S. 277 [1983]) the Court held that a mandatory life sentence *without possibility of parole* constituted cruel and unusual punishment for a five-time non–violent felony offender.

3. Many defendants have argued that to sentence more severely those drunk drivers who cause injury is to violate the equal protection clause. The courts have had no difficulty rejecting this argument (see Mancke 1981).

4. Many states have defined a felony offense of "causing injury by means of drunken driving." For example, California Vehicle Code, sec. 23101 (Felony Drunk Driving), states that

any person who, while under the influence of intoxicating liquor, or under the combined influence of intoxicating liquor and any drug, drives a vehicle and when so driving does any act forbidden by law or neglects any duty imposed by law in the driving of such vehicle, which act or neglect proximately causes bodily injury to any person other than himself is guilty of a felony and upon conviction thereof shall be punished by imprisonment in the state prison for not less than one year nor more than five years or in the county jail for not less than 90 days nor more than one year and by fine of not less than two hundred fifty dollars ($250) nor more than five thousand dollars ($5000).

In states without such specialized laws, drunk driving resulting in personal injury can be prosecuted as aggravated assault (see Spencer 1985). For example, in *State v. Hill* (692 P.2d 100 [1984]), the Oregon Supreme Court held that a drunk driver whose passenger was injured in a collision could be held guilty of third-degree assault defined as recklessly causing serious physical injury to another by means of a deadly or dangerous weapon.

5. Involuntary manslaughter consists of the killing of a human being either by (1) the consequences of an unlawful act or (2) the doing of a lawful act in an unlawful manner.

6. For example, Karaba (1951) asserted in a law review article that

juries are frequently unwilling to condemn as a felon one who is guilty only of some act of negligence even though that act has resulted in the death of another. It has been said that the term "manslaughter" imports a degree of brutality which jurors do not care to place upon a merely negligent driver. Moreover, the penalty in manslaughter cases is often greater than that which jurors feel is warranted in auto death cases. The obstacles to manslaughter convictions appear not only at the trial stage but also at the appellate level. The judges themselves exhibit a good deal of reluctance in auto death manslaughter convictions.

The author provides no empirical support for these assertations. However, in their famous jury study Harry Kalven and Hans Zeisel (1966) did find that in 27 percent of drunk-driving-cases judge would have convicted when juries acquitted and that in 3 percent of the cases the judge would have acquitted when the jury convicted. This was greater "net jury leniency" than was shown for most other offenses.

7. The current Nebraska Drunk Driving Homicide Law carries stiffer fines but lesser prison sentences than the 1919 Vehicular Manslaughter statute. Sec. 39-669.07 (Neb. Supp. 1986) contains provisions for driving while under the

influence of alcohol and for the BAC 0.10 standard. Sec. 28-306(3) provides that "if the proximate cause of the death of another is the operation of a motor vehicle in violation of section . . . 39-669.07, motor vehicle homicide is a Class IV felony" (Laws 1977, LB 38, sec. 21; Laws 1979 LB 1, sec. 1). Under Nebraska's sentencing laws a Class IV felony is punishable by a maximum sentence of five years imprisonment or a $10,000 fine or both; there is no statutory minimum. See sec. 28-105(1), Neb. (1984).

8. Some recent decisions are *People v. Olivas,* 172 Cal. App. 3d 984, 218 Cal. Rptr. 567 (Calif. Ct. App. 1st district [1985]) (upholding a second-degree murder conviction of a PCP-intoxicated driver who killed an infant after a high-speed chase with police); *State v. Omar-Muhammad,* 694 P.2d 922 (S.Ct. New Mexico 1985) (a defendant who struck and killed a person while driving an automobile was properly charged with first-degree murder under the depraved-mind murder statute rather than under the vehicular homicide statute); *Pears v. State,* 698 P. 2d 1198 (Alaska S. Ct. [1985]) (the defendant was considered properly convicted of murder for two deaths arising from a drunk driving episode; but concurrent twenty-year sentences were vacated as being excessive); *Essex v. Commonwealth,* 322 S.E. 2d 216 (S. Ct. Virginia 1984) (second-degree murder conviction for three deaths arising from a drunk driving episode was reversed; to elevate the crime to second-degree murder, the defendant must be shown to have willfully or purposely—rather than negligently—embarked on a course of wrongful conduct likely to cause death or great bodily harm).

Chapter Eight

1. Highway Safety Act of 1966 as amended, 28 U.S.C., sec. 408 (1982). The regulation specific to roadblocks is found at 23 C.F.R., sec. 1309.6(11) (1984).

2. Several courts have disapproved of specific sobriety checkpoints because of lack of adequate protections against arbitrary enforcement (see, e.g., *State ex. rel. Ekstrom v. Justice Court,* 663 P. 2d 992 [Ariz. 1983]; and *Jones v. State,* 459 So. 2d 1068 [Fla. 1984]).

3. Once accepted in the drunk driving context, this dragnet technique could be extended to other pressing law enforcement problems, such as possession of narcotics or firearms, mugging, shoplifting, or bank robbery. There is a strong parallel between a drunk driving roadblock investigation based on the statistical likelihood that a certain number of passing drivers will be under the influence of alcohol and, for example, a requirement that all pedestrians on a certain street submit to a frisk or magnetometer search because of the statistical likelihood that some of them will be carrying a gun or knife illegally.

4. Some statutes, however, give suspects the right to consult with counsel by phone, as long as contact can be made within the short time period before the BAC level begins to dissipate. Until 1981 Illinois's implied-consent law required that a suspect be given ninety minutes in which to consult with an attorney to decide whether to take the test. Ill. Rev. Stat. ch. 95 1/2, sec. 11-501.1a (1979), repealed and superseded by P.A. No. 82-311, sec. 11-501–11-501.2 (1981). The Minnesota Supreme Court held that a state law providing suspects the right to counsel gave DWI suspects facing a decision whether to take the Breathalyzer

test the right to contact an attorney within a reasonable amount of time (*Prideaux v. State Dept. of Public Safety,* 247 N.W. 2d 385 [Minn. 1976]).

5. Thus, for example, criminal defendants have a right to counsel at a *post*-indictment lineup, but not at a *pre*indictment lineup.

6. The New York statute is typical (New York Vehicle and Traffic Law, sec. 1194):

Chemical Tests: Any person who operates a motor vehicle in this state shall be deemed to have given his consent to a chemical test of his breath, blood, urine, or saliva for the purposes of determining the alcoholic or drug content of his blood provided that such test is administered at the direction of a police officer:

1) having reasonable grounds to believe such person to have been driving in an intoxicated condition or, while his ability to operate such motor vehicle or motorcycle was impaired by the consumption of alcohol or the use of a drug as defined in this chapter. . . .

If such person having been placed under arrest or after a breath test indicates the presence of alcohol in his system and thereafter having been requested to submit to such chemical test refuses to submit to such chemical test, the test shall not be given, but the commissioner shall revoke his license or permit to drive and any non-resident operating privilege.

7. Nationwide adoption of implied-consent laws was encouraged by NHTSA requirements that must be met for a state to qualify for highway safety funds. See Highway Safety Program Standard No. 8, "Alcohol in Relation to Highway Safety," 23 C.F.R., sec. 204.4-8: "An approved program must provide that: Any person placed under arrest for operating a motor vehicle while intoxicated or under the influence of alcohol is deemed to have given his consent to a chemical test of his blood, breath, or urine for the purpose of determining the alcohol content of his blood."

8. See Alaska Statute 28.35.032(f) and *State v. Jensen,* 667 P. 2d 188 ([Alaska Ct. App. 1983]).

9. In June 1987 the 5th Circuit Court of Appeals ruled that a state DWI defendant is entitled to a jury trial even though the maximum punishment is less than six months because "even though DWI is classified as a petty offense according to Louisiana's statutory scheme, and even though the penalty may reflect a considered legislative judgment, we are not persuaded that DWI should not be classified as a 'serious' offense triable to a jury. However, the offense is truly malum in se. Recent statistics indicate that nearly one of every two people in this country will be involved in an alcohol-related automobile collision. The loss of life, impairment of body and destruction of property present a devastating social problem in America today" (*Landry v. Hoepfner,* 818 F.2d 1169 [5th Cir. 1987]).

10. NHTSA's August 1979 summary of the ASAP initiative contains the following revealing statement about how criminal procedure is regarded by anti–drunk driving advocates: "A major element in making the increased enforcement activity effective must be a rapid, low cost flow of the apprehended drivers through the courts. Unless there is a high proportion of 'satisfactory'

outcomes of court prosecutions, an increased arrest rate cannot be maintained. This puts an emphasis upon finding streamlined procedures that permit rapid processing of first offenders."

Part III

1. Neither of these studies has been published in a scholarly journal or subjected to critique or replication, illustrating once again a major problem in accumulating knowledge about drunk driving.

Chapter Nine

1. Zimring and Hawkins (1973) have effectively shown that the distinction between general and special deterrence is more apparent than real. In effect, legal threats are aimed at the general audience, although a particular subgroup (such as those who have been arrested previously) might be especially sensitive and attentive (or the opposite).

2. This is different from saying that people generally do not know the dividing line between petit and grand larceny or between third- and fourth-degree sexual assault. Those are grading distinctions. What we are talking about is failure to know the threshold of criminality between drinking/driving and drunk driving. This threshold should be of particular interest to students, most of whom are drinkers and drivers.

3. Admittedly, the same concern about the capacity of the offender for rational decision making arises in other crimes, but it is central to drunk driving. Many offenses—for example, assaults in taverns and spousal abuse—are committed by people under the influence of alcohol. For the reasons stated in the text, it might well be difficult to achieve marginal deterrence of these offenses by escalations of legal threats.

4. Professor Robert Borkenstein (more than twenty years ago) guestimated that a drunk driver could expect to be arrested once in every two thousand trips. Over time and countless repetitions, this statistic has attained an unjustified authoritativeness.

5. For example, the Report Every Drunk Driver Immediately (REDDI) hotline in Soldetene, Alaska, was instituted in 1983 with the assistance of a federal grant. Wallet cards with the number of the police hotline were distributed throughout the Kenai Peninsula. The police promised to dispatch a patrol car to pursue the suspected drunk driver. Program administrators estimate that the hotline received about sixty calls per month between 1983 and 1985. Currently, with the termination of the federal grant funds, only about twelve calls per month are received.

6. Some recent initiatives have cut down police processing time to between two and two and one-half hours.

7. For example, New York Vehicle and Traffic Law, sec. 1193-a, states that "every person operating a motor vehicle which has been involved in an accident or which is operated in violation of any of the provisions of this chapter shall, at the request of a police officer, submit to a breath test to be administered by the

police officer." A preliminary breath test constitutes a search and therefore cannot be compelled without probable cause or at least reasonable suspicion. Therefore, sec. 1193-a as applied to accident-involved drivers who show no signs of intoxication would, in my opinion, be unconstitutional under the Fourth Amendment. Two New York lower courts have so held: *People v. Pecora,* 123 Misc.2d 259, 473 N.Y.S.2d 320 (1984) and *People v. Hamza,* 109 Misc.2d 1055, 441 N.Y.S.2d 579 (1981).

8. I have encountered a puzzling police resistance to targeting taverns and bars, on the ground that this would amount to entrapment or discrimination. Neither of these objections makes sense in terms of the legal definition of these concepts.

9. Although thousands of cars are stopped, only a few drunk driving arrests are made. In *State ex rel. Ekstrom v. Justice Court,* 136 Ariz. 1, 663 P.2d 992 (1983), the Arizona Supreme Court pointed out that 5,763 vehicles were stopped at the drunk driving roadblocks under consideration but that only 14 drivers were arrested for driving under the influence. Similarly, the dissenting opinion in *State v. Deskins,* 234 Kan. 529, 673 P.2d 1174 (1983), pointed out that of the 2,000–3,000 motorists stopped at the drunk driving roadblock in question, only 15 were arrested for driving while under the influence of alcohol. A DWI strike force that operated sobriety checkpoints in Bergen County, New Jersey, from May 31, 1983, to October 30, 1983, reported that 17,824 motor vehicles were stopped and that 276 DWI arrests were made. During its twenty-two weekends of operation, the strike force made one DWI arrest for every 5.2 hours of enforcement. During the July 4, 1983, weekend, the Massachusetts State Police maintained roadblocks at which 11,863 cars were stopped and 66 DWI arrests made.

10. More specifically, in the HGN test, the driver is asked to cover one eye and focus the other on an object held by the officer at the driver's eye level. As the object is moved out of the driver's field of vision, the officer watches the driver's eyeball to detect involuntary jerking. By observing (1) the inability of each eye to track movement smoothly, (2) pronounced nystagmus at maximum deviation, and (3) onset of nystagmus at less that forty-five degrees in relation to the center point, the officer can estimate whether the driver's BAC exceeds the legal limit of 0.10.

11. On the horizon is also the possibility of "passive alcohol detectors," devices that can measure the presence of alcohol inside a vehicle without requiring the driver's voluntary cooperation. There might still be a live issue of constitutionality, depending on whether, with respect to the Fourth Amendment, testing the alcoholic content of the air in the vehicle constitutes a search.

12. The UCRs provide the following (estimated) arrest data: 1978, 1,268,700; 1979, 1,324,800; 1980, 1,426,700; 1981, 1,531,400; 1982, 1,778,400; 1983, 1,921,100; 1984, 1,779,400; 1985, 1,778,400.

13. For example, The National Institute of Justice's (1984, P. 18) recent study of anti–drunk driving initiatives in Seattle found that "over the 4-year period, there was an increase of about 33 percent in drunk-driving arrests by the Seattle police Department, both for the special "DWI Squad" and for regular

police patrol units. The DWI Squad increase was attributed by police officials to a reduction in routine assignments for squad members, increased use of radar, and improved supervision." Interestingly, the increase for regular patrol-force officers was actually larger than for the DWI squad and was attributable to actions initiated by the officers themselves. It appears that increased public concern over drunk driving played an important role in the increased level of enforcement activity by the police.

14. "These tendencies [to think of research only in terms of evaluating countermeasures] have stifled imaginative research and led to a monotonous repetition of studies designed to prove, and prove once again, that some particular countermeasure is effective, or that some particular program is working" (Haight 1985, Pp. 13–14).

15. Admittedly, Ross's methodology is quite conservative in its capacity to pick up reductions in drunk driving. Because there are no accurate data on the amount of drunk driving, Ross uses single-vehicle nighttime fatalities as a surrogate dependent variable on the ground that if drunk driving has decreased, this fatality category, which is known to be disproportionately associated with drunk driving, will show a greater decrease than daytime vehicle fatalities. Ross deploys interrupted-time-series analysis in order not to mistake a momentary perturbation or a regression to the mean for a true effect (see Campbell and Stanley 1963). This methodology requires data on daytime and nighttime fatalities over a reasonably substantial time period before and after the passage of a new law or implementation of an enforcement crackdown. Even if a real decline is identified (and calculated as statistically significant), it cannot be attributed to the anti–drunk driving intervention if all other categories of traffic fatalities have decreased by the same amount during the same time. In that case, some other factor(s), such as better emergency medical care, must be at work. Only if single-vehicle nighttime fatalities declined more than other kinds of vehicle fatalities would Ross be able to confirm a marginal deterrent effect. This methodology may underestimate the effect of DWI countermeasures on drunk driving because it assumes that a drunk driving decline will be reflected in reduced single-vehicle nighttime fatalities (see Heeren et al. 1985). But what if, as seems plausible, drivers involved in fatal accidents are a peculiar subset of all drunk drivers—that is, severely alcoholic, highly dangerous, and highly troubled—who may be particularly resistant to deterrent measures? It is possible that run-of-the-mill drunk drivers (e.g., social drinkers) are being deterred and that alcohol-related nonfatal crashes would show a much greater decline than fatal accidents if appropriate data were available (see Andenaes 1984; Simpson 1985).

16. In a cursory review of recent initiatives ("Deterring Drinking Driving: An Analysis of Current Efforts," 1985. *Journal of Studies on Alcohol,* suppl. 10 [1985], Pp. 122–128), Ross confirmed his previous conclusions.

17. In New York City, for example, a decision to hold a drunk driver for criminal court arraignment and bail determination means twenty-four to forty-eight hours of pretrial detention.

18. Most states have statutes authorizing the police to impound auto-

mobiles for safekeeping when a vehicle operator is arrested. Thus, for example, it is routine for police agencies to enter into contracts with towing companies to provide services along different sections of a highway. If a driver is stopped for DWI, the vehicle will either be left in the possession of a sober passenger or towed away by the private contractor. When arrests are made on back roads, the police may be more willing to leave the vehicle secured alongside the curb.

19. I suspect that many observations of low conviction rates reflect a failure to take diversion programs and plea bargains into account. While diversion or plea negotiation may produce a disposition other than a DWI conviction, they cannot be considered acquittals.

20. For example, Arkansas law prohibits prosecuting attorneys from reducing drunk driving charges. California law provides that when a drunk driving charge is reduced to reckless driving, the prosecuting attorney is required to note the defendant's alcohol involvement on the record, and this reduced charge is counted as a prior conviction if the defendant is subsequently charged with drunk driving. The reason for judicial dismissal or reduction of a drunk driving charge must be noted on the record, and it becomes part of the defendant's driving record. See Cal. Veh. Code, sec. 13352 et seq. and 23152 et seq. (West Supp. 1985). Connecticut law requires the prosecutor to give reasons on the record for the reduction or dismissal of a drunk driving charge. See Conn. Gen. Stat. Ann., sec. 14-227a. Florida prohibits plea bargaining if the BAC is 0.20 or higher. See Fla. Stat. Ann., sec. 316.656. Wisconsin requires court approval for all plea bargaining that would result in the reduction of a drunk driving charge to a non-alcohol-related offense.

21. Section 408 of the Highway Safety Act provides that, to qualify for certain highway funds, a state must have a law that mandates two days of jail (forty-eight consecutive hours of confinement) or ten days of community service for *second* offenders.

22. Further National Institute of Justice research noted the stress that carrying out these jail sentences caused for jails that already were overcrowded: "In Memphis, the use of mandatory confinement has severely strained Penal Farm operations on all days and especially on weekends when most drunk drivers serve their sentences. Cincinnati also uses weekend confinement for convicted drunk drivers, and this practice caused an enormous backlog, with offenders forced to wait as long as 6 or 7 months before serving their sentences. In Seattle, less than 18 months after the new sanctions were implemented, the county was obliged to open a new incarceration facility to handle all first-offender drunk drivers" (National Institute of Justice 1984).

23. For example, in a December 27, 1984, page-one *Wall Street Journal* article entitled "Jail for Drunk Driving Becoming Harsh Reality For Middle Americans," Julie Solomon wrote:

Not all communities have adopted Phoenix's policy of jailing drunk drivers alongside other offenders. In Hamilton County, Ohio, which includes Cincinnati, "judges were reluctant to take John Q. Citizen, who had had a few too many at the office Christmas party, and put him in with hard-core criminals," says county prosecutor Terry Gaines. So the warden outfitted an abandoned annex of the county's Drake hospital with alarms and window grilles. Some 3,700 first offenders served sentences there last year, about three times the number in 1980. . . . [The offenders] spend part of their three day sentences watching films on alcoholism and meeting the president of the local MADD chapter.

24. Other states provide for the following fines: Arizona—mandatory minimum fine $250 for first offense, $500 for second offense, maximum for first or second offense $1000, maximum for third offense $150,000; California—mandatory minimum fine $390 for first offense, $375 for second offense, $390 for third and subsequent offense; Florida—no mandatory minimum fine; first offense $250–$500, second offense $500–$1,000, third and subsequent offenses $1,000–$5,000; Illinois—no mandatory minimum fine, no more than $1,000 for any DWI offense; Oregon—no mandatory minimum fine, no more than $1,000 for any DWI offense, $100,000 maximum for motor vehicle homicide or driving while license suspended or revoked on account of DWI; South Dakota—mandatory minimum fine $1,000 for first and second offense, $2,000 for third and subsequent offenses.

25. This may result from the all too often accurate belief that they will not be apprehended for scofflaw violations. While it is true that the chance of apprehension is low, so is the cost of compliance. At a minimum, so much scofflaw violating indicates that the threat of license suspension does not produce enormous fear and anxiety.

26. See, for example, West Ann. California Codes, Vehicle, sec. 14601.2 (driving while license was suspended or revoked, when the basis was a DWI offense punishable by ten days to six months and a fine of not more than $1,000 for first offense, revoked).

27. From 1975 to 1980 the U.S. Department of Transportation sponsored survey research on the safety attitudes, behaviors, and reported actions of drivers and potential drivers. Respondents were asked which interventions they had taken that year to prevent friends and acquaintances from driving drunk. Unfortunately, the surveys have never been published and have been discontinued.

Intervening Action Taken	1975	1976	1978	1979	1980
Drove person home	62.0	63.0	62.1	61.6	63.8
Took keys	19.0	20.0	11.5	12.1	15.2
Had person stay over	6.0	19.0	10.4	10.5	11.6
Called a taxi	3.0	2.0	1.1	2.7	1.7
Called police	NA	NA	2.3	2.0	1.4
Physical restraint	3.0	3.0	2.6	1.4	2.8
Other	NA	NA	4.6	17.9	15.3

28. In a comparative study by Snortum, Hauge, and Berger (1986), 88 percent of the Norwegian sample and 55 percent of the American sample said yes to the statement, "I never drink before driving."

29. Those driving with BAC greater than 0.15 may be jailed for two weeks to one month. In Norway all drinking/drivers with BAC greater than 0.05 are given nonsuspended jail sentences.

Chapter Ten

1. An increase in the number of secondary insureds on a policy will cause upward variance in an important insurance-pricing variable—frequency rate (reflecting the probability of careless driving). See report of the Federal Trade Commission to the U.S. Department of Transportation, "Price Variability in the Automobile Insurance Market" (1970), Pp. 38–39; see also J. Ferreira, "Quantitative Models for Automobile Accidents and Insurance," sec. 4.3 (1970), P. 69.

2. This is not meant to minimize the carnage and economic loss suffered on America's roadways. We have already noted that motor vehicles are the most common cause of accidental death in the United States. Although most drivers are both accident free and claim free over the multiyear period pertinent to insurance rating, over a lifetime virtually every motorist will be involved in an accident. See New York State Insurance Department (1970).

3. Insurance companies could, for example, require their insureds to provide a copy of driver licenses with the insurance application, or they could lobby for laws requiring courts or departments of motor vehicles to report drunk driving convictions to the defendant's insurance company.

4. See U.S. Bureau of the Census, "1980 Census of Population Occupation by Industry," PC80-2-7c (Washington, D.C., May 1984), Pp. 555–557 (statistics demonstrating that the insurance companies employ a far greater number of people in the categories of financial managers, other financial officers, and managers of properties and real estate than in the categories of actuaries and statisticians).

5. It is interesting that (to my knowledge) no one has yet proposed requiring applicants for insurance to produce medical or psychiatric statements concerning apparent alcohol consumption. Such medical and psychiatric assessments might be better indicators of future drunk driving risk than is a previous arrest or conviction. However, such a requirement would severely strain the traditional doctor-patient relationship.

6. In some states, privacy laws prevent the department of motor vehicles from providing this information. See in general, All-Industry Research Advisory Council (1981). This important study found that (1) accident information is not available to automobile insurers in ten states—and in the remaining states only 36.9 percent of the serious accidents were reflected on motor vehicle records and (2) on a countrywide basis, only 22.3 percent of serious accidents resulted in a violation being recorded on motor vehicle registrations.

7. Equifax is a private company headquartered in Atlanta, Georgia, that collects data on individual driving records and makes this information available, for a fee, to public or private customers.

8. Most states regulate insurance surcharging. New York State, for in-

stance, strictly limits points and surcharges. Personal injury damage caused by an insured can only trigger a surcharge if the driver was at fault. See NYCRR, sec. 169.1(c) (1985). Additionally, there is a threshold of $400 for surcharges predicated on property damage, unless the insured has had two or more prior accidents involving property damage. See NYCRR, sec. 169.1(a). Section 169.0(a)(2) allows insurance companies to add surcharges for drunk driving convictions. In New York State, the amount of the surcharge is governed by NYCRR, sec. 169.1(e). Under "additive" plans, surcharges can increase by as much as three times the total limits premium per base class for liability coverage and by as much as three times the base for collision coverage. Under "multiplicative" plans, insureds can be surcharged at twice the premium, for both liability and collision coverage.

9. In 1984 New York State suspended or revoked 25,362 licenses because the license holders were driving without insurance.

10. It is difficult to identify a general trend favoring either drivers or insurance companies in New York State arbitration proceedings. See, for example, NF-1178, 7 N.Y. No-Fault Arb. Rep. 7-8 (no. 12, 1983) (0.20 BAC not enough to suspend policy); NF-1075, 7 N.Y. No-Fault Arb. Rep. 4-5 (no. 3, 1983) (BAC of 0.11 and arrest for drunk driving not conclusive); but see NF-1098, 7 N.Y. No-Fault Arb. Rep. 6 (no. 5, 1983) (0.14 BAC is sufficient); NF-1102, 7 N.Y. No-Fault Arb. Rep. 7 (no. 5, 1983) (same).

11. The traditional view is that intoxication does not obviate proof of negligence. See Dolley and Mosher, "Alcohol and Legal negligence," *Contemporary Drug Problems* 7 (1978), Pp. 145, 154–156; see also, *Mckenna v. Volkswagenwerk A.G.,* 57 Hawaii 460, 558 P.2d 1018 (1977); *Cain v. Houston Gen. Ins. Co.,* 327 So. 2d 526 (La. App.), cert. refused, 330 So. 2d 279 (La. 1976). Thus far, no jurisdiction has imposed strict liability for DWI, although it was proposed by Professor Ehrenzweig during the 1950s. See Ehrenzweig (1955) ("tort fines" for drunk drivers). More recently, the New York State Insurance Commission proposed strict liability for drunk drivers. See NYS Insurance Commission, "In Whose Benefit?" (1970). Neither negligence per se nor traditional strict liability is synonymous with absolute liability. Negligence per se usually permits the defendant to raise excuses. See Prosser, *Law of Torts,* 4th ed. (1971). Even under so-called strict liability, the defendant may plead the plaintiff's contributory negligence.

12. Commentators have frequently criticized punitive damages (see, e.g., 1 Long, sec. 1.27; Walther 1965; Duffy 1969). A major criticism is that punitive damages blur the distinction between criminal law, which seeks to achieve social control through punishment and deterrence, and tort law, whose primary goal, according to some theorists, is to determine who should bear the loss when some social activity results in an injury. Judge Richard Posner believes that the purpose of tort law should be deterrence of uneconomical accidents or, to put it differently, to produce the socially efficient number of accidents. Nevertheless, in his view, punitive damages should play a limited role because "if the defendant's liability exceeded accident cost, he might have an incentive to incur

prevention costs in excess of accident cost, and this would be uneconomical" (R. Posner, 2d ed. [1977], P. 143).

13. States that permit punitive damages for drunk driving characterize it variously as either gross negligence, culpable disregard, or willful and wanton conduct. See, for example, *Ross v. Clark*, 35 Ariz. 60, 274 P. 639 (1929); *Homes v. Hollingsworth*, 234 Ark. 347, 352 S.W.2d 96 (1961); *Infield v. Sullivan*, 151 Conn. 506, 199 A.2d 693 (1964); *Taylor v. Superior Court*, 24 Cal. 3d 890, 598 P.2d 854, 157 Cal. Rptr. 693 (1979); *Busser v. Sabalasso*, 143 So. 2d 532 (Fla. App. 1962); *Madison v. Wigal*, 18 Ill. App. 2d 564, 153 N.E.2d 90 (1958); *Sebastion v. Wood*, 246 Iowa 94, 66 N.W.2d 841 (1954); *Southland Broadcasting Co. v. Tracy*, 210 Miss. 836, 50 So. 2d 572 (1951); *Svejcara v. Whitman*, 82 N.M. 739, 487 P.2d 167 (N.M. App. 1971); *Colligan v. Fera*, 76 Misc. 2d 22, 349 N.Y.S. 2d 306 (1973); *Harrell v. Ames*, 265 Or. 183, 508 P.2d 211 (1973); *Focht v. Rabada*, 217 Pa. Super. 35, 268 A.2d 157 (1970); *Pratt v. Duck*, 28 Tenn. App. 502, 191 S.W. 562 (1945); *Higginbotham v. O'Keefe*, 340 S.W.2d 350 (Tex. Civ. App. (1960).

14. A typical dram shop law is Ill. Rev. Stat. ch. 43, 135 (supp. 1981): "Every person who is injured in person or property by an intoxicated person has a right of action . . . against any person who by selling or giving alcoholic liquor, causes the intoxication of such person; Mich. Comp. Laws, sec. 436.22 (1978), provides: Every wife, husband, parent, child, guardian, or other person who shall be injured . . . by a visibly intoxicated person by reason of the unlawful selling, giving, or furnishing to such persons of any intoxicating liquor . . . shall have a right of action."

15. Twenty-three states have enacted some form of dram shop law. Of those, eighteen states use dram shop laws only. There are eighteen states that apply common law liability principles against the suppliers of alcoholic beverages; of those, thirteen states use common law principles only. Five states have both dram shop laws and common law liability. See Insurance Information Institute (August 1984), Pp. 1–2. In stark contrast to this trend, Tennessee recently amended its dram shop act to all but immunize taverns and their owners (Humphrey 1986).

16. In March 1985 the South Dakota legislature abrogated the dram shop liability created by *Walz*. See S.D. Comp. Laws Ann., sec. 35-4-78 (1985). The Wisconsin Supreme Court established dram shop liability in *Sorenson v. Jarvis*, Wis. 2d, 350 N.W.2d 108 (1984).

17. This is due, in great part, to the incredibly high turnover in bar personnel. See American Bartenders' Association, *Annual Report* (1984), Pp. 3–4 (turnover impossible to precisely ascertain, but is "undeniably large").

18. In civil cases, bartenders and waiters are not normally held to the level of an expert in intoxicated behavior. See *Coulter v. Superior Court*, 21 Cal. 3d 144, 577 P.2d 675, 145 Cal. Rptr. 534 (1978); *Kyle v. State*, 366 P.2d 961 (Okla. Crim. App. 1961). The customer must be drunk enough to raise the suspicion of a reasonable person of ordinary experience. See *State v. Morello*, 169 Ohio St. 213, 158 N.E.2d 525 (1959). Negligence suits based on violation of an alcohol beverage act may involve heightened standards of care, such as the

"reasonable bartender" or even the "reasonable bartender of like experience." See Prosser, *Law of Torts,* 4th ed. (1971), Pp. 161–166 (explaining higher standards of conduct).

19. The city of Boca Raton, Florida, for instance, has outlawed oversized drink glasses, such as those used in many establishments to serve margaritas. See Boca Raton, Fla. Ord. 35-23.5 (1985). Many of these glasses exceed thirty-two-ounce capacity and resemble fishbowls more than cocktail glasses.

20. A growing number of states have banned or strictly curtailed special liquor promotions; among them are Nebraska, New Jersey, Texas, Michigan, Ohio, Rhode Island, Arizona, and Oklahoma. See *Dram Shop & Alcohol Reporter* 3(2)[1985]: 1.

21. Russ and Geller (1987) report a fascinating field experiment to test the effectiveness of server intervention training. The subjects were seventeen waiters and waitresses at two local taverns; half received TIPS training and half did not. Student "pseudopatrons" were instructed to spend an evening in the bars, consuming beverages at a specified rate up to and beyond the point of intoxication. A sober (light-drinking) companion of the pseudopatron recorded the number of intervention efforts by the various waiters and waitresses. When the drinking pseudopatron left the bar, his or her BAC was tested. The TIPS-trained waiters and waitresses far exceeded the untrained waiters and waitresses in interventions, and those who were served by the former had BACs much lower than those of patrons served by the untrained waiters and waitresses; in fact, not one of the TIPS-served pseudopatrons had a BAC greater than 0.10. While this field experiment is nothing like a definitive evaluation, and while there are many reasons to doubt its realism, it is an important first effort to determine the efficacy of the server intervention programs; and its results are encouraging.

22. Such a proposal has been suggested to the Vermont legislature:

Under the proposed legislation, liquor sellers and providers would have to demonstrate proof of financial responsibility as follows:
1. A certificate that there is in effect for the period covered by the license an insurance policy or pool providing the following minimum coverages:
(a) $100,000 because of bodily injury to any one person in any one occurrence, and subject to the limit for one person, in the amount of $200,000 because of bodily injury for two or more persons in any one occurrence, and in the amount of $10,000 for injury to or destruction of property of others in any one occurrence.
(b) $100,000 for loss of means of support of any one person in any one occurrence, and, subject to the limit for one person, $200,000 for loss of means of support of two or more persons in any one occurrence; or BAC less than .15; "visibly intoxcated" would mean a state of intoxication accompanied by a perceptible act indicative of that intoxication.

23. See, for example, *Congini v. Petersville Valve Co.,* 470 A. 2d 515 (1983); *Brokett v. Kitchen Boyd Motor Co.,* 100 Cal. Rptr. 752 (1972); *Brattain v. Herron,* 309 N.E. 2d 150 (1974); *Thaut v. Finley,* 213 N.W. 2d 820 (1973).

24. In *Coulter v. Superior Court,* 21 Cal. 3d 144, 577 P.2d 675, 145 Cal. Rptr. 534 (1978), the California Supreme Court held that social hosts could be

liable for the drunk driving injuries of their guests. The California legislature soon reversed the court. See Cal. Bus. & Prof. Code Ann., sec. 25602(b)(c) (West Supp. 1979) (eliminating all dram shop liability for commercial sellers and social hosts).

25. The New Jersey legislature passed a bill that would limit a social host's liability to those situations in which the social host continued to serve alcohol to the guest even though the guest was "visibly intoxicated." Governor Kean did not sign the bill.

26. Comprehensive personal injury policies would certainly cover suits based on social host liability, absent express contractural language to the contrary. Such policies cover the insured's legal obligation to honor personal injury judgments. See 7A W. Berdal, Appelman on Insurance Law and Practice 4501.4 (Supp. 1983). Coverage under homeowner policies may be more problematic. Service of alcohol is not what is traditionally thought of as a condition of the premises. However, nonpremises interests are occasionally protected under homeowner contracts. Thus far, homeowner policies do not expressly cover social host liability, but this is probably due to the current rarity of the theory.

Chapter Eleven

1. But see Corpus Juris Secundum, sec. 146a. Driver's licenses are privileges regulated under the state legislature's police power. The license exists to protect public safety and to assure a sufficient level of driving competency.

2. Some states, however, do provide for hearings to determine whether drivers who have been involved in fatal accidents or who have been convicted of serious traffic offenses should retain their licenses. Such drivers may be required to take a safe-driving course and/or convince departmental personnel that they can drive safely.

3. Uniform Vehicle Code, sec. 6-103: "The Department shall not issue any license hereunder . . . to (4) any person, as an operator or chauffeur, who is an habitual drunkard, or who is an habitual user of narcotic drugs, or is an habitual user of any other drug to a degree which renders him incapable of safely driving a motor vehicle."

4. The federal government's National Driver Register (NDR) is a computerized system constituting a national data base on license revocations and suspensions. Unfortunately, the system has not lived up to its promise. Many states do not report revocations and suspensions to it, and requests for information are very episodic. For a description of NDR, see 23 C.F.R., sec. 1325.

5. The Uniform Vehicle Code, sec. 6-112, states that a person must carry his or her license at all times while operating a motor vehicle, *but* it is a defense if the person can later demonstrate to a court that he or she had a valid license.

6. In New York State, driving without a valid license is a misdemeanor punishable by up to one year jail term and a $1,000 fine.

7. CPLR, sec. 13-A, Forfeiture Actions: "A civil action may be commenced by the appropriate claiming authority against a criminal defendant to recover the property which constitutes the proceeds of a crime, the substituted proceeds

of a crime or *an instrumentality of a crime* or to recover a money judgment in an amount equivalent in value to the property which constitutes the proceeds of a crime, the substituted proceeds of a crime, or an instrumentality of a crime" (emphasis added). For discussion of New York forfeiture law, see *District Attorney of Queens County v. McAuliffe,* 493 N.Y.S. 2d 406 (1985).

8. Under traditional civil forfeiture law, the owner's innocence is not a defense. See *United States v. one Mercedes Benz 380 SEL,* 604 F. Supp. 1307 (S.D.N.Y. 1984), aff'd 762 F.2d 991 (1985). But civil forfeiture rules allow innocent third parties to petition the attorney general for return of their property. Under the Comprehensive Crime Control Act of 1984, the government cannot forfeit the property of someone who paid value for an asset and who was without reason to know that the asset was forfeitable. Congress evinced an intent to forfeit property that is transferred to third parties via "sham transactions"—but not to penalize innocent owners of forfeitable assets.

9. New York Vehicle and Traffic Law, sec. 318 (12a), provides for impoundment when a vehicle owner involved in an accident fails to demonstrate insurance or financial security.

10. If a defendant knows he may be facing a forfeiture or impoundment on conviction for DWI, he may transfer the vehicle to a third party or otherwise put it beyond the reach of the court. Therefore it is important either to seize the vehicle immediately on arrest or put in place mechanisms that prevent the vehicle from being sold, transferred, or hidden. The 1984 Comprehensive Crime Control Act allows a federal prosecutor to obtain an ex parte temporary restraining order freezing the defendant's assets under certain circumstances, and the courts are given broad power to freeze assets or to require adequate collateral.

11. During the mid 1960s, the Schwitzgebels (1964) outlined a system of electronic monitoring that would enable criminal justice and mental health personnel to monitor the location of parolees and mental patients. Nothing much came of the idea until 1983, when an electronic bracelet was invented and tested in New Mexico (Niederberger and Wagner 1985; Lilly, Ball, and Wright 1986).

12. Some states have "habitual traffic offender" laws, which punish the accumulation of serious traffic offenses with license revocation and a jail term. For example, Wisconsin Vehicle Code ch. 351 (Habitual Traffic Offenders) states: "Habitual traffic offender means any person, resident or non-resident whose record, as maintained by the department, shows that the person has accumulated the number of convictions for separate and distinct offenses . . . under parts 9(a) and (b) within a five year period. a. Four or more convictions [of serious offenses, including vehicular homicide and DUI]. b. Twelve or more convictions [for lesser moving violations]." The maximum punishment is only ninety days in jail. It is hard to see why "habitual traffic offender" statutes have not become more popular. When license forfeiture, rehabilitation, fines, brief jail terms, and home detention all have failed, a lengthy incarceration may not be undeserved—and may be the only effective means of incapacitation.

Chapter Twelve

1. Comptroller General, Report to the Congress of the United States, "The Drinking-Driver Problem—What Can Be Done About It?" (February 1979) P. i: "Society's general acceptance of drinking and driving is the main obstacle to solving the drinker-driving problem. Before any significant reduction in alcohol-related traffic accidents will occur, a long term continuous educational commitment must be made. Governments, educational institutions and the general public need to work together to change attitudes about drinking and driving."

2. Interestingly, mandatory seat belt laws backed up by the threat of small fines have had a positive effect on usage. This might be a good example of what Andenaes refers to as the use of the criminal law as a "moral eye opener." Once it became a crime not to wear a seat belt, many people had an excuse for doing what they wanted to do all along.

3. For example, Aetna Life and Casualty presented thirty-second commercials in support of SADD during the 1987 World Series.

4. MADD accepts funds from the beverage alcohol industry, but RID does not. This is a major difference of opinion within the anti–drunk driving movement. RID contends that in retaliation for its support of the movement to remove alcohol advertising from the air, radio and television stations refuse to donate or sell air time.

5. This may not always have been true. Every so often I see old movies in which drunk driving is portrayed humorously and even positively, as an aspect of good times and hard living.

6. During the mid-1980s the Washington-based Center for Science in the Public Interest, joined by many other national organizations and PTAs, led a drive to ban the advertising of beer and wine on television. The campaign, under the slogan SMART (Stop Merchandizing Alcohol on Radio and Television), obtained one million signatures on a petition that it presented to Congress. It is now campaigning to obtain equal time for antialcohol PSAs.

7. Indeed, the disease model of alcoholism has been criticized as unwittingly supplying alcohol abusers with just this excuse.

Chapter Thirteen

1. The report appeared in the August 23, 1985, issue of *Drinking/Driving Law Letter* (vol. 4, no. 17), P. 8.

2. The Cincinnati program claims that none of the 200 have been rearrested for DWI, while 17 of 693 controls recidivated.

3. But see medical historian Dr. David Musto's contrasting view in Sheron (1986), arguing that a new temperance movement is upon us.

4. "Death rates from cirrhosis were 29.5 per 100,000 in 1911 for men, and 10.7 in 1929; admissions to state mental hospital for disease classified as alcoholic psychosis fell from 10.1 in 1919, to 3.7 in 1922, rising to 4.7 by 1928. In two predominantly wet states, the decline in alcoholic psychosis was even more

dramatic. In New York, it fell from 11.5 in 1910, to 3.0 in 1920, to 6.5 in 1931, and in Massachusettes, from 14.6 in 1910, to 6.4 in 1922, to 7.7 in 1929" (Aaron and Musto 1981, P. 165). National records of arrest for drunkenness and disorderly conduct declined 50 percent between 1916 and 1922. Reports from welfare agencies around the country overwhelmingly indicated a dramatic decrease in alcohol-related family problems (Aaron and Musto 1981, P. 165).

5. It is noteworthy that the anti–drunk driving movement does not advocate a return to Prohibition, especially in light of society's inclination to prohibit so many other drugs, including heroin, cocaine, and marijuana. In fact, the citizen's anti–drunk driving groups are anxious to dispel suspicion that they are a temperance movement.

6. Any such effort would no doubt be compared with the crusade of the Anti-Saloon League, which was formed during the 1890s for the purpose of abolishing saloons (Lender and Martin 1982).

7. Some bars are purchasing this type of equipment on their own. The *New York Times* (December 29, 1985 [sec. I]) reports that regular customers at Belmont Park Inn, a bar in Elmont, New York, try to ignore a new machine that for a quarter will tell them if they are sober enough to drive home.

8. The *New York Times* (November 3, 1985 [sec. I]) reports that New York State's Division of Alcoholism and Alcohol Abuse has recommended that happy hours be barred, that alcoholic beverages be required to carry warning labels, and that a moratorium be imposed on new liquor licenses.

9. In December, 1984, Massachusettes became the first state in the nation to adopt a ban on virtually all bar and restaurant promotion gimmicks. The new regulation prohibits establishments from offering free drinks, two-for-ones, happy hours with reduced prices, drinks as contest prizes, drinking competitions, and even the sale of pitchers of beer to solitary drinkers. Violators can be fined up to $5,000 and lose their liquor license for thirty days. Apparently, bar owners applauded the law, saying that they had resorted to drink promotions only to remain competitive.

10. The most prominent of these studies, a multistate study conducted by the Insurance Institute of Highway Safety, showed that vehicular fatalities, especially those that are alcohol related, decreased (Williams et al. 1983). This study and a few others were cited again and again during the congressional debates over whether to make the minimum purchase age twenty-one-years.

11. 23 U.S.C., sec. 158 (Surface Transportation Assistance Act of 1984). The law provides a 5 percent reduction in highway funds if, after fiscal year 1987, the state does not make illegal all public possession or purchase of alcoholic beverages by a person less than twenty-one years of age. In fiscal year 1988 the penalty increases to 10 percent.

12. In her dissenting opinion, Justice Sandra Day O'Connor argued that while Congress has very wide latitude to legislate under the spending power, the conditions it sets must be reasonably related to the purposes of the programs it has chosen to fund. In her view, it is not reasonable to condition receipt of highway safety funds on a minimum drinking age.

When Congress appropriates money to build a highway, it is entitled to insist that the highway be a safe one. But it is not entitled to insist as a condition of the use of highway funds that the State impose or change regulations in other areas of the State's social and economic life because of an attenuated or tangential relationship to highway use or safety. Indeed, if the rule were otherwise, the Congress could effectively regulate almost any area of a State's social, political or economic life on the theory that use of the interstate transportation system is somehow enhanced.

13. "It is logically possible that alcoholic or problem drinkers could be relatively insensitive to alcohol prices in their consumption decisions, so that price-induced changes in aggregate consumption could result exclusively from a subset of drinkers who do not in any case cause or experience drinking problems. This logical possibility was examined and rejected for the Canadian province of Ontario, and similar findings, consistent [with the Ontario study] have been derived from other data series" (Moore and Gerstein 1981, P. 69).

Chapter Fourteen

1. Richard Schwartz's essay on "Rehabilitation" in the *Encyclopedia of Crime and Justice* states: "As used in the field of crime and justice, the word rehabilitation means the purposeful reduction or elimination of an offender's subsequent criminal behavior through a program of planned intervention" (P. 1364). The National Research Council's Panel on Research on Rehabilitative Techniques (see Sechrest, White, and Brown 1979, P. 20) has offered the following definition, which seems quite workable for purposes of this chapter: "Rehabilitation is the result of any planned intervention that reduces an offender's further criminal activity, whether that reduction is mediated by personality, behavior, abilities, attitudes, values, or other factors. The effects of maturation and the effects associated with fear or intimidation are excluded, the result of the latter having traditionally been labeled as specific deterrence."

2. The most recent edition of *Diagnostic and Statistical Manual* (American Psychiatric Association 1980) distinguishes between alcohol abuse and alcohol dependence. Diagnostic criteria for alcohol abuse include drinking non-beverage alcohol, going on binges (remaining intoxicated throughout the day for at least two days), occasionally drinking a fifth of spirits (or its equivalent in wine or beer), and having had two or more blackouts, as well as impaired social or occupational functioning, due to alcohol. In addition, problems must have existed for a month or more. The diagnostic criteria for alcohol dependence, traditionally referred to as alcoholism, include the criteria for alcohol abuse and two additional criteria: tolerance and withdrawal. Tolerance is defined as "the need for markedly increased amounts of alcohol to achieve the desired effect, or diminished effect with regular use of the [same] amount. 'Withdrawal' includes morning shakes and malaise relieved by drinking."

3. "The most compelling empirical evidence against the existence of a sharp distinction between alcohol use and the disorder, alcoholism, has been Cahalan's (*Problem Drinkers: A National Survey,* [San Francisco: Josey Bass, 1970]) study of a national panel of alcohol users, which suggests that drinkers

cannot be divided into social drinkers and alcoholics, but that the categories of alcohol users and alcohol abusers merge with each other depending upon one's definition of abuse. Alcohol abuse is not black and white; it is gray" (Vaillant 1983, P. 4).

4. The National Research Council's Panel on Research on Rehabilitative Techniques (Sechrest, White, and Brown 1979) concluded that "Martinson and his associates were essentially correct. There is no body of evidence for any treatment or intervention with criminal offenders that can be relied upon to produce a decrease in recidivism. Where there are suggestions of efficacy, they are just that—suggestions. They prove to be elusive, not replicable, not quite statistically significant, working now only with one group, then only with another. The Panel does not believe that it would be possible on the basis of the literature available to Martinson . . . to put together an intervention that could be counted on to reduce recidivism rates in any group of offenders."

Bibliography

Aaron, Paul, and David Musto. 1981. "Temperance and Prohibition in America: A Historical Overview." In *Alcohol and Public Policy: Beyond the Shadow of Prohibition*, edited by Mark H. Moore and Dean R. Gerstein. Washington, D.C.: National Academy Press.

Albonetti, Celesta A. 1987. "Prosecutional Discretion: The Effects of Uncertainty." *Law and Society Review* 71(2): 291–314.

"Alcohol Abuse and the Law." Note. 1981. *Harvard Law Review* 94:1660–1712.

All-Industry Research Advisory Council. 1981. *State Motor Vehicle Records as a Source of Driver Performance Information*. Oak Brook, Ill.: All-Industry Research Advisory Council.

———. 1985. *A Survey of Public Attitudes toward the Civil Justice System, Trends in Personal Injury Suits, Drunk Driving, Automobile Crash Protection, and Other Insurance Topics*. Mimeographed. Oak Brook, Ill.: All-Industry Research Advisory Council.

American Law Institute. 1960. *Model Penal Code and Commentaries*. Draft 10. Philadelphia: American Law Institute.

———. 1979. *Restatement (Second) of Torts*. Philadelphia: American Law Institute.

American Law Reports (ALR) 3d ed. 1968. "Homicide by Automobile as Murder." 21:116–163. Rochester, N.Y.: The Lawyers Cooperative Publishing Co.

American Medical Association Committee on Medico-Legal Problems. [1970] 1976. *Alcohol and the Impaired Driver: A Manual on the Medico-Legal Aspects of Chemical Tests for Intoxication with Supplement on Breath/Alcohol Tests*. Chicago: National Safety Council.

American Psychiatric Association. 1980. *Diagnostic and Statistical Manual of Mental Disorders*. 3d ed. Washington, D.C.: American Psychiatric Association.

"An Analysis of Drunken Driving Statutes in the United States." Note. 1955. *Vanderbilt Law Review* 8:888–896.

Andenaes, Johannes. 1984. "Drinking-and-Driving Laws in Scandinavia." *Journal of Scandinavian Studies in the Law*, pp. 13–23.

———. 1988. "The Scandinavian Experience." Pp. 43–63 in *Social Control of the Drinking Driver,* edited by Michael Laurence, John Snortum, and Franklin Zimring. Chicago: University of Chicago Press.

Atkin, Charles, and Martin Block. 1980. *Content and Effect of Alcoholic Beverage Advertising.* East Lansing: Michigan State University. Prepared for the Bureau of Alcohol, Tobacco and Firearms, Federal Trade Commission, Department of Transportation, and NIAAA.

————. 1981. *Contents and Effects of Alcohol Advertising.* NTIS PB82-123142. Washington, D.C.: Bureau of Alcohol, Tobacco and Firearms.

A.T.O., Inc. 1980. *The Figgie Report on Fear of Crime: America Afraid.* Willoughby, Ohio: A.T.O.

Ball, Richard A., and J. Robert Lilly. 1986. "The Potential Use of Home Incarceration for Drunken Drivers." *Crime and Delinquency* 32(2): 224–247.

Barrow, Roscoe. 1975. "The Fairness Doctrine: A Double Standard for Electronic and Print Media." *Hastings Law Journal* 26:659–708.

Beauchamp, D. E. 1980. *Beyond Alcoholism: Alcohol and Public Health Review.* Philadelphia: Temple University Press.

Beitel, G., M. Sharp, and W. Glauz. 1975. "Probability of Arrest While Driving under the Influence of Alcohol." *Journal of Studies on Alcohol* 36:237–256.

Beitman, Ronald S., ed. *Dram Shop and Alcohol Reporter.* Falmouth, Mass.: Seak.

Beyer, Janice M., and Harrison M. Trice. 1978. *Implementing Change: Alcoholism Policies in Work Organizations.* New York: Free Press.

Blane, Howard T., and Linda E. Hewitt. 1977. "Mass Media, Public Education and Alcohol: A State-of-the-Art Review." Final Report. Washington, D.C.: National Institute on Alcohol Abuse and Alcoholism.

Blum, Walter, and Harry Kalven. 1965. *Public Law Perspectives on a Private Law Problem—Auto Compensation Plans.* Boston: Little, Brown.

Blumstein, Alfred, Jacqueline Cohen, and Daniel Nagin, eds. 1978. *Deterrence and Incapacitation: Estimating the Effects of Criminal Sanctions on Crime Rates.* Washington, D.C.: National Academy of Sciences.

Blumstein, Alfred, Jacqueline Cohen, Jeffrey Roth, and Christy Visher, eds. 1986. *Criminal Careers and Career Criminals.* 2 vols. Washington, D.C.: National Academy Press.

Bonnie, Richard J. 1985. "Regulating Conditions of Alcohol Availability: Possible Effects on Highway Safety." *Journal of Studies on Alcohol,* suppl. 10:129–143.

Borkenstein, Robert F. 1960. "The Evolution of Modern Instruments of Breath Alcohol Analysis." *Journal of Forensic Sciences* 5:395–444.

————. 1985. "Historical Perspective: North American Traditional and Experimental Response." *Journal of Studies on Alcohol,* suppl. 10:3–12.

Borkenstein, Robert F., R. F. Crowther, R. P. Shumate, W. P. Ziel, and R. Zylman. [1964] 1974. "The Role of the Drinking Driver in Traffic Accidents (the Grand Rapids Study)." In *Blutalkohol: Alcohol, Drugs, and Behavior.* Vol. 11, suppl. 1. 2d ed. Hamburg: Steintor.

Brown, Peggy, Paul Zelhart, and Bryce Schurr. 1975. "Evaluating the Effectiveness of Reduction Programs for Convicting Impaired Drivers." Pp. 749–763 in *Alcohol, Drugs, and Traffic Safety,* edited by S. Israelstam and S. Lambert. Toronto: Alcoholism and Drug Addiction Research Foundation of Ontario.

Bulduc, Ann. 1985. "Jail Crowding." *Annals of the American Academy of Political and Social Science* 478:47–57.

Burrell, Robert B., and Mark S. Young. 1978. "Insurability of Punitive Damages." *Marquette Law Review* 62:1–33.

Cahalan, Don, Ira H. Cisin, and Helen Crossley. *American Drinking Practices.* New Brunswick, N.J.: Rutgers University Center for Alcohol Studies.

Calabresi, Guido. 1970. *Costs of Accidents: Legal and Economic Analysis.* New Haven: Yale University Press.

Cameron, Tracy. 1979. "The Impact of Drinking-Driving Countermeasures: A Review and Evaluation." *Contemporary Drug Problems* 8:495–566

Campbell, D., and J. Stanley. 1963. *Experimental and Quasi-Experimental Designs for Research* Chicago: Rand McNally.

Carpenter, R. 1962. "The Effects of Alcohol on Some Psychological Processes: A Critical Review with Special References to Automobile Driving Skill." *Quarterly Journal of Studies on Alcohol* 23:274–281.

Casale, Silvia, and Sally Hillsman. 1985. *The Enforcement of Fines as Criminal Sanctions: The English Experience and Its Relevance to American Practice.* Unpubl. review draft. Available from author.

Clark, N. H. 1976. *Deliver Us from Evil: An Interpretation of American Prohibition.* New York: Norton.

Cohen, Jacqueline. 1983. "Incapacitation as a Strategy for Crime Control: Possibilities and Pitfalls." Pp. 1–84 in *Crime and Justice: An Annual Review of Research,* vol. 5, edited by Michael Tonry and Norval Morris. Chicago: University of Chicago Press.

Collins, J. J., Jr., ed. 1981. *Drinking and Crime: Perspectives on the Relationship between Alcohol Consumption and Criminal Behavior.* New York: Guilford.

Colon, I. 1981. "Alcohol Availability on Cirrhosis Mortality Rates by Gender and Race." *American Journal of Public Health* 71:1325–1328.

Comptroller General. 1979. Report to the Congress of the United States. *The Drinking-Driver Problem: What Can Be Done about it?* Washington, D.C.: Government Printing Office.

Connecticut Governor's Task Force on Driving While Intoxicated. November 1983. *Report to the Governor, State of Connecticut, William A. O'Neill.*

Cook, Phillip. 1980. "Research in Criminal Deterrence: Laying the Groundwork for the Second Decade." In *Crime and Justice: An Annual Review of Research,* vol. 2, edited by Norval Morris and Michael Tonry. Chicago: University of Chicago Press.

———. 1981. "The Effect of Liquor Taxes on Drinking, Cirrhosis, and Auto Accidents." In *Alcohol and Public Policy: Beyond the Shadow of Prohibi-*

tion, edited by Mark Moore and Dean Gerstein. Washington, D.C.: National Academy Press.

Cook, Phillip, and G. Tauchen. 1982. "The Effect of Liquor Taxes on Heavy Drinking." *Bell Journal of Economics* 13(a): 379–390.

————. 1984. "The Effect of Minimum Drinking Age Legislation on Youthful Auto Fatalities: 1971–1977. *Journal of Legal Studies* 13:169–190.

Cramton, Roger. 1969. "Driver Behavior and Legal Sanctions: A Study of Deterrence." *Michigan Law and Review* 67, pt. 1:421–454.

Cressey, Donald. 1974. "Law, Order, and the Motorist." In *Crime, Criminology, and Public Policy,* edited by R. Hood. London: Heinemann.

Crime Control Institute. 1986. *Drunk Driving Tests in Fatal Accidents.* Washington, D.C.: Crime Control Institute.

"Curbing the Drunk Driver under the Fourth Amendment: The Constitutionality of Roadblock Seizures." Note. 1983. *Georgetown Law Journal* 71:1457–1486.

Dillon, J. *Christian Science Monitor,* June 30 and July 1, 2, 11, 1975.

DiMaio, V. J. M., and J. C. Garriott. March 1985. "How Valid Is the 0.10 Percent Alcohol Level as an Indicator of Intoxication?" *Pathologist,* pp. 31–33.

Distilled Spirits Council of the United States (DISCUS). 1975. *If You Choose to Drink, Drink Responsibly.* Washington, D.C.: DISCUS.

Dix, M. C., and A. D. Layzell. 1983. *Road Users and the Police.* London: Police Foundation.

Dooley, D., and J. F. Mosher. 1978. "Alcohol and Legal Negligence." *Contemporary Drug Problems* 7:145–179.

Douglas, Richard L. 1979–1980. "The Legal Drinking Age and Traffic Casualties: A Special Case of Changing Alcohol Availability in Public Health Context." *Alcohol Health and Research World* 4(2): 101–117.

Douglas, R. L., L. D. Filkins, and F. A. Clark. 1982. *The Effect of Lower Legal Drinking Age on Youth Crash Involvement.* Ann Arbor, Mich.: University of Michigan, Highway Safety Research Institute.

Douthwaite, Graham. 1981. *Jury Instructions on Damages in Tort Actions.* Indianapolis, Ind.: A. Smith Co.

Dowie, Mark. 1985. "Pinto Madness: How the Ford Motor Company Built a Car That Could Burst into Flames on Impact." In *Crisis in American Institutions,* 6th ed., edited by Jerome Skolnick and Elliot Currie. New York: Little, Brown.

Dowling, Noel T. 1932. "Compensation for Automobile Accidents: A Symposium." *Columbia Law Review* 32:785–824.

"Driving While Intoxicated and the Right to Counsel: The Case against Implied Consent." Note. 1980. *Texas Law Review* 58:935–960.

Dunham, Roger G., and A. L. Mauss. 1982. "Reluctant Referrals: The Effectiveness of Legal Coercion in Outpatient Treatment for Problem Drinkers." *Journal of Drug Issues* 12:4–20.

Durkheim, Emile. 1947. *The Division of Labor in Society,* translated by George Simpson. New York: Free Press.

Eastman, Joel. 1984. *Styling vs. Safety: The American Automotive Industry and the Development of Automotive Safety, 1900–1966.* New York: University Press of America.

Economos, James P., and David C. Steelman. 1983. *Traffic Court Procedure and Administration.* Chicago: American Bar Association Committee on the Traffic Court Program.

Ehrenzweig, Albert A. 1955. "Full Aid Coverage for the Traffic Victim." *California Law Review* 43:1–48.

Ehrlich, N. J., and M. L. Selzer. 1967. "A Screening Procedure to Detect Alcoholism." In *Traffic Offenders in the Prevention of Highway Injury,* edited by M. L. Selzer, P. W. Gikas, and F. F. Hueke. Ann Arbor, Mich.: University of Michigan, Highway Safety Research Institute.

Ellingstad, Vernon S., and T. J. Springer. 1976. *Program Level Evaluation of ASAP Diagnosis Referral and Rehabilitation Efforts.* Vol. 3. *Analysis of ASAP Rehabilitation Countermeasures Effectiveness.* NHSTA contract DOT-H5-191-3-759. Vermillion, S.D.: University of South Dakota, Human Factors Laboratory.

"Employer Liability for Drunken Employees' Actions Following an Office Party: A Cause of Action under Respondeat Superior." Comment. 1982. *California West Law Review* 19:107–140.

Ennis, J. 1977. "General Deterrence and Police Enforcement: Effective Countermeasures against Drinking and Driving." *Journal of Safety Research* 9:15–25.

Enno Foundation for Highway Traffic Control. 1949. *The Motor-Vehicle Driver: His Nature and Improvement.* Saugatuck, Conn.: Enno Foundation.

Epstein, Richard. 1980. "Is Pinto a Criminal?" *Regulation: AEI Journal on Government and Society* 4:15–21.

Evans, Richard. 1987. "3-Year Target For Random Breath Tests." *New York Times,* August 24.

Fagen, R. W., and N. M. Fagen. 1982. "Impact of Legal Coercion on the Treatment of Alcoholism." *Journal of Drug Issues* 12(1): 103–114.

"Fallacy and Fortuity of Motor Vehicle Homicide." Comment. 1962. *Nebraska Law Review* 41:793–815.

Farmer, P. J. 1975. "The Edmonton Study: A Pilot Project to Demonstrate the Effectiveness of a Public Information Campaign on the Subject of Drinking and Driving." In *Alcohol and Highway Safety,* edited by S. Israelstam and S. Lambert. Toronto: Alcoholism and Drug Addiction Research Foundation of Ontario.

Farris, R., T. B. Malone, and H. Lilliefors. 1976. *A Comparison of Alcohol Involvement in Exposed and Injured Drivers: Phases I and II.* NHTSA Tech. Rep. DOT-HS-801-826. Washington, D.C.: National Highway Traffic Safety Administration.

Federal Bureau of Investigation. 1983. *Uniform Crime Reports: Crime in the United States.* Washington, D.C.: Department of Justice.

——. 1985. *Uniform Crime Reports: Crime in the United States.* Washington, D.C.: Department of Justice.

Federal Trade Commission. 1970. Report to the Department of Transportation: *Price Variability in the Automobile Insurance Market*. Washington, D.C.: Government Printing Office.

Federal Trade Commission, Bureau of Economics. 1979. *Staff Report on Consumer Responses to Cigarette Health Information*. Washington, D.C.: Government Printing Office.

Fee, D. 1975. "Drunk Driving: Outline of a Public Information and Education Program." Pp. 789–798 in *Alcohol and Highway Safety*, edited by S. Israelstam and S. Lambert. Toronto: Alcoholism and Drug Addiction Research Foundation of Ontario.

Feeley, Malcolm M. 1983. *Court Reform on Trial: Why Simple Answers Fail*. New York: Basic Books.

Fell, James C. 1983. "Tracking the Alcohol Involvement Problem in U.S. Highway Crashes." Paper presented at the Twenty-seventh Annual Proceedings, American Association of Automobile Medicine, San Antonio, Texas, October 3–6.

Ferreira, J. 1970. *Quantitative Models for Automobile Accidents and Insurance*. Washington, D.C.: Department of Transportation.

Fileding, J. E. 1977. "Health Promotions: Some Notions in Search of a Constituency." *American Journal of Public Health* 67:1082–1086.

Filkins, L. D., C. D. Clark, C. A. Rosenblatt, W. L. Carlson, M. W. Kerlan, and H. Manson. 1970. *Alcohol Abuse and Traffic Safety: A Study of Fatalities, DWI Fatalities, DWI Offenders and Alcoholics and Court-related Treatment Approaches*. Prepared for U.S. Department of Transportation, Publ. FH-11-6555 and FH-11-7129. Ann Arbor: University of Michigan, Highway Safety Research Institute.

Finklestein, R., and J. McGuire. 1971. *An Optimum System for Traffic Enforcement and Control*. Mountainview, Calif.: GTE Sylvania.

Fitzpatrick, James F., Michael N. Sohn, Thomas E. Silfen, and Robert H. Wood. 1974. *The Law and Roadside Hazards*. Charlottesville, Va: Michie Co.

Flanagan, N. G. 1983. "Effects of Low Doses of Alcohol on Driving Performance." *Medical Science Law* 23:203–208.

Fletcher, George. 1978. *Rethinking Criminal Law*. Boston: Little, Brown.

Flink, James J. 1975. *The Car Culture*. Boston: MIT Press.

Force, Robert. 1979. "The Inadequacy of Drinking Driving Laws: A Lawyer's View." In *Proceedings of the Seventh International Conference on Alcohol, Drugs and Traffic Safety*. Canberra: Australian Government Publishing Service.

Ford, A. B., N. B. Rushforth, N. Rushforth, C. S. Hirsch, and L. Adelson. 1979. "Violent Death in a Metropolitan County. II. Changing Patterns of Suicides (1959–1974)." *American Journal of Public Health* 69(5):459–464.

Freimuth, H. C., S. R. Watts, and R. S. Fisher. 1958. "Alcohol and Highway Fatalities." *Journal of Forensic Science* 3:66–71.

Gallup, George. 1977. *Four in Ten Drive after Boozing*. Princeton, N.J.: Gallup Poll.

————. 1982. *Alcohol Abuse: A Problem in One of Three American Families.* Princeton, N.J.: Gallup Poll.

Gardiner, John. 1969. *Traffic and the Police: Variations in Law Enforcement Policy.* Boston: Harvard University Press.

Gerstein, Dean. 1981. "Alcohol Use and Its Consequences." In *Alcohol and Public Policy: Beyond the Shadow of Prohibition,* edited by Mark Moore and Dean Gerstein. Washington, D.C.: National Academy Press.

Goldstein, Herman. 1985. *Early Impressions of the Impact of Increased Sanctions on the Arrest, Prosecution, Adjudication, and Sentencing of Drinking Drivers in Madison, Wisconsin.* Madison: University of Wisconsin School of Law.

Goldstein, Herman, and C. Susmilch. 1982. *The Drinking Driver in Madison: A Study of the Problem and the Community's Response.* Madison: University of Wisconsin School of Law.

Graham, Kathy T. 1979. "Liability of the Social Host for Injuries Caused by the Negligent Acts of Intoxicated Guests." *Willamette Law Journal* 16:561–589.

Grass, Jeffrey. 1984. "Drunk Driving Murder and *People v. Watson:* Can Malice Be Implied?" *Southwestern Law Review* 14:477–520.

Greenwood, Peter, and Allan Abrahamse. 1982. *Selective Incapacitation.* Report to the National Institute of Justice. Santa Monica, Calif.: Rand Corporation.

Grey Advertising, Inc. 1975a. *Communications Strategies on Alcohol and Highway Safety.* Vol. 1. *Adults 18–55.* U.S. Department of Transportation publ. DOT-HS-801-400. Springfield, Va.: U.S. National Technical Information Service.

————. 1975b. *Communications Strategies on Alcohol and Highway Safety.* Vol. 2. *High School Youth: Final Report.* U.S. Department of Transportation publ. DOT-HS-801-400. Springfield, Va.: U.S. National Technical Information Service.

Gusfield, Joseph. 1963. *Symbolic Crusade: Status Politics and the American Temperance Movement.* Urbana: University of Illinois Press.

————. 1981. *The Culture of Public Problems: Drinking-Driving and the Symbolic Order.* Chicago: University of Chicago Press.

Gusfield, Joseph, P. Rasmussen, and J. Kotarba. 1984. "The Social Control of Drinking-Driving: An Ethnographic Study of Bar Settings." *Law and Policy* 6:45–66.

Haberman, P. W., and M. M. Baden. 1978. *Alcohol, Other Drugs, and Violent Death.* New York: Oxford University Press.

Hacker, George, and Michael Jacobson. 1986. "Raising the Cost of Drinking: Higher Taxes Save Lives and Cut Abuse." *New York Times,* May 25.

Haddon, William, Jr. 1981. *Policy Options for Reducing the Motor Vehicle Injury Cost Burden.* Washington, D.C.: Insurance Institute for Highway Safety.

Haddon, William, Jr., Edward Suchman, and David Klein. 1964. *Accident Research: Methods and Approaches.* New York: Harper & Row.

Haddon, William, Jr., P. Valion, J. R. McCarroll, and C. J. Umberger. 1961. "A Controlled Investigation of the Characteristics of Adult Pedestrians Fatally Injured by Motor Vehicles in Manhattan." *Journal of Chronic Diseases* 14:555–578.

Haight, Frank. 1985. "Current Problems in Drinking Driving: Research and Intervention." *Journal of Studies on Alcohol*, suppl. 10.

Halberstam, David. 1986. *The Reckoning: The Challenge to America's Greatness*. New York: Morrow.

Hall, Jerome. 1944. "Intoxication and Criminal Responsibility." *Harvard Law Review* 57:1045–1084.

Hamilton, C. J., and J. J. Collins. 1981. "The Role of Alcohol in Wife Beating and Child Abuse: A Review of the Literature." Pp. 70–109 in *Drinking and Crime: Perspectives on the Relationship between Alcohol Consumption and Criminal Behavior*, edited by J. J. Collins, Jr. New York: Guilford.

Harford, Thomas C., Douglas A. Parker, Charles Paulter, and Michael Wolz. 1979. "Relationship between the Number of On-Premise Outlets and Alcoholism." *Journal of Studies on Alcohol* 110(11): 1053–1057.

Harrington, D. M. 1972. "The Young Driver Follow-up Study: An Evaluation of the Role of Human Factors in the First Four Years of Driving." *Accident Analysis and Prevention* 4:191–240.

Hart, H. L. A. 1968. *Punishment and Responsibility*. New York: Oxford University Press.

Haskins, J. B. 1969. "Effects of Safety Communication Campaigns: A Review of Research Evidence." *Journal of Safety Research* 1:58–66.

Hedlund, J., R. Arnold, E. Cerrilli, S. Partyka, P. Hoxie, and D. Skinner. 1983. *An Assessment of the 1982 Traffic Fatality Decrease*. Staff Report. Washington, D.C.: National Highway Traffic Safety Administration.

Heeren, T., A. R. Williams, A. Smith, S. Morelock, and R. W. Hingson. 1985. "Surrogate Measures of Alcohol Involvement in Fatal Crashes: Are Conventional Indicators Adequate?" *Journal of Safety Research* 16(3): 127–134.

Henderson, Roger C. 1977. "No Fault Plans for Automobile Accidents." *Oregon Law Review* 56:287–329.

Henk, William A., Norman Stahl, and James R. King. 1984. "The Readability of State Drivers' Manuals." *Transportation Quarterly* 38:507–520.

Highway and Vehicle Safety Report. March 17, 1986. 12(13): 5.

Hingson, Ralph. 1987. "Effects of Maine's 1981 and Massachusetts' 1982 Driving-under-the-Influence Legislation." *American Journal of Public Health* 77(5): 593–597.

Hlstala, Michael. 1985. "Physiological Errors Associated with Alcohol Breath Testing." *Champion* 9(6): 15–19, 39.

Hochheimer, John. 1981. "Reducing Alcohol Abuse: A Critical Review of Educational Strategies." Pp. 286–335 in *Alcohol and Public Policy: Beyond the Shadow of Prohibition*, edited by Mark H. Moore and Dean R. Gerstein. Washington, D.C.: National Academy Press.

Holcomb, R. L. 1938. "Alcohol in Relation to Traffic Accidents." *Journal of the American Medical Association* 3:1076–1085.

Holden, Robert T. 1983. "Rehabilitative Sanctions for Drunk Driving: An Experimental Evaluation." *Journal of Research in Crime and Delinquency* 20:55–72.

Hubbard, J. C., M. L. DeFleur, and L. B. DeFleur. 1975. "Mass Media Influences on Public Conceptions of Social Problems." *Social Problems* 23:22–34.

Humphrey, Tom. 1986. "Tennessee Sharply Cuts 'Dram Shop' Liability." *National Law Journal* 8(19): 3.

Hunvald, Edward H., Jr., and Franklin Zimring. 1968. "Whatever Happened to Implied Consent?: A Sounding." *Missouri Law Review* 33:323–399.

Hurst, P. M. 1973. "Epidemiological Aspects of Alcohol in Driver Crashes and Citations." *Journal of Safety Research* 5:130–148.

Hyman, Merton H., Marilyn A. Zimmerman, Carol Gurioli, and Alice Helrich. 1980. *Drinkers, Drinking and Alcohol-related Mortality and Hospitalizations: A Statistical Compendium.* New Brunswick, N.J.: Rutgers University Center for Alcohol Studies.

"Insurance Coverage of Punitive Damages." Note. 1980. *Dickinson Law Review* 84:221–240.

Insurance Information Institute. 1984. *Fact Sheet.* New York: Insurance Information Institute.

Insurance Institute for Highway Safety. 1981. "Promoting Belt Use: Lessons from the Past." *Highway Loss Reduction Status Report* 16(9): 1–3.

————. 1982. *The Year's Work 1981–1982.* Washington, D.C.: Insurance Institute for Highway Safety.

————. 1987a. "The Public Prefers Air Bags." *Status Report* 22(1): 1–6.

————. 1987b. *Teenage Drivers.* 2d ed. Washington, D.C.: Insurance Institute for Highway Safety.

"Insurance for Punitive Damages: A Reevaluation." Note. 1976. *Hastings Law Journal* 28:431–475.

Jacobs, James B. 1988. "The Impact of Insurance and Civil Law Sanctions on Drunk Driving." In *The Social Control of the Drinking Driver,* edited by Michael Laurence, John Snortum, and Franklin Zimring. Chicago: University of Chicago Press.

Jacobs, James B., and Nadine Strossen. 1985. "Mass Investigations without Individualized Suspicion: A Constitutional and Policy Critique of Drunk Driving Roadblocks." *U.C. Davis Law Review* 18:595–680.

Jacobson, Michael, Robert Atkins, and George Hacker. 1983. *The Booze Merchants: The Inebriating of America.* Washington, D.C.: Center for Science in the Public Interest.

Janowitz, Morris. 1976. "Military Service and Citizenship in Western Societies." *Armed Forces and Society* 2:185–204.

Jellinek, E. M. 1960. *The Disease Concept of Alcoholism.* New Haven: College and University Press.

Jerome, John. 1972. *The Death of the Automobile: The Fatal Effects of the Golden Era, 1955–1970.* New York: Norton.

Johnson, Daniel E. 1962. "Drunken Driving: The Civil Responsibility of the Purveyor of Intoxicating Liquor." *Indiana Law Journal* 37:317–333.

Johnson, P., P. Levy, and R. Voas. 1976. "A Critique of the Paper 'Statistical Evaluation of the Effectiveness of Alcohol Safety Action Projects.'" *Accident Analysis and Prevention* 8:67–77.

Johnson, Delmas M. 1984. Classification and Estimation of Alcohol Involvement in Fatalities." *Traffic Safety Evaluation Research Review* 3(3):23–33.

Johnston, L. D., P. M. O'Malley, and J. G. Bachman. 1985. *Drugs by America's High School Students, 1975–1984.* DHHS publ. (ADM) 85-1394.

Jones, A. W. 1978. "Variability of the Blood: Breath Alcohol Ratio in Viva." *Journal of Studies on Alcohol* 39(11): 1931–1939.

Jones, R., and K. Joscelyn. 1979. *Alcohol and Highway Safety: A Review of the State of Knowledge.* Tech. Rep. DOT-HS-803-714. Washington, D.C.: National Highway Traffic Safety Administration.

Kalven, Harry, and Hans Zeisel. 1966. *The American Jury.* New York: Little, Brown.

Karaba, Frank A. 1951. "Negligent Homicide or Manslaughter: A Dilemma." *Journal of Criminal Law, Criminology and Police Science* 41:183–189.

Keenan, Alexander. 1973. "Liquor Law Liability in California." *Santa Clara Law Review* 14:46–81.

Keeton, Robert E. 1971. *Basic Text On Insurance Law.* St. Paul: West Publishing Co.

Keeton, Robert and Jeffrey O'Connell. 1965. *Basic Protection for the Traffic Victim: A Blueprint for Reforming Automobile Insurance.* Boston: Little, Brown.

Keeton, W. Page., Dan B. Dobbs, Robert E. Keeton, and David G. Owen. 1984. *Prosser and Keeton on the Law of Torts.* 5th ed. Minneapolis: West Publishing Company.

Kelly, Michael A., and John A. Tarantino. 1983. "Radio Frequency Interference and the Breathalyzer: A Case Analysis." *Rhode Island Bar Journal* 31:6–8.

King, J., and M. Tipperman. 1975. "Offense of Driving While Intoxicated: The Development of Statutes and Case Law in New York." *Hofstra Law Review* 3:541–604.

Kobler, J. 1973. *Ardent Spirits: The Rise and Fall of Prohibition.* New York: Putnam's.

Kohn, P. M., and R. G. Smart. 1984 "The Impact of Television Advertising on Alcohol Consumption: An Experiment." *Journal of Studies on Alcohol* 45:295–301.

Kornhauser, Lewis A. 1985. "Review: Theory and Fact in the Law of Accidents." *California Law Review* 73:1024–1042.

LaFave, Wayne R. 1987. *Search and Seizure: A Treatise on the Fourth Amendment.* 2d ed. St. Paul: West Publishing Co.

LaFave, Wayne R., and Jerome Israel. 1985. *Criminal Procedure.* St. Paul: West Publishing Co.

LaFave, Wayne R., and Austin W. Scott, Jr. 1985. *Handbook on Criminal Law.* St. Paul: West Publishing Co.

Laurence, Michael, John Snortum, and Franklin Zimring. 1988. *Social Control of the Drinking Driver.* Chicago: University of Chicago Press.

Lazersfeld, Paul, B. Berelson, and H. Gaudet. 1948. *The People's Choice.* 2d ed. New York: Duell, Sloan & Pearce.

Lender, Mark E., and James K. Martin. 1982. *Drinking in America: A History.* New York: Free Press.

Lerblance, Penn. 1978. "Implied Consent to Intoxication Tests: A Flawed Concept." *St. Johns Law Review* 53:39–64.

Levine, Harry G. 1978. "The Discovery of Addiction: Changing Conceptions of Habitual Drunkenness in America." *Journal of Studies on Alcohol* 39(1): 143–177.

Levy, Paul, Robert Voas, Penelope Johnson, and Terry M. Klein. 1978. "An Evaluation of the Department of Transportation's Alcohol Safety Action Projects." *Journal of Safety Research* 10(4): 162–176.

Lewis, David, and Lawrence Goldstein. 1983. *The Automobile and American Culture.* Ann Arbor: University of Michigan Press.

Lilly, J. Robert, Richard A. Bell, and Jennifer Wright. 1986. "Home Incarceration with Electronic Monitoring in Kenton County Kentucky: An Evaluation." Unpublished report.

"Liquor Advertising: Resolving the Clash between the First and Twenty-first Amendments." Note. 1984. *New York University Law Review* 59(1): 157–186.

Little, Joseph. 1973. "An Empirical Description of Administration of Justice in Drunk Driving Cases." *Law and Society Review* 7:473–496.

Long, Rowland H. 1976. *The Law of Liability Insurance.* New York: Mathew Bender.

McClelland, David, William N. Davis, Rudolph Kalin, and Eric Wanner. 1972. *The Drinking Man.* New York: Free Press.

Maccoby, N., J. W. Farquhar, P. D. Wood, and J. Alexander. 1977. "Reducing the Risk of Cardiovascular Disease: Effects of a Community Based Campaign on Knowledge and Behavior." *Journal of Community Health* 3:100–114.

McDonald, Douglas C. 1986. *Punishment without Walls: Community Service Sentencing in New York City.* New Brunswick, N.J.: Rutgers University Press.

McEwen, W. J., and C. J. Hanneman. 1974. "The Depiction of Drug Use in Television Programming." *Journal of Drug Education* 4(3): 281–293.

McFarland, R. A., and R. C. Moore. 1957. "Human Factors in Highway Safety: A Review and Evaluation." (Three-part article.) *New England Journal of Medicine* 256: 792–799, 837–845, 890–897.

McGuinness, T. 1979. *An Econometric Analysis of Total Demand for Alcoholic Beverages in the U.K., 1956–1975.* Edinburgh: Scottish Health Education Unit.

McNeely, Mary, C. 1941. "Illegality as a Factor in Liability Insurance." *Columbia Law Review* 41:26–60.

Males, Mike. 1986. "The Minimum Purchase Age for Alcohol and Young-Driver Fatal Crashes: A Long-Term View." *Journal of Legal Studies* 15:181–211.

Malin, H., J. Coakley, C. Koelber, N. Murrch, and W. Holland. 1982. "An Epidemiological Perspective on Alcohol Use and Abuse in the United States." In *Alcohol and Health: Alcohol Consumption and Related Problems.* Monograph 1. Washington, D.C.: Department of Health and Human Services.

Mancke, John. 1981. "Homicide by Vehicle in Pennsylvania." *Dickinson Law Review* 85:180–190.

Marco, Corey, and Joni Michel Marco. 1980. "Antabuse: Medication in Exchange For a Limited Freedom—Is It Legal?" *American Journal of Law and Medicine* 5:295–330.

Massachusetts Department of Public Health. 1984. "An Evaluation of Drunk Driving in Massachusetts under Chapter 373, Acts of 1982." Boston: Massachusetts Department of Public Health, Office of the Commissioner of Probation and the Division of Alcoholism. Mimeographed.

Medicine in the Public Interest. 1979. *The Effects of Alcohol Beverage-Control Law.* Washington, D.C.: Medicine in the Public Interest.

Meyer, J., and J. Gomez-Ibanez. 1981. *Autos, Transit and Cities: A Twentieth Century Fund Report.* New York: Twentieth Century Fund.

Michelson, Larry. 1979. "The Effectiveness of an Alcohol Safety School in Reducing Recidivism of Drinking Drivers." *Journal of Studies on Alcohol* 40(11): 1060–1064.

Monaghan, John. 1981. *Predicting Violent Behavior: An Assessment of Clinical Techniques.* Beverly Hills, Calif.: Sage.

Moore, Mark H., and Dean R. Gerstein, eds. 1981. *Alcohol and Public Policy: Beyond the Shadow of Prohibition.* Washington, D.C.: National Academy Press.

Morris, Norval. 1974. *The Future of Imprisonment.* Chicago: University of Chicago Press.

Mosher, James. 1979. "Dram Shop Liability and the Prevention of Alcohol Related Problems." *Journal of Studies on Alcohol* 40(9): 773–798.

———. 1980. "The History of Youthful-Drinking Laws: Implications for Current Policy." Pp. 11–38 in *Minimum Drinking Age Laws,* edited by H. Wechsler. Lexington, Mass: D. C. Heath.

———. 1983. "Server Intervention: A New Approach for Preventing Drinking and Driving." *Accident Analysis Prevention* 15:483–497.

Moynihan, Daniel P. 1966. "The War against the Automobile." *Public Interest* 3:10–26.

"Murder Convictions for Homicides Committed in the Course of Driving While Intoxicated." Comment. 1978. *Cumberland Law Review* 8:477–494.

Murphy, Joseph P., and Ross D. Netherton. 1959. "Public Responsibility and the Uninsured Motorist." *Georgia Law Journal* 47:700–745.

Myers, M. L., C. Iscoe, C. Jennings, W. Lenox, E. Minsky, E. Sacks, and A. Sacks. 1981. *Staff Report on the Cigarette Advertising Investigation*. Washington, D.C.: Federal Trade Commission.

Nader, Ralph. 1964. *Unsafe At Any Speed: The Designed-in-Dangers-of the American Automobile*. New York: Grossman.

National Highway Traffic Safety Administration. 1978. *Review of the State of Knowledge*. Washington, D.C.: National Highway Traffic Safety Administration.

National Institute of Alcohol Abuse and Alcoholism. 1978. *Third Special Report to the U.S. Congress on Alcohol and Health*. Washington, D.C.: Government Printing Office.

National Institute of Justice. 1984. *Jailing Drunk Drivers: Impact on the Criminal Justice System*. Washington, D.C.: Department of Justice.

National Safety Council. 1985. *Accident Facts*. Chicago: National Safety Council.

National Transportation Safety Board. 1984. *Safety Study, Deterrence of Drunk Driving: The Role of Sobriety Checkpoints and Administrative License Revocation*. Washington, D.C.: National Transportation Safety Board.

New York City Criminal Justice Agency. 1988. *DWI Arrests in New York City (July 1, 1983, to June 30, 1985)*. New York: New York City Criminal Justice Agency.

New York State Insurance Department. 1970. *Automobile Insurance . . . For Whose Benefit?* Albany: New York State Insurance Department.

Nichols, Donald H. 1983. "Toward a Coordinated Judicial View of the Accuracy of Breath Testing Devices." *North Dakota Law Review* 59:329–348.

———, ed. 1984. "New Device Prevents Intoxicated Driving." *Drinking/Driving Law Letter* 4(17): 8.

Nichols, James, Elaine Weinstein, Vernon Ellingstad, and David L. Struckman-Johnson. 1978. "The Specific Deterrent Effects of ASAP Education and Rehabilitation Programs." *Journal of Safety Research* 10(4): 177–187.

———. 1979. "The Effectiveness of Education and Treatment Programs for Drinking Drivers: A Decade of Evaluation." Pp. 1293–1395 in *Alcohol, Drugs and Traffic Safety*, vol. 3, edited by L. Goldberg. Stockholm: Almquist & Wiksell.

Niederberger, W. V., and W. F. Wagner. 1985. *Electronic Monitoring of Convicted Offenders: A Field Test*. Washington, D.C.: National Institute of Justice.

O'Connell, Jeffrey and Roger Henderson. 1976. *Tort Law, No-Fault and Beyond*. Abridged ed. New York: Mathew Bender.

O'Connell, Jeffrey, and Arthur Myers. 1965. *Safety Last: An Indictment of the Auto Industry*. New York: Random House.

O'Donnell, Mary A. 1985. "Research on Drinking Locations of Alcohol Impaired Drivers: Implications for Prevention Policies." *Journal of Public Health Policy* 6:510–525.

Ogborne, A. C., and R. G. Smart. 1980. "Will Restrictions on Alcohol Advertising Reduce Alcohol Consumption?" *British Journal of Addictions* 75: 293–296.

O'Hagen, John. 1983. "The Rational for Special Taxes on Alcohol: A Critique." *British Tax Review* 1983:370–380.

Olson, Steve, and Dean Gerstein. 1985. *Drinking in America: Taking Action to Prevent Abuse.* Washington, D.C.: National Academy Press.

Ornstein, Stanley I. 1980. "The Control of Alcohol Consumption through Price Increases." *Journal of Studies on Alcohol* 41(a): 807–818.

Palmer, John W., and Paul E. Tix. 1985. "Minnesota Alcohol Roadside Survey." Minneapolis: St. Cloud University, Department of Health Education. Typescript.

Peele, Stanton. 1987. "The Limitations of Control-of-Supply Models for Explaining and Preventing Alcoholism and Drug Addiction. *Journal of Studies on Alcohol* 48(1): 61–77.

"*People v. Watson:* Drunk Driving Homicide-Murder or Enhanced Manslaughter?" Comment. 1983. *California Law Review* 71:1298–1323.

Perrine, M. W. 1975. "The Vermont Driver Profile: A Psychometric Approach to Early Identification of Potential High-Risk Drinking Drivers." In *Alcohol, Drugs, and Traffic Safety,* edited by S. Israelstam and S. Lambert. Toronto: Alcohol and Drug Addiction Research Foundation of Ontario.

Perrine, M. W., J. A. Waller, and L. S. Harris. 1971. *Alcohol and Highway Safety: Behavioral and Medical Aspects.* Burlington: University of Vermont.

Petersilia, Joan. 1987. *Expanding Options for Criminal Sentencing.* Santa Monica: Calif.: Rand.

Polich, J. Michael, David J. Armor, and Harriet B. Braiker. 1980. *The Course of Alcoholism: Four Years after Treatment.* Santa Monica, Calif.: Rand.

Posner, Richard A. 1977. *Economic Analysis of Law.* 2d ed. Boston: Little, Brown.

Presidential Commission on Drunk Driving. 1983. *Final Report.* Washington, D.C.: Government Printing Office.

Preusser, David, Robert Ulmer, and James Adams. 1976. "Driver Record Evaluation of a Drinking Driver Rehabilitation Program." *Journal of Safety Research* 8(3): 98–105.

Proceedings of the Second International Conference on Alcohol and Road Traffic. 1955. Toronto: Garden City.

Prosser, William. 1971. *Handbook of the Law of Torts.* 4th ed. St. Paul: West Publishing Co.

Prosser, William, and Robert Keeton. 1984. *On the Law of Torts.* 5th ed. St. Paul: West Publishing Co.

Rauss, Nason W., and E. Scott Geller. 1987. "Training Bar Personnel to Prevent Drunk Driving." *American Journal of Public Health* 7(8): 952–954.

Reagan on the Road: The Crash of the U.S. Auto Safety Program. 1982. Washington, D.C.: Public Citizen.

Reed, David R. 1981. "Reducing the Costs of Drinking and Driving." In *Alcohol and Public Policy: Beyond the Shadow of Prohibition,* edited by Mark H. Moore and Dean R. Gerstein. Washington, D.C.: National Academy Press.

Reese, John H. 1971. *Power, Politics, People: A Study of Driver Licensing Administration.* Washington, D.C.: National Research Council.

Reinerman, Craig. 1985. *Social Movements and Social Problems: Mothers against Drunk Drivers, Restrictive Alcohol Laws and Social Control in the 1980's.* Unpubl. ms. School of Public Health, University of California, Berkeley.

Richman, Alex. 1984. "Human Risk Factors in Alcohol-Related Crashes." *Journal of Studies on Alcohol,* suppl. 10:21–31.

Robertson, Leon S. 1983. *Injuries-Causes, Control, Strategies and Public Policy.* Lexington, Mass.: Lexington.

Robertson, Leon S., Albert B. Kelley, William Haddon, Jr., Brian O'Neill, Charles Wixom, Richard S. Eisworth. 1980. "A Controlled Study of the Effect of Television Messages on Seat Belt Use." *American Journal of Public Health* 64:1071–1080.

Robertson, Leon S., and Paul L. Zador. 1978. "Driver Education and Fatal Crash Involvement of Teenage Drivers." *American Journal of Public Health* 68:959–965.

Robinson, James J. 1938. "Manslaughter by Motorists." *Minnesota Law Review* 22:755–788.

Robinson, Paul H. 1985. "Causing the Conditions of One's Own Defense: A Study on the Limits of Theory in Criminal Law Doctorine." *Virginia Law Review* 71:1–63.

Room, Robin, and James Mosher. 1979–1980. "Out of the Shadow of Treatment: A Role for Regulatory Agencies in the Treatment of Alcohol Problems." *Alcohol Health and Research World* 4(2): 11–17.

Ross, H. Laurence. 1973. "Law, Science and Accidents: The British Road Safety Act of 1967." *Journal of Legal Studies* 2:1–78.

―――. 1975. "The Scandinavian Myth: The Effectiveness of Drinking-and-Driving Legislation in Sweden and Norway." *Journal of Legal Studies* 4:285–310.

―――. 1982. *Deterring the Drinking Driver: Legal Policy and Social Control.* Lexington, Mass.: Lexington.

―――. 1984. "Social Control through Deterrence: Drinking-and-Driving Laws." *Annual Review of Sociology* 10:21–35.

―――. 1985. "Deterring Drunk Driving: An Analysis of Current Efforts." *Journal of Studies on Alcohol,* suppl. 10:122–128.

Ross, H. Laurence, and Murray Blumenthal. 1974. "Sanctions For the Drinking Driver: An Experimental Study." *Journal of Legal Studies* 3:53–61.

Ross, H. Laurence, and James P. Foley. 1987. "Judicial Disobedience of the

Mandate to Imprison Drunk Drivers." *Law and Society Review* 21:315–334.

Russ, N. W., and E. S. Geller. 1987. "Training Bar Personnel to Prevent Drunken Driving: A Field Evaluation." *American Journal of Public Health* 77(8): 952–954.

Saffer, Henry, and Michael Grossman. "Beer Taxes and the Legal Drinking Age, and Youth Motor Vehicle Fatalities." *Journal of Legal Studies* 16:351–374.

Saxe, Leonard, Denise Dougherty, Katherine Esty, Michelle Fine. 1983. *The Effectiveness and Costs of Alcoholism Treatment*. Washington, D.C.: Office of Technology Assessment.

Schulhoffer, Stephen. 1974. "Harm and Punishment: A Critique of Emphasis on the Results of Conduct in the Criminal Law." *University of Pennsylvania Law Review* 122:1497–1607.

Schumaier, Steven G., and Brian A. McKinsey. 1986. "The Insurability of Punitive Damages." *American Bar Association Journal* 72:68–72.

Schwartz, Gary T. 1987. "The Ethics and Economics of Tort Liability Insurance." Unpubl. paper.

Schwartz, Richard. 1983. "Rehabilitation." Pp. 1364–1374 in *Encyclopedia of Crime and Justice*. New York: Free Press.

Schwitzgebel, R. K., and Schwitzgebel, R. L. 1964. "A Program of Research in Behavioral Electronics." *Behavioral Science* 9:233–238.

Sechrest, L. B., S. O. White, and E. D. Brown. 1979. *The Rehabilitation of Criminal Offenders: Problems and Prospects*. Washington, D.C.: National Academy Press.

Selzer, Melvin L. 1969. "Alcoholism, Mental Illness, and Stress in 96 Drivers Causing Fatal Accidents." *Behavioral Science* 14:1–10.

———. 1971. "The Michigan Alcoholism Screening Test: The Quest for a New Diagnostic Instrument." *American Journal of Psychiatry* 127:1653–1658.

Selzer, Melvin L., and E. Barton. 1974. "The Drinking Driver: A Psychosocial Study." *Drug and Alcohol Dependence* 2:239–253.

Selzer, Melvin L., and Charles Payne. 1962. "Automobile Accidents, Suicide, and Unconscious Motivation." *American Journal of Psychiatry* 119:237–240.

Selzer, Melvin L., Charles Payne, Franklin Westervelt, and James Quinn. 1967. "Automobile Accidents as an Expression of Psychopathology in an Alcoholic Population." *Quarterly Journal of Studies on Alcohol* 28:505–516.

Selzer, M. L., J. E. Rogers, and S. Kern. 1968. "Fatal Accidents: The Role of Psychopathology, Social Stress, and Acute Disturbance." *American Journal of Psychiatry* 124:1028–1036.

Sheingold, Stuart. 1974. *The Politics of Rights*. New Haven: Yale University Press.

Sheron, Georgia. 1986. "New Temperance Movement Seen by Historian." *New York Times,* March 16.

Simpson, Herbert M. 1985. "Human Related Risk Factors in Traffic Crashes: Research Needs and Opportunities." *Proceedings of the North American*

Conference on Alcohol and Highway Safety, edited by Thomas B. Turner, Robert F. Borkenstein, Ralph K. Jones, and Patricia Santora. *Journal of Studies on Alcohol,* Suppl. no. 10:32–39.

Singer, Richard G. 1979. *Just Deserts: Sentencing Based upon Equality and Desert.* Cambridge, Mass.: Ballinger.

Smart, R. G., and R. E. Cutler. 1976. "The Alcohol Advertising Ban in British Columbia: Problems and Effects on Beverage Consumption." *British Journal of Addictions* 71:13–21.

Smart, Reginald G. 1977. "Changes in Alcoholic Beverage Sales after Reduction in the Legal Drinking Age." *American Journal of Drug and Alcohol Abuse* 4(1): 101–108.

Smart, S. N., and C. R. Sanders, 1976. *The Costs of Motor Vehicle Related Spinal Injuries.* Washington, D.C.: Insurance Institute For Highway Safety.

Smith, R. A., R. W. Hingson, S. Morelock, T. Hereen, M. Mucatel, T. Mangione, and N. Scotch. 1984. "Legislation Raising the Legal Drinking Age in Massachusetts from 18 to 20: Effect on 16 and 17 Year Olds." *Journal of Studies on Alcohol* 45:534–539.

Snortum, John. 1988. "Deterrence of Alcohol-impaired Driving: An Effect in Search of a Cause." In *Social Control of the Drinking Driver,* edited by Michael Laurence, John Snortum and Franklin Zimring. Chicago: University of Chicago Press.

Snortum, John, Ragnar Hauge, and Dale Berger. 1986. "Deterring Alcohol-Impaired Driving: A Comparative Analysis of Compliance in Norway and the United States." *Justice Quarterly* 3(2): 139–165.

"Social Host Liability for Injuries Caused by Acts of an Intoxicated Guest." Note. 1983. *North Dakota Law Review* 59:445–447.

Spencer, J. R. 1985. "Motor Vehicles as Weapons of Offense." *Criminal Law Review* 1985:29–41.

Steinbock, Bonnie. 1985. "Drunk Driving." *Philosophy and Public Affairs* 14(3): 278–293.

Stewart, Ernest I., and James L. Malfetti. 1970. *Rehabilitation of the Drunken Driver.* New York: Teachers College Press.

"The Surface Transportation Assistance Act: Federalism's Last Stand?" Note. 1986. *Vermont Law Review* 11:203–232.

Survey Research, Consultants International. 1986. *Index to International Public Opinion.* Hastings on Hudson, N.Y.: Greenwood.

Tabachnik, Norman. 1973. *Accident or Suicide: Destruction by Automobile.* Springfield, Ill.: Charles C Thomas.

Tarrants, William E. 1984. "Evaluation News and Notes." *Traffic Safety Research and Evaluation Review* 3:1–6.

Taylor, Jerry. 1987. "Study Reports Fewer 1st-Time Drivers Repeat Offense." *Boston Globe,* April 1, 1987.

Teknetron Research, Inc. 1979. *1979 Survey of Public Perceptions on Highway Safety.* Washington, D.C.: Department of Transportation.

Tillman, W. A., and G. E. Hobbs. 1949. "The Accident-Prone Automobile

Driver: A Study of Psychiatric and Social Background." *American Journal of Psychiatry* 106:321–33.

Tittle, Charles. 1980. *Sanctions and Social Deviance: The Question of Deterrence.* New York: Praeger.

Transportation Research Board. 1984. "55: A Decade of Experience." Washington, D.C.: National Research Council.

Turner, Thomas B., Robert F. Borkenstein, Ralph K. Jones, and Patricia B. Santona, eds. 1985. "Alcohol and Highway Safety: Proceedings of the North American Conference on Alcohol and Highway Safety." *Journal of Studies on Alcohol,* suppl. 10.

U.S. Department of Health and Human Services 1983. *Fifth Special Report to U.S. Congress on Alcohol and Health from the Secretary of Health and Human Services.* Washington, D.C.: National Institute on Alcohol Abuse and Alcoholism.

U.S. Department of Transportation. 1968. *Alcohol and Highway Safety.* Report to the United States Congress. Washington, D.C.: Department of Transportation.

———. 1974a. *Alcohol Safety Action Projects: Evaluation of Operations—1972.* Washington, D.C.: National Highway Traffic Safety Administration.

———. 1974b. *The Uses of Mass Media for Highway Safety.* DOT-HS-801-209. Washington, D.C.: National Highway Traffic Safety Administration.

———. 1978. *Alcohol and Highway Safety: A Review of the State of Knowledge 1978.* Washington, D.C.: National Highway Traffic Safety Administration.

———. 1979. *Alcohol Safety Action Projects Evaluation of Operations: Data, Tables of Results and Formulations.* Washington, D.C.: National Highway Traffic Safety Administration.

———. 1981. *Alcohol and Highway Safety Laws: A National Overview,* Washington, D.C.: National Highway Traffic Safety Administration.

———. 1982. *Report on Traffic Accidents and Injuries in the United States—1981.* Washington, D.C.: National Highway Traffic Safety Administration.

———. 1983. *DWI Sanctions: The Law and the Practice.* Washington, D.C.: National Highway Traffic Safety Administration.

———. 1985a. *Alcohol and Highway Safety: A Review of the State of Knowledge 1984.* Washington, D.C.: National Highway Traffic Safety Administration.

———. 1985b. *Digest of State Alcohol-Highway Safety Related Legislation.* 3d ed. Washington, D.C.: National Highway Traffic Safety Administration.

———. 1986a. *The Drunk Driver and Jail: The Drunk Driver and Jail Problem.* Washington, D.C.: National Highway Traffic Safety Administration.

———. 1986b. *DWI Charge Reduction Study.* Washington, D.C.: National Highway Traffic Safety Administration.

U.S. General Accounting Office. 1984. *Status of Two Department of Transportation Air Bag Projects.* Report to the Chairman, Subcommittee on Oversight and Investigations, Committee on Energy and Commerce, House of Representatives B-212740.

"U.S. National Roadside Breath-testing Survey and Several Local Surveys."

1975. In *Alcohol, Drugs and Traffic Safety,* edited by S. Israelstam and S. Lambert. Toronto: Addiction Research Institute of Ontario.

"*United States v. Fleming:* When Drunk Drivers Are Guilty of Murder." Note. 1985. *American Criminal Law Review* 23:135–149.

Vaillant, George. 1983. *The Natural History of Alcoholism.* Boston: Harvard University Press.

Valverius, M., ed. 1982. "Roadside Surveys." In *Proceedings of the Eighth International Conference on Alcohol, Drugs, and Traffic Safety.* Stockholm: Swedish Council on Information on Alcohol and Other Drugs.

Vingilis, E. 1983. "Driving Drinkers and Alcoholics: Are They from the Same Population?" In *Research Advances in Alcohol and Drug Problems,* vol. 7, edited by R. G. Smart, F. B. Glaser, Y. Isreal, H. Kalant, R. E. Potham, and W. Schmidt. New York: Plenum.

Voas, R. B., and J. M. Hause. 1984. *Deterring the Drinking Driver: The Stockton Experience.* Report prepared by the National Public Service Research Institute for the NHTSA. Washington, D.C.: National Highway Traffic Safety Administration.

Voas, Robert. 1981. "Results and Implications of the ASAPS." In *Alcohol, Drugs, and Traffic Safety,* vol. 3, edited by L. Goldberg. Stockholm: Almquist & Wiksell.

"Void for Vagueness Doctrine." Note. 1960. *University of Pennsylvania Law Review* 109:67–116.

Von Hirsch, Andrew. 1976. *Doing Justice: The Choice of Punishments.* New York: Hill & Wang.

———. 1985. *Past or Future Crimes.* New Brunswick, N.J.: Rutgers University Press.

Von Hirsch, Andrew, and Donald Gottfredson. 1983–1984. "Selective Incapacitation: Some Queries about Research Design and Equity." *Review of Law and Social Change* 12:11–51.

Votey, Harold L., Jr. 1982. "Scandinavian Drinking-Driving Control: Myth or Intuition?" *Journal of Legal Studies* 11:93–116.

Wagenaar, Alexander C. 1983. *Alcohol, Young Drivers, and Traffic Accidents.* Lexington, Mass.: Lexington.

Wald, Patricia. 1974. "Alcohol, Drugs, and Criminal Responsibility." *Georgetown Law Journal* 63:69–86.

Wallach, L. 1984. "Drinking and Driving; Toward a Broader Understanding of the Role of the Mass Media." *Journal of Public Health Policy* 5:471–496.

Wallach, Lawrence, Warren Breed, and John Cruz. 1987. "Alcohol on Prime Time Television." *Journal of Studies on Alcohol* 48(1): 33–38.

Waller, Julian. 1967. "Identification of Problem Drinking among Drunken Drivers." *Journal of American Medical Association* 200:114–120.

———. 1976. "Alcohol Ingestion, Alcoholism and Traffic Accidents." In *The Legal Issues in Alcoholism and Alcohol Usage.* Boston: Boston University, Law-Medicine Institute.

Walther, David L., and Thomas A. Plain. 1965. "Punitive Damages—A Critical Analysis." *Marquette Law Review* 49:369–386.

Warner, Kenneth E. 1977. "The Effects of the Anti-Smoking Campaign on

Cigarette Consumption." *American Journal of Public Health* 67(7): 645–650.

Wasserstrom, Richard. 1960. "Strict Liability in the Criminal Law." *Stanford Law Review* 12:731–745.

Wasserstrom, Silas J. 1984. "The Incredible Shrinking Fourth Amendment." *American Criminal Law Review* 21:257–401.

Wechsler, H., ed. 1980. *Minimum-Drinking-Age Laws*. Lexington, Mass: D. C. Heath.

Weed, Frank J. 1987. "Grass-Roots Activism and the Drunk Driving Issue." *Law and Policy* 9:259–278.

Weisner, C., and Robin Room. 1984. "Financing and Ideology in Alcohol Treatment." *Social Problems* 32:167–184.

Wiener, Carolyn. 1981. *The Politics of Alcoholism: Building an Arena around a Social Problem*. Camden, N.J.: Transaction.

Wilkinson, Rupert. 1970. *The Prevention of Drinking Problems: Alcohol and Cultural Influences*. New York: Oxford University Press.

Willett, T. C. 1973. *Drivers after Sentence*. London: Heinemann.

Williams, Allan F., Adrian K. Lund, and David F. Presser, 1986. "Drinking and Driving among High School Students." *International Journal of Addictions* 21(6): 643–655.

Williams, Allan F., Michael A. Peat, Dennis Crouch, Joann Wells, and Bryan Finkle. 1985. "Drugs in Fatally Injured Male Drivers." *Public Health Reports* 100(1): 19–25.

Williams, Allan F., R. F. Rich, and P. L. Zador. 1975. "The Legal Minimum Age and Fatal Motor Vehicle Crashes." *Journal of Legal Studies* 4:219–239.

Williams, Allan F., Paul L. Zador, Sandra S. Harris, and Ronald S. Karpf. 1983. "The Effect of Raising the Legal Minimum Drinking Age on Involvement in Fatal Crashes." *Journal of Legal Studies* 12:169–179.

Wolfe, A. C. 1975. "Characteristics of Late-Night Weekend Drivers: Results of the U.S. National Roadside Breath-testing Survey and Several Local Surveys." In *Alcohol, Drugs, and Traffic Safety: Proceedings of the Sixth International Conference on Alcohol, Drugs, and Traffic Safety*, edited by S. Israelstam and S. Lambert. Toronto: Addiction Research Foundation of Ontario.

Worden, J. K., J. A. Waller, and T. J. Riley. 1975. *The Vermont Public Education Campaign in Alcohol and Highway Safety: A Final Review and Evaluation*, CRASH Rep. I-5. Waterbury: Vermont Department of Mental Health, Project CRASH.

Yoder, Richard, and Robert Moore. 1973. "Characteristics of Convicted Drunken Drivers." *Quarterly Journal of Studies on Alcohol* 34:927–936.

Zador, Paul. 1976. "Statistical Evaluation of the Effectiveness of Alcohol Safety Action Projects." *Accident Analysis and Prevention* 8:51–66.

———. 1977. "A Rejoinder to a Critique of the Paper 'Statistical Evaluation of the Effectiveness of Alcohol Safety Action Projects' by Johnson, et al." *Accident Analysis and Prevention* 9:15–19.

Zimring, Franklin. 1978. "Policy Experiments in General Deterrence: 1970–1975." In *Deterrence and Incapacitation: Estimating the Effects of Criminal Sanctions on Crime Rates,* edited by Alfred Blumstein, Jacqueline Cohen, and Daniel Nagin. Washington, D.C.: National Academy of Sciences.

————. 1982. *The Changing Legal World of Adolescence.* New York: Free Press.

Zimring, Franklin, and Gordon Hawkins. 1973. *Deterrence: The Legal Threat in Crime Control.* Chicago: University of Chicago Press.

Zoffer, H. J. 1959. *The History of Automobile Liability Insurance Rating.* Pittsburg: University of Pittsburg Press.

Zylman, Richard. 1971. "The Alcohol Highway Safety Program: A Panacea or a Pandora's Box?" *Traffic Digest and Review* 19(4): 16–24.

————. 1972. "Drivers' Records: Are They a Valid Measure of Driving Behavior?" *Accident Analysis and Prevention* 4:333–349.

————. 1973. "Youth, Alcohol and Collision Involvement." *Journal of Safety Research* 5(2): 51–72.

————. 1974. "A Critical Evaluation of the Literature on Alcohol Involvement in Highway Deaths." *Accident Analysis and Prevention* 6:163–204.

————. 1975a. "DWI Enforcement Programs: Why Are They Not More Effective?" *Accident Analysis and Prevention* 7:179–190.

————. 1975b. "Mass Arrests for Impaired Driving May Not Prevent Fatal Crashes." Pp. 225–235 in *Proceedings of the Sixth International Conference on Alcohol Drugs, and Traffic Safety.* Toronto: Alcohol and Drug Addiction Research Foundation.

————. 1976. "All Alcoholics Are High Risk Drivers: A Myth." *Journal of Traffic Safety Education* 23(2): 7–10.

Index

Accident Facts (National Safety Council), 16, 29, 32

Accidents, vehicular, xiii, 27–41, 60, 108, 192; and BAC levels, 76; crackdown effects on, 112–14; exaggeration of drunk driving role in, 27–29; and insurance surcharges, 131; and minimum drinking age, 177; problems in estimating drunk driving role in, 29–37; statistics on, 16–19; strategies for estimating drunk driving role in, 37–40; strategies for reducing, 20–26. See also Fatalities

Actus reus, of drunk driving, 65–68

Administrative model of drunk driving, 63–64, 75

Advertising, of alcohol, 5–8, 161, 165

Age: and drunk driving, 47–48, 54; and traffic fatalities, 17. See also Youth

Aggravated drunk driving, 60, 64, 78–89, 195; definition of, 78–79; procedural implications of, 82–83; and recidivism, 80–81; resulting in death, 83–89; resulting in injury, 83; in Scandinavia, 125

Aiken, Doris, xv

Air bags, 19, 21–22, 26, 171, 196

Alaska, vehicle forfeiture in, 152–54

Alcohol: advertising of, 5–8, 161, 165; ambivalence toward, 13; business of, 5–7; role of, in U.S., 3–4; and youth, 7

Alcohol abuse, xiii, 109, 191–92; concept of, 9–10; and disease model of alcoholism, 10–11; and drunk driving patterns, 48–49, 54; and public education, 162–63, 166–67; and rehabilitation, 11, 181; by youth, 176. See also Alcoholism; Problem drinking

Alcohol Abuse and Alcoholism Prevention, Treatment, and Rehabilitation Act of 1970, 12

Alcohol and Health (report), 43

Alcohol and Highway Safety (report), xiv–xv, 27–28, 32, 40

Alcohol consumption, xiii, 68–69, 165; pattern of, 4–5; restrictions on, 171–80

Alcohol dispensers, commercial: education strategy with, 165–66; legal liability of, xviii, 139–47, 165–66, 196; state regulation of, 172–73

Alcoholic Beverage Control (ABC) laws, 172–73

Alcoholic psychosis, 172

Alcoholic Rehabilitation Act of 1968, 11–12

Alcoholics Anonymous (AA), 10, 167, 182, 185, 186

Alcoholism: concept of, 9; and disease, 9–10; disease model of, 10–11; driver's license screening for, 149–50; and drunk driving patterns, 48–49, 52; and public education, 166; and recidivism, 109; and rehabilitation, 11–12, 181, 188. See also Alcohol abuse; Problem drinking

Alcohol Safety Action Project (ASAP), xv, xvii, xviii, 46, and antabuse, 182; on deterrence, 107, 112–13; and drinking/driver programs, 186–87; on drinking habits, 49

Alco-sensor, 92, 111

American Medical Association, xix

Antabuse, 182–83, 190

Arrests, drunk driving: effect of increased, 112–14; number of, xviii, 24–25; perceived probability of, 108–9; and right to counsel, 95; and roadblocks, 111–12. See also Recidivism

ASAP. See Alcohol Safety Action Project (ASAP)

253